Dear Ann Landers

Dear Ann Landers

Landers

Our Intimate and Changing Dialogue with America's Best-Loved Confidante

DAVID I. GROSSVOGEL

CONTEMPORARY
BOOKS, INC.
CHICAGO ▪ NEW YORK

Library of Congress Cataloging-in-Publication Data

Grossvogel, David I., 1925–
  Dear Ann Landers.

  1. Landers, Ann—Interviews.   2. Journalists—United
States—Interviews.   3. American newspapers—Sections,
columns, etc.—Advice.   4. United States—Social
conditions—1945–   I. Landers, Ann.   II. Title.
PN4874.L23G76   1987   070'.92'4   87-15547
ISBN 0-8092-4675-9

For the original Zelig 15

Published by Contemporary Books, Inc.
180 North Michigan Avenue, Chicago, Illinois 60601
Manufactured in the United States of America
Library of Congress Catalog Card Number: 87-15547
International Standard Book Number: 0-8092-4675-9

Published simultaneously in Canada by Beaverbooks, Ltd.
195 Allstate Parkway, Valleywood Business Park
Markham, Ontario L3R 4T8 Canada

Contents

Preface

The three or so letters a day published in the Ann Landers column, multiplied by 365 days a year for more than thirty years works out to more than 35,000 letters. To investigate what these letters say about American life of the fifties through the eighties, I have attempted a methodical approach to a necessarily subjective analysis. I read each letter, tried to summarize it fairly, then entered it into a computer for accurate location, retrieval, comparative analysis, and determination of statistical and historical frequency.

The nearly four years required to do this suggest that it was more than a do-it-yourself project. Many people helped along the way. First and foremost I must thank Eppie, Ann Landers herself, for her assistance and the right to quote from her columns. She was most generous with her time (of which she has precious little), and with her resources, knowledge, and encouragement. Many of those resources were made available to me through her able assistant, Kathy Mitchell, who was unfailingly helpful, responsive, and optimistic.

Reading, classifying, and analyzing the letters would

have been an even longer task had it not been for the modern miracles of electronics. That electronic wizardry was available to me thanks to the creation of Project Ezra, the result of fruitful negotiations between IBM and many people at Cornell, among whom should be mentioned the Dean of the College of Arts and Science, Geoffrey V. Chester.

Anil Nerode, Chair of Cornell's mathematics department and a genius in many fields, was unsparing of his time in teaching me much more than the little I retained about PCs, computer systems, floppy disks, hard disks, and what to do when the machine becomes temperamental. When he wasn't around, Cynthia Frazier, the humanities liaison for Project Ezra, devised ingenious ways of circumventing a sophisticated instrument that can unaccountably turn into an unmanageable tangle of negative signals.

And then there are those on the Cornell Humanities Faculty Research Grants Committee who assisted in funding a part of the project's expense by advocating its worth.

Glenn Altschuler, whose name appears at this same place in so many books, helped me as an American historian to read our times and to find facts essential to that reading. Maurice Neufeld, of the New York State School of Industrial and Labor Relations, reviewed the entire manuscript, giving me the benefit of a pitiless and keen eye, whether in the area of his special competence, the contemporary sociological scene, or on small points of syntax.

Ferris Mack, who had been Ann Landers's editor when they were preparing her monumental *Encyclopedia*, then went over this manuscript once again and translated it from academic prose to a more generally recognized language.

Darlene Flint, the personification of the ideal secretary, helped with old-fashioned typing and new-fangled word processing. She also remained good-humored and patient when all those phone calls started coming in.

And throughout, there was my wife, Jill, who has not only been a very good proofreader, but was always there to remind me that *women* has now replaced *girls*, that green vegetables are good for you, to smile on days that seemed to be especially bleak, and to share the sunshine of the rest.

All these, as well as the many others whose comments and ideas are incorporated in some part of this work unacknowledged, I acknowledge now, and with sincere gratitude.

Introduction:
Who Is Speaking Here?

In recent times, American newspapers have gone in for personal instruction—recipes, gardening tips, health hints, financial guidance, and horoscopes. But especially vital and tenacious has been what Nathaniel West called, in a classical American novel of the thirties, the "Miss Lonelyhearts" column—the column whose advice is directed to the specific troubles of a single reader.

Before Ann Landers, the most famous of these columnists was Elizabeth Meriwether Gilmer, who wrote "Dorothy Dix Talks." Like Ann, Dorothy Dix was out to help people who needed assistance because of domestic problems, affairs of the heart (from puppy love to extramarital liaisons), or superfluous hair. Like Ann Landers, too, Dorothy Dix favored a hard-headed realism, kept pace with changing values and social standards, and built up a huge readership. According to the *Dictionary of American Biography*, she was syndicated by some 300 papers at the start of the Second World War, and had a readership of around sixty million.

There are, of course, differences between Dorothy Dix and Ann Landers because of the times during which each

1

woman wrote. One may hesitate to say that Ann's readers live in more difficult times (although there is really no reason for hesitating to say so), but she undoubtedly lived through years of progressively freer expression in the family newspaper. The gradual disappearance of various kinds of censorship encouraged confession of more intimate, more diverse questions, which required a proportionally greater array of answers and called into question the very concept of a norm—whether moral or social. But regardless of its necessary changes, the idea of the advice column is an enduring fixture of the American scene.

Ann Landers took over the column that already bore that name in 1955, when she was still Esther Pauline Lederer. By what feats of raw determination she powered her way from Lake Shore Drive to the inner sanctum of the *Chicago Sun-Times* we will learn in Chapter 6.

The year 1955 may not seem all that long ago when so much of our electronic gadgetry is used to store and preserve documents. But a third of a century is a long time nevertheless, and the variety of changes that have occurred is remarkable. This review of thirty years of Ann Landers's columns documents and measures aspects of those changes.

When Ann Landers began writing, the guns of the Second World War had been stilled for only a decade, and its tremors continued to be felt. Although in 1955 a treaty was signed establishing the independence of Austria, across the border troops still occupied Germany. The United States fought another war in Korea, and that one had been over for two years. But more than thirty thousand American lives were lost because of it, and the memory was still fresh. The political temper of the country was conservative. John Foster Dulles, as Secretary of State, made the Cold War against the Soviet Union an instrument of policy. His was a voice of the fifties, a time that had been dominated by the anti-Communism of Joseph McCarthy. It wasn't until 1954 that the senator from Wisconsin was censured and his influence began to wane.

Network television, born in 1947, was in its infancy. In 1955, Arthur Godfrey was newsworthy in a country where almost every home had a radio but only two-thirds had television sets. Even so, cinema screens felt threatened by the arrival of the new small screen in so many living rooms and countered with the huge VistaVision and Cinemascope. That year, *Marty* won the Academy Award, as did its star, Ernest Borgnine—while an Italian woman, Anna Magnani, won the award for best actress. Sacred idols who had made Hollywood legendary were still around. One of them, Clark Gable, married Kay Williams, while Carmen Miranda, "the Latin bombshell," died at the age of 41. Albert Einstein died also, and Winston Churchill resigned as Prime Minister of Great Britain.

The Brooklyn Dodgers won the World Series against the Yankees with stars whose names would live on—Pee Wee Reese, Duke Snider, and Jackie Robinson, the man who just a few years earlier had been the first to break the color barrier. Until 1947, no black athlete had ever worn a major-league uniform.

In 1955, it cost three cents to mail a letter, and Dwight D. Eisenhower, the Republican president, blocked an attempt to raise that price.

When Esther Pauline Lederer became Ann Landers, the country was feeling itself tested. Self-confidence and optimism had carried it through previous crises to predictable and satisfactory ends, but an inconclusive war in Korea and political stalemates in other parts of the world now made Americans uneasy. In time, the very virtues that sustained American confidence would start to be questioned.

Ann Landers thus began her column at a time of self-doubt. Americans were to endure the Sputnik challenge, the Cuban missile crisis, the assassinations of John F. Kennedy and Martin Luther King, Jr., the Vietnam War, and the social turmoil of the late sixties and early seventies, capped by the Watergate trauma, when nearly usual politics produced nearly disastrous results. These were to be part of the cataclysmic backdrop against which individuals were enacting the crises of their private lives, even as society was altering gradually the ways in which they would respond to their personal quandaries. And Ann Landers, who was at once their counselor, their own voice, and the measure of normal expectations, reflected and embodied that alteration.

Still, to speak of "the voice of Ann Landers" is to oversimplify. Her voice, responding as it does to her reader's voice, comes into being as the result of a complex relationship. The reader's act of writing to Ann Landers is itself not the simplest of acts—as we can infer from the many writers whose letter begins with versions of the formula most often used: "I never thought I would find myself writing to Ann Landers."

The complex relationship begins with the diversity of letter writers. There are those who have become excited because of an idea or an event. There are others who write in the name of a constituency—and those who are opposed to a constituency. There are also the solitary ones with something weighing on their mind. The writer with a private complaint has isolated an area of his or her life that causes dissatisfaction; the problem area falls short of some standard. Thus, writing letters to Ann Landers assumes a consensus of what is normal.

The relationship continues when Ann Landers edits the letters that show stylistic or grammatical aberrations and contributes to giving them a similar voice, however different each problem may be. Lastly, the letter writer assumes that Ann Landers's response represents the standard of normalcy—whose attainment will dissipate the writer's unhappiness.

Ann Landers echoes and extends the expectations that problems are avoided when people live up to standards for appropriate behavior. The language of, and references to, psychiatrists entered her column fairly early (it is pretty well standard fare by the seventies, and is increasingly relied on thereafter). Still, unlike psychiatrists, she is not particularly interested in the clinical causes of an individual leaving the beaten track. Instead, she is a social moralist; she measures behavior against generally agreed-upon standards. She therefore usually takes the letters at face value, as an outline of the apparent causes of the reader's trouble. And she responds according to the standards of an orderly society.

In responding to her writers' expectations of commonly accepted values, Ann Landers certifies those values. The moment of personal distress described in a letter becomes a symbol of a more general problem. She thus raises a moment already arrested in time and separated from its circumstances to an iconic level—one husband's affair comes to stand for masculine infidelity, a violation of the prevalent morality.

In articulating generally accepted values, Ann Landers is a mirror rather than an analyst. She does not set the standards but finds them in the aspirations of those who write to her. Confirmation of those values comes from the authorities to whom she appeals—ministers, marriage counselors, school advisers, therapists, doctors, lawyers. Even though irritated readers suggest now and then that she "cops out" by referring to these arbiters, she has continued to do so because she and they speak with the same voice.

The language of Ann Landers is clear and simple. She says, "I write as I talk" and believes that the virtue of plain language matches the precision of moral explicitness. Even when her words are humorous, their message is plain. So even though there is a voice that is unmistakably that of a writer called Ann Landers, her voice also has a mythical resonance, since it is, for many of her readers, the voice of a social culture.

The filtering voice of Ann Landers also filters out the person Eppie Lederer might have been. As described by her daughter, Margo Howard, in her book *Eppie*, Ann Landers would have had, at her grandest, the proper qualifications for being the Jewish mother of America. She seems to have been strong on traditional moral principles to the point of naïveté, heavily relying on euphemisms to avoid offense in social mores or everyday language (with particular ostracism directed at the "S word" and the "F word"). The family euphemism for women's breasts was "hermans," a concealment born of the kind of prudishness that finally led Ann to misunderstand the activities of Linda Lovelace. When informed by her daughter of *Deep Throat*'s significance, Eppie was for once at a loss for words; "then, not quite believing the whole thing, she had a final question. 'You can really see her hermans?' "

The high priority Ann Landers gave to appearances may have led her to marry Jules Lederer, who satisfied a perhaps half-forgotten consciousness: He was Jewish but, to quote Margo, also "looked like *goyim*." She reenacted this ambivalence in her role as Jewish mother of America by addressing the mainstream concerns of a huge readership while reminding her readership now and then that she was indeed Jewish.

It was Esther Pauline's enormous energy that propelled her out of the world of affluent Jewish housewives to which her workaholic husband's success would otherwise have consigned her. She was a force looking for a purpose; inherited values made up for the education she missed as an adolescent, and those values combined with her drive to succeed in whatever she undertook. Those values also gave her something against which to measure many of the unfortunate departures imposed by the times—before she too had to abandon them. Her values were widely shared since, true to the morality of Benjamin Franklin himself, they posited material rewards for a life properly lived. It seems emblematic of a younger Eppie's aspirations and conformities that she acquired a taste for furs early on, but that the monograms in the linings of those furs were not her own initials but "Jules's Wife."

What Esther Pauline might not have bargained for when she took over the Ann Landers column in 1955 was that American society's basic standards would undergo increasingly rapid transformations. The standards she needed to uphold and reflect have been subject to nearly constant redefinition. These changes are reflected in Ann's correspondence with her many readers.

Because of the huge number of readers—some eighty-five million—and the complex process involved in giving them voice, this book is necessarily subjective. The subjectivity begins with the original letter writer. Ann Landers, too, is subjective when she picks and chooses from among hundreds the three or so letters to run each day, and when she edits the letters. The subjectivity has been enhanced by the decisions involved in writing this book. Nevertheless, the intent of this work is to reflect, as accurately as possible, the changing nature of American society over the last thirty years.

1
Ann Landers: Her Ways and Her World

The very first column Ann Landers turned out for the *Chicago Sun-Times*, on October 16, 1955, already contained much of what would one day be identifiable as her style. From the start, her advice was breezy and crackled with one-liners. In her initial answer, she told an auto racetrack lothario, "Time wounds all heels, and you'll get yours." (This line, too good to waste on a single column, would reappear.) To the woman who had fallen for a philandering and deceitful delivery boy, she commented, "What this man is delivering to your home sounds like baloney."

Most of the tone and not a few of the expressions that would become the coin of exchange between her and millions of readers were born in those earliest days. In 1956, she commented that unless a woman who smoked in bed gave up that dangerous practice, the ashes on the floor might be her own. When in October of the following year an irate reader concluded, "I feel better now that I have given you a piece of my mind," she responded, "I hate to take the last piece, but thank you for your letter."

Early on, she referred to alimony as "the high cost of leaving" (another pun worth repeating, at least until men, in changing times, began to be vocal about the unfairness of alimony awards). Also early were the first of many warnings to the easily seduced: "Compliments are like perfume. It's all right to take a whiff, but you're not supposed to swallow it."

Her skill with a snappy phrase suggests that from the start her main justification for running some letters is the fun of answering. In 1957, responding to a trained singer whose friends never thought of paying for her services, Ann advised, "The musical scale begins and ends with dough." That suspicion of Ann's occasional practice of making humor the key ingredient is confirmed throughout thirty years of writing.

The fun in many answers is superior to the content of the letter that occasioned it. During the eighties, she even responded to letters asking her to share the funniest line she had heard lately—a practice she occasionally repeated without the excuse of the inquiring letter.

Also from the start, Ann Landers introduced some of the expressions that would be her trademarks, advising readers to "wake up and smell the coffee" or offering to submit to lashes with a wet noodle for errors she had made.

And equally soon, millions of readers accepted Ann Landers on her own terms. They not only confided in her, but even learned her language. By January 1957, after less than a year and a half, certain of her expressions had become household words. For example, a dumb but assiduous "Interested Prospect" asked her how she could join her "Old-Too-Soon, Smart-Too-Late Club." Mrs. Shiny-Pate, who wanted a clever reply her bald husband could use on smart alecks, asked her to "please 'noodle this out' (as you say)." (Readers learned nearly from the first that Ann also catered wisecracks.)

That intimacy quickly made countless people feel as if they were entering into a discussion with a member of the family. Readers began butting into arguments that had nothing to do with them. That same month, a teen-ager who felt that Ann was "all wet" on some dating advice, asked her, "Why don't YOU wake up and smell the coffee?" And a few days later, another irritated reader took the initiative and advised her to "get out the wet noodle and give yourself twenty lashes."

Part of her language became nearly at once a kind of code. In September 1957, Nobody's Fool inveighed against her husband who "had a 'side-dish' (as you call it)." Three months later, there was evidence that her words had already attained sufficient resonance to confer a seal of approval she might not have intended, as when L.C.A. complained, "Ever since my husband started to read your column, he has been calling me 'Buster,' " which was indeed one of Ann's customary forms of address for those she wished to reprove.

One of Ann Landers's main gifts, and an underlying cause of her huge and nearly instant success, was this ability to foster an intimate dialogue between herself and her readers. The caring Jewish mother appeared very soon and regularly. From the start, she was able to turn the huge apparatus of a syndicated column into an expression of concern for the dilemma or pain of a single individual. Many were comforted by expressions such as "I'm betting on you," "write to me in six months and let me know how it turned out," and "good luck, honey." These expressions made countless people feel they knew someone who was close enough to yell at in moments of anger or frustration and sympathetic enough to turn to in moments of need.

The fact that Ann Landers was also a source of knowl-edge on matters ranging from etiquette to legal or health problems added to her usefulness. However, it was sec-ondary from the very start, and remained secondary even as her battery of specialists and authorities became more and more formidable. Her repeatedly stated conviction is that those who write do so more to air their feelings than to ask for specific advice.

If Ann Landers's correspondents felt nearly from the first that they could let off steam, she felt just as quickly that this kind of exercise took place on a two-way street. She further reduced the impersonality of the syndicated column by occasionally speaking with the irritated voice of someone who had been nettled. If Ann Landers ever felt she had to bite her tongue so as not to offend her readers, the feeling was no more than fleeting. Before long, readers learned that she could turn sharp, even nasty. In 1957, she told T.A., who wanted to marry the married woman by whom he had twins, to "get lost." Two months later, to Antiseptic Al complaining about his wife's mania for orderliness, she advises, "When you've finished reading this, clip it out and hand it to her . . . and leave the papers on the floor."

Even with those who became her special constituency—teens—she can be pretty rough. In December 1957, to Not Ashamed, who thought "cuddling up with a nice guy" wasn't all that bad, she answers, "A lemon that's been squeezed too many times is considered garbage." That same month, to In the Dark, who had written about a dipsomaniacal friend, she wrote, "Turn on the light, Stupid. This woman is talking dry and drinking wet."

From the earliest, Ann came on as the tough cookie who called a spade a spade, and a stupid reader Stupid. But this toughness could turn to unexpected prickliness when readers responded in kind. In July 1956, A.R.R. made the mistake of telling her, "You have holes in your head." Ann was sufficiently vexed to respond, "It's YOU who have holes in your head, not me, Lady." This capacity to rouse the ire of her readers and to be wounded in turn by the familiarity of a dialogue whose intimacy she had been able to foster, contributed to the phenomenal growth of her readership. By March 1960, she claims to have thirty-five million readers. The following December, responding to an open letter on shock treatment, she assures the writer her letter will reach forty million people.

In July 1964, Ann informs her public that she gets

24,000 letters a month; that figure jumps to 350,000 a year (or 29,000 a month) by March 1967. By the end of 1975, she is carried by 812 papers, both here and abroad. In June 1978, she has a readership of 60 million (from the ages of 6 to 103). By the eighties, she receives a thousand pieces of mail a day and over 300 daily requests for her pamphlets. In March 1986, she mentions a readership of 85 million. One can only assume that she was able to find nearly instantly a tone to which an overwhelming part of the population would respond, and that she succeeded in maintaining that tone through rapidly changing times.

Ann Landers has never drawn her readership from any particular class or group. Eminent doctors, members of the clergy, and statesmen (including the Great Communicator, Ronald Reagan) have availed themselves of her megaphone in order to reach the widest possible audience. Less eminent doctors have also written, simply to complain that their relatives were using them for free consultations. And beauticians, mail carriers, truckers, fire fighters, teachers, switchboard operators, cashiers, people in all kinds of professions and trades have written to put their case before a boss, customers, or the public at large.

To address this enormously diverse public, Ann Landers found a voice that was middle-class in its suspicion of intellectual or aesthetic excess, frequently liberal in its political views, and generally conservative in its morality. In 1957, Want to Help, a thirteen-year-old, wrote about a boy in her class, "I am sure he has an inferiority complex brought on by a dominating mother. Do you think if I could get him to talk over his problem with me it would remove his guilt feelings and he'd be more friendly and take me to a movie?" That letter might have been thought of as cute or even interesting, given the writer's youth; in any event, it could have been handled with gentle humor. But Ann chose to read the letter as pretentious. Responding "Dear Miss Freud" (one of the rare occasions she invented a name for a correspondent), she advised the teen "don't meddle with his complexes."

Although many of her authorities eventually would be drawn from the field of mental health, the Ann Landers of the early years commonly implied that writers' references to psychoanalysis were signs of intellectual affectation. Her sense of a common touch displaced a science that had yet to find its way into the mainstream. A 1957 response to an unpublished letter (which again addressed the author as Freud) observed, "Your thesis on the conscious versus the subconscious was fascinating. What does it mean?" And at the end of 1975, to the distressed mother of a graduate student in psychology who had discovered among her son's term papers a harsh analysis of herself as parent, Ann replied, "When students write papers (especially psychology majors), they often dramatize, distort, and even fabricate, to illustrate a point."

Ann Landers's distrust of mental abstractions derives in part from a firm belief in the work ethic. The sweat on one's brow is a more immediate indication of inherent virtue than what might be at work behind that brow, and the claim made for the mind will never be as convincing.

In 1957, Worried Aunt writes about her nephew, a college graduate "with honors" who refused a job as grease monkey in her husband's garage because of his qualifications. That letter might have been read as the legitimate refusal of a job by someone who was overqualified and trained in another area, or it could be read as a form of intellectual arrogance. Ann chose the latter reading and advised the nephew to "get off his qualifications."

Though firmly convinced about the value of "education," she favors the vocational kind. In this respect, an exchange with J.F.S. in November 1970 is representative. The letter thanked her for saying "Not everyone belongs in college" and went on to complain, "Too many parents have the idea that vocational education is O.K. for somebody else's children." To which Ann replied, " 'The dignity of work.' A beautiful phrase."

The conviction that it is better to have a job, even if that job denies the individual's intellectual training or needs, fuels Ann's misgivings about indulgences of the mind. Early on she makes light not only of the amateurs who venture into psychoanalytic jargon but of psycho-analysis itself. A week after Ann Landers's blast at the intellectual nephew, Scorpio's Wife writes to complain that her husband "has gone overboard on astrology [and as a result] hasn't worked in three weeks." Ann opines that the husband is "sick, sick, sick" (a rather strong conclusion, since the letter seemed to complain about the husband's refusal to work rather than about his addiction to astrology). Ann Landers suggests a doctor, adding, "and you know what kind." Her advice thus restates her opinion (your husband is mentally ill) but at the same time includes psychoanalysis in its mockery.

Ann's own language provides early evidence of her distrust of the highbrow. In September 1956, one of her answers cites the conclusions of a "motivation research study," but feels compelled to add in parentheses "(in English this means 'why people do certain things')." In time, her sense of the culture allowed her, whenever necessary, to use more technical language, but many ways remained for her to stress her location squarely in middle America.

At the end of January 1965, she shows little sympathy for the wife who complains about being starved intellec-tually after marrying a man who dropped out of school in the tenth grade, and whose friends (together with their wives) are boring. Ann appears to blame the woman for attempting to step out of her wifely world: "Maybe these dull wives can't distinguish between a Picasso and a hole in the rug, but you might pick up some useful hints on how to remove an ink spot from a white damask table-cloth." And to drive her point home, Ann calls the woman "kiddo," another term reserved for those she rebukes. Eventually, as women became more articulate and conscious of their status, Ann would become more cautious; but she remained suspicious of those professing to cultivate taste or mind too exclusively.

This mainstream approval of visible labor found its political equivalence in beliefs that defined her for hostile readers as a "liberal"—someone too far to the left for conservatives but a stubborn preserver of traditional values for those who were impatient with them. Her dislike of smoking and drinking changed, over a period of time, from simple expressions of a personal distaste to a crusading intensity. By 1960, she was a firm and constant booster of Alcoholics Anonymous, and her allergy to smoking ("that filthy habit") was becoming sufficiently well-known to get the hackles up on more than a few individuals.

Similarly, before becoming a columnist, she had, as a suburban Chicago housewife, once found in local Democratic politics a channel for part of her considerable energies. That old-time liberal endures and surfaces in her eventual espousal of gun control, prochoice movements, rehabilitation centers, and halfway houses. Since a number of Ann Landers's causes have been controversial, and since a nonpolitical column seeks to avoid offending as many readers as possible, it is remarkable that any political subjects should have found their way into her column. In fact, her writing does on the whole steer clear of politics.

However, the ease with which she can be provoked, and the oscillations in her tone that result from such provocations, emerge occasionally as full-fledged political statements. In February 1960, an unsuspecting friend of Earl Long wrote that the politician from Louisiana had been done in by press photographers who made him look mentally deranged. The writer asked her to abandon her defense of overly critical media. This piqued Ann as a journalist, and it also piqued the liberal in her who must not have been particularly fond of Earl Long. She bristled, "Speak for yourself and don't make any package statements for me, Bub. I am not qualified to pass judgment on the mental condition of Mr. Long. The voters of Louisiana expressed themselves in the recent election."

When in March 1965, Miss 62.4 wrote about her father ("a conservative type, financially and politically") who disliked her politically active boyfriend because he had been passing out campaign literature outside her father's club, Ann's answer managed to combine her political liberalism with her dislike of drink: "I think if more young people would stand on street corners and pass out campaign material instead of just sitting in bars and passing out, this country would be in better shape." Conservative excess could always be counted on to arouse the swift, retaliatory liberal in Ann. In 1969, Confused, who had heard that the Sex Information and Education Council of the United States might be part of the Communist conspiracy, was treated to a whole column outlining the merits of Mary Calderone and SIECUS.

To balance her occasionally voiced suspicion of right-wingers, Ann Landers periodically affirmed her faith in God and even prayer. When Committee Chairman wrote in 1958, "Some of us feel that prayer is out of place on the football field," Ann responded, "It all depends on what the boys pray for." Nor were her views so liberal as to prevent her from being a loyal advocate of business and capital, even during the crisis days of the seventies, when both were viewed more suspiciously than before.

In this respect, her 1972 answer to Utica Gripe was representative. Ann's answer to a complaint about the "loony public" that keeps salespeople busy after closing time sounded as if it had been lifted from one of management's less-relaxed handbooks: "A competent employee is interested in moving merchandise. He doesn't resent staying with a customer who is buying, or even looking. . . . I don't know how old you are or how long you've been a sales clerk but I suggest you look for another job." Nor did she believe that employees should get too familiar with their bosses. In 1975, she contradicted a survey that said bosses prefer to be called by their first name. Ann noted peremptorily that her own survey showed the opposite (a hint of her relative indifference to polls?). And, on several occasions, she tried to come to the rescue of Procter and Gamble against the accusation of those who were convinced that the firm's logo meant that it was being taken over by the Moonies.

Ann's political liberalism included racial and religious tolerance, as one might expect, as well as the approval of aliens absorbed into the great melting pot. After just a few months on the job, she advised the parents of Teen-Ager, who would let their daughter date only boys with "American-sounding" names, that they'd better start combing their "social set for Sitting Bull or Rain-in-the-Face. All the other names are of foreign extraction." The month before, she had urged the wife who felt left out of her husband's family because of the foreign language they spoke to request that her husband teach her some of the foreign words.

But let one of those aliens be so bold as to criticize the United States, and the angered patriot in Ann Landers found instant voice. In 1956, an alien who had lived in this country for twelve years made the mistake of suggesting that "American women are a breed of parasites— thanks to American men." Ann Landers shot back, "There's a plane or boat leaving every hour. Be my guest." Even Americans tainted by foreign prejudice misspoke at their peril, as when, four months later, Air Force man Robert B., who had stated a preference for European women as against the U.S. brand of "pampered, selfish parasites," was hit with the identical counterpunch: "There's a plane or boat leaving every hour. Be my guest." This would be a reflex whenever the derogation assumed foreign superiority.

It may have been this gut-level, old-fashioned Americanism that influenced her 1980 response to A Connecticut Yankee. This writer expressed his "nagging suspicion that our prestige has slipped not only abroad but at home." Ann Landers replied that he may have been right previously, but Iran and Afghanistan signaled a turn: "Trouble abroad promotes patriotism at home."

That old-fashioned patriotism was matched by a set of old-fashioned moral values, and it is here that Ann Landers had to perform the most delicate of high-wire acts—balancing a need to preserve time-honored principles against the awareness of what a rapidly changing culture would accept. She analyzed and adapted to those changes through certain moral assumptions.

When Ann began writing her column, middle-class values had not yet been challenged as they would be in the following decades. It was therefore possible to walk through the social landscape with relative security by following its well-marked roads. For Ann, the paths were obvious enough. They involved questions of decorum, an acceptance of established roles, the evidence of certain hierarchies. Parents, children, men, women, husband, wives were defined by relatively fixed duties and privileges.

In 1955, boys and girls "dated" and, regardless of circumstances, the boy paid. It was better, if the boy was broke, to go on a date that cost nothing than to have the girl pay for any part of it, even if she happened to have money that evening. In this ritualized encounter, the boy acted like a "gentleman," helping her with her coat, opening doors, and the like. (If the girl did not allow him to do so, it was she who would "need educating.") Dress was important. Whatever the temperature, you did not cruise around in your car "bare-chested," any more than a "young lady" wore slacks on a train. As Marilyn was told in 1956, "Rare indeed is the woman who looks well [sic] in slacks."

Hair was becoming a source of controversy, in part because of the influence of Elvis Presley. Ann frowned on both long hair and Elvis, to the extent of referring to Elvis only as "you know who." She advised readers to "stick reasonably close to the conventional hairstyles," because "a fellow with a full head of waves and curls is out of order. A girl who chops off her hair and wears sideburns like You-Know-Who looks like You-Know-What."

Together with long hair, and perhaps because of the

same pernicious influence, jeans worn "low" were not allowed (jeans, generally speaking, were less than desirable). But then, in 1959, Ann didn't like teens meeting at each other's homes in their bathing suits, even if they were on their way to the beach. And in 1960, she objected to young women's bare legs and painted toenails in town (older women simply didn't do such things). After all, these were the days when dating couples weren't supposed to walk arm-in-arm, a woman didn't visit a stranger without being accompanied by her mother, and for a woman to take a lighted cigarette from her husband's lips and put it to hers was "unappetizing and vulgar."

To be proper, dating remained casual, and diversified (as opposed to going steady) until the participants attained legal age and became engaged. Until then, it was an encounter fraught with the perils of sex. Although the Margaret Sanger-like liberal in Ann always reserved a place for the health of normal sexuality (she delighted in never sympathizing with parents who had caught their children playing doctor—"it's natural curiosity"), she remained opposed to sex outside marriage. However, safety and social decorum set the bounds for her, rather than moral imperatives. Sometimes, it appears that for her, decorum *is* a moral imperative.

In June 1965, B.Cal wrote that her twenty-two-year-old daughter dashed out to see her fiance whenever he called at night, and this worried her. He lived "across town [in] a bad neighborhood"; her letter expressed her concern but raised no moral question. Still, Ann answered, "As parents, you have an obligation to speak up. A young man cannot respect a girl who has no self-respect. He demeans her by asking her to come to his place. And she degrades herself by caving in to his selfish demands." Twenty years later, nearly to the day, Ann Landers was still voicing her opposition to unmarried couples living together, even though she was not prepared to "judge" those who acted differently.

In 1957, when Just a Mother wrote that her sixteen-

year-old daughter was "wild" for wanting to date and
wear lipstick, Ann cautioned her, "Upbringing that is too
strict is as damaging as no discipline." She suggested that
the "chaperoned" high school party is the best place for
these first encounters between boys and girls, their
sexual nature being safely absorbed by social propriety.

This willingness to acknowledge the sexual reality of
the teen's world provided it was contained within social
conventions made Ann dangerously advanced for some
worried parents. In March 1957, Disgusted Dad wrote,
"Well, you've done it again. For the second time you've
recommended to parents that they permit teen-age
daughters to neck in the parlor." In her answer, Ann
again stressed propriety and safety: "This column does
NOT condone unrestrained, uncontrolled, unsupervised
necking for kids"; but she again acknowledges the unmis-
takable nature of the encounter: "Old-fashioned philosophy is fine, Dad, but don't overlook old-fashioned
chemistry."

The letter to Disgusted Dad put the responsibility for
whatever problems might arise in that parlor on the
parents: "If the moral principles have been instilled early
and there is love and understanding in the home, this
training will act like the brakes on an automobile."
Throughout the permissive seventies, Ann stuck to that
line. Love and sweet reason were better than corporal
punishment (except for a swift slap on the rear when the
sinner was still young), and discipline was a form of love.

Parents who were spineless, indifferent, or otherwise
lax were the guilty ones. In April 1957, she devoted for
the first time a whole column to a single letter. That
letter described the teen scene and the peer pressure
that kept teens in it. Miss A.C. was thirteen but said she
and her peers could pass for eighteen. They wore makeup
and high heels and went out of town on dates. They drove
cars without having a license, were bored by school,
smoked (cigarettes in those days), and drank. Miss
A.C.'s mother "got tired of fighting [her] and just gave
up." It was on this part of the letter that Ann zeroed in:

"Reckless and irresponsible behavior isn't the sickness, it's the symptom. Parents who feel they've lost control can't just give up and say 'The kid is no good, I can't do anything with him' . . . and then turn him loose on society. . . . Mom and Dad owe it to their youngsters, to the community and to themselves to try to get these boys and girls on the right track."

Thirteen years later (March 1970), the same subject required two columns. It was triggered this time by hair, a topic still very much alive, but one on which Ann Landers had crossed over. A mother who signed herself Had It wrote to rebut Ann's statement that "hair is not important," countering with, "Hair is the most singularly important thing in our son's life. . . . It is a symbol of his loathing for me and his father and everything we stand for." In her response, Ann allowed that generation gaps have occurred in every generation, but once again placed the responsibility where she thought it belonged—on the parents charged with inculcating moral values: "If you and your husband had hoped to be pals with your son, this may well be the key to your unhappy relationship. Children need parents more than they need pals. Pals cannot administer discipline."

In her answer to Had It, Ann aligned herself with tradition: "We are the Wax Works Set. The Antediluvian Creeps. The Doddering Old Squares. Anybody over 39." Throughout the years, Ann did not go too long against the prevailing moral sense of her readers, accepting it sooner or later in its constant change. She sometimes used self-conscious, conservative rhetoric: "If that labels me as hopelessly out of date, move over," and, "If this labels me a narrow-minded prude, so be it." These statements may well have been the mask hiding her receptivity to change.

Still, she never felt comfortable about significant age differences in marriage, nor about marriages between partners of different religious faiths. The idea of women frequenting bars repelled her. Even during the sexual revolution, she cautioned that tavern-haunting men are "interested in something a bit more horizontal" than dancing—disregarding the likely possibility that the women there were, too. (As late as 1974, some of the women patronizing those bars tried to make her see the light, but she remained unrelenting.)

There were always signs of feminism in the woman who went from being an energetic housewife to the writer of the most widely syndicated column in the nation. (In the fifties, she was among the first to coin the phrase that a woman's body is her own.) Nevertheless, she began with a concept of social conventions, and of the woman's place within them, that was summarized by an early blast directed at R.R., a complaining "working wife": "The reason you gals got married was to be wives and mothers, wasn't it?" That conviction—encapsulated in a 1960 exclamation, "it's a man's world, sugar!"—remained at the core of her advice, even as the times forced her to recognize that the social articulation was changing far more dramatically than she might have wished.

However supportive she was of women, and however harsh she might be with men, the one who had once been "Jules's wife" tended to see women in traditional roles and seemed to believe that most were more comfortable in those roles. To the teen who complained in June 1957 that she could not smoke, date, drive a car, wear three-inch heels and take trips alone like her friends, Ann suggested that she try helping her tired mother and get a little experience in what would probably be her "life's work." That same year, she told Ambitious for Him the "most damaging thing a wife can do is interfere in [her husband's] business and appear to be 'the boss.' " Two days later, she was reminding Mrs. Thru-the-Mill that "The male is the hunter . . . it's the nature of the beast." (This idea was to be repeated in 1960 as "give him the pleasure of chasing you until you catch him.") The following day, answering Muddled-Up, whose stubborn fiancee refused to refrain from flirting, Ann wrote, "If she resents taking orders tell her you aren't making any demands, that it's merely a suggestion, and she doesn't have to take it—unless she wants the engagement to end up in marriage."

In 1959, a woman who complained because her husband wanted her to iron the sheets was told to do so—to please him. Pleasing the husband remains one of her standard pieces of advice (even though the ways of doing so changed over time). As late as 1971, she tells women not to wear something their spouse might dislike. In her advice about keeping the home together (a fundamental need, which she tempered but did not displace over the years), a recurring image is of sexual warmth, for which the woman is responsible. This image can be found as readily in 1965 ("men, like fires, will go out if left unattended") as in 1982 (to the woman whose marriage is going stale, the oft-repeated "turn on the heat"). She thus finds herself asking women to be more aggressive sexually, especially when married, while at the same time assuming a "hunting" instinct in men.

At other times, Ann's sense of norms contradicts the newer thought she endorses, as when an occasional stereotype unexpectedly dates her idiom. (An example is her advice to Nick of Time in April 1960; she observes that the best way to spread the news is to "telephone, telegraph and telawoman.") She kept on insisting, "Anyone who can read can cook." (In punishment for this dismissive view, she was visited with the great meatloaf disaster of 1970, described in the Afterword.) In 1975, emerging consciousness among women does not prevent her from repeating the quaint "vanity, thy name is woman." And two months before she had responded to a question about whether a woman could rape a man by saying that even though rape might be too strong a word, it described rather well the present-day aggressiveness of females.

At a time when social forms were evolving rapidly, Ann's moral conservatism could make her lose step temporarily. In 1957, she appeared to be conceding to the times when she noted, "Females who are now competing with men in business must also compete for that seat in the bus." But a closer look at her exchange with the letter writer gives her words another meaning. D.J.K., whose letter elicited the reply, was complaining that her aging mother (a fifty-three-year-old working woman) had to travel fifty-five minutes on the bus to work and back again in the evening, often standing all the way "because American men are such skunks." This hardly conjures up the picture of an aggressive female competing in the men's marketplace. Ann's decision to misinterpret it may have stemmed from her lingering sense that women belonged primarily in the home. She confirms this two weeks later in response to A Mother-in-Law, who had exclaimed, "I'd like to know what is so disgraceful about hating housework? It's the most uninteresting, thankless, lowest-paid job in the world." Ann replied, "Your sad story gets me right here, pal."

Hobbled by beliefs that sometimes caused her to fall behind in the fast-changing scene, she had to be educated by readers about the "shocking" things that went on at coed pajama parties in the sixties. ("Of course, I attended college back around the time earth's crust cooled.") Her old typewriter, by which she continued to swear, became an emblem of the old virtues, in contrast to the electronic instrument, to which she remained unalterably opposed. In 1970, she refused a plea to speak up for data processors and called their machines "monsters." In 1957, she was even able to link this dislike of technology to the sins of delinquent parents, through her dismissal of something known as an exclusion key meant to ensure telephone privacy: "Once upon a time a word from a parent would have been sufficient. Exclusion key indeed!" In 1983, she was still waging a battle with computers whose misdeeds contrived a "sad commentary on what we call progress."

The dependable and recognizable typewriter was of course the credential of the traditionalist that allowed another part of Ann Landers to move with the restless times of her writing. But on any given day, she could discover that more than just old-fashioned typewriters might suddenly turn out to be obsolete. Longer than she should have, she advised mothers to teach their daughters to sew, cook, fix hems, and make beds, prompting Over 30 to ask her in 1974, "Where have you been these last ten years, Annie?" And the same year she said, "I prefer 'Negro,' but of course that dates me because the 'in' word is definitely 'black' "—which brought on the predictable avalanche of outraged mail.

Keeping in step with erratic times could not be easy; Ann won a few and lost a few. Although the new conservatism on campuses would not set in until the eighties, she surmised a decade earlier (one short year after the 1969 riots) that even the Ivies were getting fed up, "and it's about time." But her liberal belief in the boon of sex for everyone left her unexpectedly stranded after the nation swung back to a more conservative position. In 1981, she found herself being assaulted on the left for having said "count your blessings" to the woman who complained about her husband's sexual importuning. But in 1983, a hitherto silent majority suddenly found a loud voice to berate her because she had assumed, in responding to a couple that was tired of coupling, that God would be disappointed if we returned unused his gift of sex. She was forced to devote two columns to hostile mail that had run thirty to one against her.

Still, though her views may not always have bent quite to the speed of the times, she kept her finger remarkably close to the pulse of her concerned readers. Because of this attention to the surface of a particular problem, large outpourings of mail may sometimes have been mistaken for national opinion when they could represent no more than the interest of readers affected by the topic in question or the specifics of her prescription.

This kind of surface identification does not mean, however, that she is superficial. Granting her the immediacy of her reading, she is a remarkably skilled reader. Of considerable help to her analysis is the knowledge that whatever the writer might or might not say, the very act of writing represents an initial statement by the reader and one that will help her interpret the more explicit message.

Writing to Ann Landers is an acknowledgement of having strayed beyond generally accepted boundaries. The letter is the first step in an attempt to reenter the fold. Ann caught on to this quickly. In 1957, Blue Note writes about a widow who has taken him under her wing—and now wants to take him to Europe as well—in order to "study serious music." In the moral climate of the fifties, Ann reads around the writer's avowal, "I've had a way with women since I was 18," and the fact that he is "pretty good on the trombone" (he had a job playing in a club), to focus instead on his comment, "I'm beginning to wonder where I'll end up." Instead of seeing simple bragging (or perhaps even the wish to live a life of music and other pleasures as a couple of consenting adults), Ann reads the evidence of writing the letter as an appeal for help and a desire to strengthen a fraying moral fiber. She accordingly advises him to get the widow "out of your hair."

The following July, Iris wrote that for five years her husband foisted her onto another man, who suddenly declared his love. She writes, "I'm shocked and upset. I'm not sure whether or not I love Jack, but I don't want to mess up my life." Perhaps because she was so patently self-delusive, the fact that Iris entertained sufficient doubts to write gives more force to "I don't want to mess up my life" than to "I'm not sure whether or not I love Jack." Ann would likely have advised Iris to remain with her husband in any event, but the hesitation evidenced by Iris's writing makes it easier for Ann to dismiss facts that might legitimately have given the writer pause: "My husband suggested Jack take me to the movies, the theater and so forth. In fact he supplied the tickets and would beg off because he was tired. [Jack and I] had much in common. He liked to browse in galleries (my husband detested this) and we had fun playing badminton together."

The letter may have provided Ann Landers with a

couple of other clues to Iris's selfishness. One was the writer's attempt to pass off parenthetically what should have been an important consideration: The husband could not play badminton "because of a slight heart condition." And there was also the part about the galleries. Ann evidently noted that while Iris's businessman husband was working hard at his office ("he'd fall asleep in the chair" when he came home), Iris was busy indulging her aesthetic propensities in art galleries (a self-indulgence that may have contaminated Jack as well).

From the start, Ann was quick to spot suspicious language, allowing her for many years to exhibit phony letters sent her by Yale students. She slanted her advice accordingly. In 1956, Mrs. J.M. wrote, "My sister Doris is losing her husband to another woman but refuses to believe it after 15 years. She's failed to develop poise and charm, yet her handsome husband has retained his youthful appearance and interesting outlook. . . . Is there any way my sister can recapture her husband's love? We've never had a divorce in the family, and my parents will be very distressed." Ann read in that declaration too little sisterly support and an undue measure of admiration for the brother-in-law. She rewarded Mrs. J.M. for her efforts with, "This grave concern for your sister's marriage is as phony as a $6 bill. My guess is you can hardly wait for the situation to crack wide open."

On occasion, Ann Landers has gone to the trouble of explaining her textual analysis. In April 1957, C.D. wrote, "I'm 18 years of age but I look older. I have an uncle by marriage who is 12 or 14 years older than I am. He has expressed fondness for me and I'm certain that I love him very much. He's hinted at marriage but several people have told me it would never work. What is your opinion?" Again reading this avowal of love through the mitigation of the letter that was nevertheless written, Ann confirmed her prejudice against age difference in marriage and then addressed the problem of blood relations, which had not been raised, by explaining, "You say this man is an uncle 'by marriage.' I hope you don't mean he's your dad's brother and married. Sometimes people phrase questions in an odd way to get a desired reply."

In the letter to Mrs. Thru-the-Mill previously referred to, the writer had said, "I'm burning over the answer you gave the 16-year-old girl who found herself in serious trouble. You told her 'an unwilling groom makes a poor husband . . .' Why didn't you advise this girl to drag the bum to the preacher by the nape of the neck, if necessary? She didn't get into this trouble alone." In her answer, Ann invited the reader to join her in a little textual analysis: "If you read the letter carefully you'll recall the boy did not want to marry her. I don't recommend putting a gun to a boy's head and dragging him to a preacher 'by the nape of his neck . . .' There isn't a law in the land that can force a boy to marry a girl if he doesn't want to. Support, yes, but marriage no."

Sometimes, readers needed Ann's help to reread their own letters. Early in 1960, Alone wrote to say she felt cheesy about having buttered up the milkman for five years: "The other day he took out his billfold and when I saw the picture of his wife and four beautiful children I felt like two cents. What is a lonesome widow to do?" Ann Landers found that the letter did not support those feelings; if Alone had been friendly with the milkman for five years, "you were whooping it up long before you were a lonesome widow." Similarly, in 1970 Suffering in Suffolk details through two paragraphs the reasons why she should be happy, assumes it is her husband's romantic neglect that is making her miserable, and concludes, "On my birthday he always buys something like a vacuum sweeper, an electric coffee maker or a power lawn mower. His love making is so cut and dried I feel like a call girl. No tender kisses, no words of love—just sex." Ann responds, "The first part of your letter was, as we both know, window-dressing. Your real complaint shows up in the last two lines."

Ann also invited people to practice reading between the lines in their own lives, as when she advised Not So Peachy in 1965 to decode her boyfriend's words: "When a fellow says 'I think you should go with other fellows to see if you are as madly in love with me as you think,' he means 'I would like to go with other girls, because I'm not sure of my feelings for you.' "

Ann understands that the first clue to the meaning of the letters she gets lies in the fact that they were written and sent. Also, her belief that those who write to her do so more for confirmation than for information allows her at times to find the writer's answer inscribed in the question. In June 1960, Phony of the Year detailed the loss of his love for his wife and his entanglement with another woman. "As if I haven't suffered enough torment and guilt, last week was the crowning blow. I was elected by our church club as 'Father of the Year.' " The letter convinced Ann that she was dealing with a pillar of society; she answered, "You know what to do but you've written to me because you need someone to tell you to go ahead and do it."

In the eighties, psychological insights were current enough for Ann Landers to use them in her own analyses. In 1982, a letter from Finally Feeling Guiltless described a problem that has been claiming increasingly explicit analysis in her column during the past several years: "As a small child I was sexually abused by a family member. . . . For years this shame ate at me. With the help of a loving husband and a therapist, I have come to deal with what happened. I no longer blame myself. I blame him. . . . Now the truth has come out to a handful of family members. How shocked I was at their reaction. They felt I was overreacting to a "harmless prank." . . . As they see it, every family has a "funny" member. . . . Please make them see who is guilty in this situation." The form of the letter is very nearly standard for this kind of confession, with its upbeat references to the husband, the therapist, and the future. But the recourse to Ann Landers for approval contradicts the claims of the text and its signature. The response, therefore, was appropriately blunt: "Who told them? You? If so, why? . . . Obviously, you wanted to punish this relative for what you perceive as a terrible act. . . . I hope you will pursue this matter with your therapist and get the anger out of your system."

That letter is interesting because *abuse*, as a word and concept, represents an area of increasing awareness. Child abuse is a sensitive issue and as such was spoken of only later; but wife abuse, though yet unnamed, was already a frequent topic in the sixties. It appears to be deeply ingrained in American culture, and that depth may be gauged in part by our language. Evidence for this can be found in Ann herself, even though her stand against every form of abuse has been strong and constant. As late as 1965, in advising Zamboanga, who bragged about how she got even with her husband for his lack of consideration, Ann used a favorite expression of hers: "If it cured him, it's all right with me, but I've known wives to get a fat lip for less." Our occasionally brutal culture sometimes informs our language as well.

Within a readership of millions, a number of sophisticated readers are bound to be reading Ann's mail over her shoulder. Some of them are occasionally moved to write, especially at a time of more vocal consciousness and involvement. In 1984, XYZ gave Ann the benefit of insights derived from a raised sensitivity of and about women:

> The woman who expressed disappointment in the privileges of adulthood said a lot about herself that you didn't pick up on. . . . She described her husband as "a lot more demanding and tougher" than her parents ever were. Is that a marriage or did her husband adopt her? . . . Her final statement was most revealing: "If I were a kid again I'd be less critical about the rules my parents laid down. I'd enjoy my childhood more and not be in such a hurry to grow up." I don't mean to be unkind, but her real problem is that she never did grow up. She merely traded dependence on her parents for dependence on her husband.

Ann Landers recognized a turn in the road and responded, "Thanks for cleaning up after me. You're right. I should have told the woman that age does not automatically confer adulthood."

But Ann Landers is more likely to do her own reading and to spot a trend in the making. Moral imperatives and social customs may slow her, but she remains sensitive to change. And since her only contact with readers is through words, she is especially sensitive to the changing forms of our speech—which are one of the changing forms of our social fabric. Her column, a central feature of the family newspaper, shied away from the word *sex* (as intercourse) until 1965. Twenty years later, chosen because it was the feature most widely read and because of the accessibility of its conversational style, that same column described the details of anal intercourse in order to educate the public about AIDS. Those extremes help measure the extent to which, along with the family newspaper, the language and the mores of the country evolved during the past two decades.

The fifties, when Eppie Lederer started writing, were a time of euphemisms. In 1958, Miserable wrote in the style of the day about the man who had loved her and left her, "I'm ashamed to say it but we became intimate." This doubly demure disavowal of carnality did not prevent Miserable from missing the man "so much I could die," a condition considerably exacerbated by the fact that "he keeps phoning, but I know that he's interested only in the physical side of our relationship." Still wreathed in poesy, the practical woman in Miserable emerged at the end nevertheless: "I plan to leave this town and go home for good in two months. Shall I relieve my aching heart and see him again? I have nothing to lose, frankly speaking, so why not enjoy a few last flings?" This kind of letter, oscillating between desire for an impossible approval and the very real hesitancy that caused its writing, was calculated to awaken Ann's sarcastic propensities, and so it did. But she herself was still bound by the times to remain within a world of euphemisms: "Those few 'last flings' could fling you right into a maternity ward. . . . This relationship is neither head nor heart. It's chemical."

Of course some who were sufficiently perverse to do so were already questioning euphemisms. In 1957, Col. Inf. U.S.A. complained, "You and other writers use the word 'lady' improperly nine times out of 10. According to Webster's dictionary a lady is 'a well-bred, refined gentlewoman.' The way you use the word, any female who wears a skirt rates the distinction. . . . Should not a cultured woman feel insulted to be called a lady, judging from the way the word is bandied about?" Ann pointed out that the American College Dictionary had a more liberal definition that extended beyond its former reference to high social position. But not one to cross hostile swords with a member of the military, she conceded, "If you want to get really technical, the origin of the word lady was the 'kneader of bread'—which means there aren't any honest-to-goodness ladies left." Not much later, a rising sense of self-awareness in women would render the term completely unusable.

Even before the end of euphemisms, sex could rear its ubiquitous head. In 1958, Westchester Husband asserted that when the wife "has frequent 'headaches' or 'backaches' or is 'very tired' [the husband may resort to pornography]. I know countless sane, respectable, well-balanced guys—many of them sitting behind mahogany desks—who get a kick out of pornography." This attempt to get a dialogue started through innuendo was met head-on by Ann, without ever breaching the decorum that still prevailed: "There are plenty of 'sick' people holding down big jobs. Many a financial giant is an emotional midget. . . . The wife who has headaches, backaches, and is always 'too tired' is also sick and should see a doctor." But then the feminist in Ann rose and delivered the parting kick: "It could be that she has developed these ailments as a defense against a husband who is clumsy, or just plain ignorant."

Little by little, freer times were freeing language. *Make out* was permissible in 1962, though *sex* still wasn't quite. *Menopause* (previously known as "that time of life" or "the change") received its proper name in 1964. *Syphilis* is spelled out the following year, as is *breast*. In 1966, a young woman says explicitly that she had an abortion. *Incest, rape, gays*, and the drug language enter with the seventies. As might be expected, the writers with a cause had toppled what few bastions of linguistic propriety remained by 1975, in the manner of Mrs. M., who wrote that year, "I am amazed [by the letter of] the woman who was thinking of having her left ovary removed . . . so she could be sure of producing a baby girl." After some scornful remarks about such a surgical procedure and anyone who would consider it, Mrs. M. concluded, "I suppose now, when that dodo reads this, she will [ask] if it's all right to have her husband's left testicle cut off."

Ann took notice of this linguistic emancipation that signaled a change in the way Americans were looking at their world. In February 1979, she ran an open letter about the use of condoms and remarked that two years earlier the paper would not have allowed its printing. The following year, a woman in her sixties complained that her husband suffered from premature ejaculation.

Linguistic freedom was affecting readers of all ages; it was also affecting the kind of amusement Ann allowed herself in her replies. A year later, in June of 1981, Tired After 40 Years complained that Ann's credo about sex— "If you don't use it, you'll lose it"—was forcing her nearly impotent husband into unnecessarily heroic efforts: "I do everything I can think of to discourage him. At bedtime I find things to do, such as washing clothes. . . . But if he wakes up in the middle of the night, he won't leave me alone until we start something. More often than not, he folds up and can't finish."

Ann responded, "Sounds like a ma-and-pa laundry. . . . You are spending your evening hours at the tub and he's folding. The challenge is to bring some starch to the scene." The following year, when another tired wife told her to blow the lid on the myth of women's enjoyment of sex, Ann gave her the usual advice about the need for women to seek enjoyment, not to remain passive; but this time she added to the advice, don't "be so laid back—if you'll pardon the expression." And six months later, she answered Once Burned (who favored the proposal that women require men to acknowledge their participation before agreeing to have sex with them), "I think such a request will turn up an awful lot of men who suddenly have no lead in their pencils."

Ann's idiom, like most of her advice, has been shaped by the times and by the huge middle-American audience to whom she has addressed herself. If this sometimes irritates purists (of nearly every kind), it is a risk she is more than willing to take. The purists who urge her to use a more correct language are reminded that her speech is part of her common touch. To Aching Ears, who complained in 1983 about her awful use of the English language, she gave an answer whose typical self-assurance (and whose perhaps deliberate incorrectness) derives from her knowledge of those for whom her words are intended: "I offer no defense of my poor English except to say I was taught to write like I talk. Some people like it."

But readers still occasionally raise the question of language. As Ann's resources required her to use a more technical vocabulary (she has relied heavily, for example, on the language of therapy), she has been criticized by those who believe as she does that plain speech is a defining and fundamental virtue. Early in 1975, Tired of Double Talk catches her using "high-brow esoteric language": "[When] asked if masturbation was harmful you replied, 'If it becomes obsessive and compulsive it can border on the pathological and, therefore, be harmful.' " Ann apologized, "I must have gotten carried away."

Four months later, she falls in with For Telling It Like It Is, who sought her endorsement of a campaign for plain speech. The letter was in fact another example of the American love of, and concomitant resistance to, euphemisms: "Instead of saying Johnny 'doesn't get along with the other kids,' the teacher writes a note to the effect that 'Johnny does not relate well with his peer group.' . . . Parents don't want to hear that their children are 'lazy,' but they don't mind being told they are 'underachievers.' Another evasion of reality is calling deviant sex behavior 'an alternate lifestyle.' "

Middle America's ambivalence toward its speech reflects the ambivalence of a culture that remains conservative even as it changes. At a time of accelerated and deep change, that culture is sometimes unable to identify the extent of its alteration. Ann Landers is occasionally caught in the bind of these conflicting tendencies. In 1981, Fort Stockton wrote,

> You told Riverside, Calif., who wrote about strange behavior at weddings, "As far as I'm concerned, people can do whatever they want, and I'm keeping my mouth shut." . . . People pretty much do what they want anyway, but when a reader asks Ann Landers for advice, she should give it. . . . Not everyone is "with it." Social amenities are usually learned from one's parents. Unfortunately, not all parents are informed. This is why so many people look to you for guidance.

Ann's answer reflected the dilemma of someone forced to identify mainstream trends while still not losing those who haven't: "Your point is well taken—but a great many readers were quick to let me know that I have no right to inflict my traditional views on people who choose to do things differently. After some soul-searching (and a few thousand letters), I decided a wedding was a private affair, and the ones who were paying the bill had a right to do as they please."

Towards the end of 1983, Ann Landers reminisced:

> My very first editor, back in 1955, was Larry
> Fanning (rest his beautiful soul)—a patient
> mentor and a marvelous teacher. He told me,
> "You can deal with any subject so long as you use
> the right words—with one caveat: Never take
> your readers into the bathroom."
>
> Twenty-five years later I departed from his
> advice and printed a letter from a woman who
> was having an argument with her cousin. Should
> the toilet paper be hung so that it goes OVER the
> roll and hangs down in front—or should it go in
> the opposite direction and hang close to the
> wall?
>
> When I received more than 15,000 letters
> from readers with opinions, I knew it was an OK
> subject.

Like so many others, the teachings of editors, however
wise, were going to change during the third of a century
following Larry Fanning's admonition. If Ann was able to
find her way into the bathrooms (and beyond other
hitherto closed doors) of her readers' worlds, it was
because she usually knew at any given moment what
doors could now be opened. She got that sense from her
readers. They were the ones who told her about the ways
in which our private (and sometimes public) worlds
were changing, about the dangers of those worlds and
their opportunities, about the parts that were to be
avoided, and about the safe and proper ways to traverse
the others. And curiously, the readers informed her in
order that she might let them know. She was the author-
itative communicator of values, whose voice remained
conservative (and therefore as trustworthy as it was
familiar), even as it spoke about new values that might
well contradict some that had been upheld previously.

2
The Faltering
Institution: Marriage

At the time Eppie Lederer, then the wife of Jules Lederer, began writing the Ann Landers column, she appeared to be enjoying a solid marriage. Many others found their marriages less satisfactory and were terminating them in numbers sufficient to indicate that the institution was less solid than it had once been. Still, the fifties were a time of relative stability: About one divorce occurred for every four marriages, and that ratio remained fairly constant through the midsixties.

By 1971, the ratio had worsened to a fraction over one divorce to three marriages. On one of the numerous occasions when Ann was compelled to address what she knew to be a less and less satisfactory state of affairs, she commented, "Two principal reasons for marriage failures are boredom and nagging." Although she did not identify the partner most likely to be bored, she placed the blame for nagging squarely on women: "Repeated nagging can sour the best marriage in the world. It's like being nibbled to death by a duck. If a wife is going to chew at her husband it should be over something . . . important."

That castigation voiced her sense that women were the

ones primarily responsible for keeping a marriage together. She seemed to believe that men's derelictions were mainly premarital. Presumably, men were temperamentally less likely to enter into such a solemn bond; once they did, their willingness represented a greater commitment that exempted them from certain blames.

Ann may have gotten that sense from her readers. The war years had seen marriages in record numbers; in 1946, they reached a high of 16.4 per thousand population. But by 1954, they had dropped to the lowest point since the midthirties (9.2 per thousand), and some readers, women especially, were beginning to be obsessed with the thought of marriage. In 1957, Miss Rip Van Winkle wrote, "How does a girl get off a 'sister kick' and get a guy to be romantic? I've known this sailor since January, 1955, and he's as sweet as molasses but I'm getting nowhere with him. . . . He has no girl friend and is as unattached as I am. How do I attach him? Please help. This is a rush job. I'm getting frantic." The letter was meant to be breezy and amusing, but Ann had read a sufficient number of similar ones to know that the ironic "frantic" hid a real concern. Accordingly, her own irony did not disguise the seriousness of her response. Noting the writer's age, she advised, "Explain that your hair is turning gray and your brow is becoming furrowed. After all, you are 20, and this is practically the wax-works set. Keep it light and airy, but get your point across."

Until the midsixties, Ann wanted all the Miss Rip Van Winkles to get married once they were truly ready. She shared with the great majority of her readership the conviction that marriage and the traditional family were the most important unit of the social structure. In fact, she maintained for many years a nearly Catholic conviction about the indissoluble integrity of marriage, for the sake of which even serious sacrifice had to be contemplated. (It may or may not be a coincidence that Father Hesburgh of Notre Dame became one of her most trusted advisers on such interpersonal problems.) Ann viewed matrimony as a solemn engagement—one that required maturity above all else. Gallons of Coffee wrote in 1966, "Andy and I are both 22. I look like 40 and I feel like 90. . . . I have been pregnant four times in the past four years." Ann's harsh response combined her dislike of those who don't consider marriage seriously with her feeling that women bear primary responsibility for making marriage work: "According to my arithmetic you grabbed the bargain when he was 18 years old. No wonder you are having trouble. He wasn't ready to settle down—and he still isn't. (Are you listening, students?)"

The message seemed clear: It was up to the woman not to force a yet immature male, and an unwilling one, into marriage. And Ann's parenthetical aside to students extended the warning. The turbulent end of the decade was fast approaching, and teen marriages were on the rise. They reflected a transitional moment between a conventional morality the teens were bending to their purpose and a freedom greater than any ever granted but not yet fully realized.

Responsibility in marriage thus depended on maturity and the ability to avoid hasty decisions based on the deceptions of "chemistry." However, for the mature, marriage was strongly advised. Girlfriends of hesitant partners in relationships of some duration were repeatedly told to issue ultimatums: Fish or cut bait. Moreover, it was never too late to contemplate entering upon such a fine institution; in fact, until the midsixties, Ann seemed to feel that marriage was a preferable choice for nearly everyone. In 1955, Puzzled wrote that, because he was in his forties, "My friends and co-workers insist I am crazy to start looking for a wife at my age. What do you think? Is it a hopeless cause?" Ann replied, "A good man your age is hard to find," and advised him merely to be sure to "get the right girl." And because women were the ones on whom the institution's burden rested, they were especially urged to settle into matrimony. The day following Puzzled's letter, Two Contented Career Girls wrote in to say that at thirteen they had entered into a pact not to marry and "at 24, we still have no intentions of marrying. (Not that we haven't had the chance)." Ann was utterly skeptical: "Write me again when you are 35 and still batching it. . . . Good gracious, can this be real life?"

Early the following year, there is a letter signed Perplexed (at the time, signatures seem to be a frequent indication of the extent to which the prospect of marriage genuinely befuddles the writers): "I'm in my late 40's and going with a man in his 50's. We've been dating 10 years and are free to marry since his children are grown and so are mine. My problem is he never mentions marriage. When I bring it up, he brushes it off with a very funny remark. Am I being a fool?"

Why did Perplexed fear being a fool? It is true that in the fifties only marriage could sanction the act of living with a man. But Perplexed did not seem to fear going against public morality by her failure to observe the ritual as much as she feared shortchanging *herself* through such an act of dereliction. Besides this sense of being short-changed, Perplexed stated no complaint. One assumes, therefore, that other aspects of her relationship were good. (After all, she *did* wish to marry the man.) But for Ann, at this time, the relationship on any terms but marriage was unsatisfactory practically by definition: "Learn what he has in mind for the future. If he insists on being a comedian, tell him to find a new audience and you should start to look for a new gentleman friend." Since Perplexed already had a "gentleman friend," one assumes that Ann meant a prospective husband.

Perplexed spoke about "dating." Whether or not the word was intended as a masking euphemism, it directed the question toward social issues. When the question was openly sexual, the fact of being an adult conferred no privileges on those involved. At twenty-three, Miss Jones was told by her thirty-year-old boyfriend, "A normal man can stand only so much and your stubbornness is getting too hard on my blood pressure." Ann answered, "These 'normal men' who propose anything but marriage should be given the bum's rush"—an answer that most likely confirmed Miss Jones's reason for writing. In the glimmering of the sixties, those who proposed to make less traditional plans were too far ahead of their times for Ann Landers, as Grown Up discovered in 1960 for having written, "We want to enter into marriage with a tacit agreement that if it doesn't work, we'll shake hands, meet in a lawyer's office and dissolve the marriage like civilized adults." Ann countered, "The mature approach is not to holler uncle and run for the exit at the first sign of trouble. Any coward can do that"—emboldened perhaps by the knowledge that if Grown Up had really lived up to his alias, he would not have written her. She reiterated the conviction on which her advice still rested: "Marriage is a promise before God and man that two people will cherish and love each other until death separates them."

In those days, Ann was willing to have her readers walk that extra mile for the sake of marriage. In February 1956, she told Lonesome to try again with the wife he divorced nine years earlier—even though "she dropped [their baby], banged his head on things 'accidentally' and [was] married and divorced twice" during their separation. The following year, Celia was told to walk an even more difficult mile: For ten years, her husband had been having an affair with a married woman. When she confronted the woman's husband, she discovered he knew already about his wife's infidelity but "had decided to do nothing because [of] their four children." Moved by such selflessness, Celia fell in love with him, and her own three children liked him too—in fact "better than their own dad." Everything seemed to conspire to ensure a logical and happy outcome, but for a single hitch: Celia's husband wanted to come back. Celia was accordingly admonished by Ann, "Wipe the slate clean and try to make something of your marriage."

Those were the days when bachelors wrote in periodically to twit Ann Landers about a conviction that might well have seemed less than logical to them (after all, a substantial portion of her mail derived from unhappiness caused by marriage). Those were likewise the days when Ann unfailingly lashed back at them with sustained gusto—and sometimes even with a certain amount of animus. When, in 1956, Single, Solvent and Smiling suggested that she pass on to her troubled readers the "magic formula" of bachelorhood, Ann matched his alliterations with a vengeance: "The young man who today congratulates himself on being single, solvent and smiling may wake up tomorrow to find he has been selfish, smug and stupid."

In those early days, Ann Landers felt that much of the wisdom necessary for a successful marriage was a function of age. While it was all right to marry at nearly any (older) age, marrying someone who was younger by more than a few years could present serious problems. In the fifties, it was mainly the older man who was discouraged from marrying the younger woman. (A typical answer was the one to Puzzled who wanted to marry his younger secretary: "Don't feel you are 'too old for her.' The trouble is she is 'too young for you.' ")

But the more interesting cases were those in which younger men wished to wed women who were their seniors. In 1956, a forty-year-old Harlan, who felt he had "developed a beautiful friendship with a magnificent lady in her late fifties," asked Ann for her opinion about such a marriage. Ann may have read a hesitation in the fact that Harlan bothered to ask in the first place; however that may be, she combined firmness with facetiousness: "Since you speak four languages fluently, I'll give it to you so you can't miss. Elle est trop vieille pour vous. . . . Es demasiado vieja para usted. . . . Sie ist zu alt fur sie. In plain English, Harlan, she's too old for you." But when a *woman* asked the same question (even though the age disparity might be less), facetiousness was likely to disappear. In 1955, Mrs. K, thirty and divorced, asked about the nineteen-year-old she had met at work. Ann's answer was peremptory: "He was born 10 years too late for you. Come down to earth."

At the time she was starting to write the column, Ann Landers identified what she considered to be another one of marriage's potential jeopardies—religious differences. In 1956, Dorothy wrote about her parents' opposition to her boyfriend because "he's of a different religion." Dorothy was twenty and had been dating the boy for five months: "We are very much in love. He earns a good living and is extremely considerate." Were it not for the fact that the letter was written at all, an act that Ann could always read as a sign of hesitancy, it would have appeared that the young people were more mature than her recalcitrant parents. But Ann answered with the kind of firmness she would maintain for many years: "A marriage has a better chance to succeed when both partners have similar backgrounds. This means educational, cultural, race, color and—most important of all—religion."

This is one of the tenets Ann hung on to with surprising tenacity, in defiance of views that would start changing in the sixties, perhaps because of the religious disaffection of more rebellious times. When Yiddisher Papa wrote a decade later (December 1964) about the successful marriage of his son who converted from Judaism to Catholicism for the sake of his wife, Ann was moved by the letter's tone of brotherly love only to the extent of prefacing her opposition with a partial concession: "While we have encountered exceptions, most interfaith marriages do not work out well." And a few months later, she said to Eunice, "I am opposed to interfaith dating. . . . Dating has been known to lead to marriage. And even marriages that have everything going for them are fairly risky these days. I advise teen-agers to stick to their own, because the records prove that marriages between individuals of the same religious background stand the best chance of survival."

So strongly and enduringly rooted was Ann's opinion

on the subject of planting a marriage in the same cultural soil that it occasionally skewed her reading, even in recent times. In 1980, Sick in Sunnyvale complained that their daughter, who had been dating "a fine young man," suddenly threw him overboard for a Lebanese—to the parents' obvious disgust. ("This guy looks like the Turk in the Camel cigarette ads. He gives me the creeps and none of our friends can stand him.") This kind of bigoted letter, deriving its prejudice from the milieu in which it was spawned, normally would have drawn Ann Landers's ire. But in this case, she had absolutely nothing to say about the parents' racism. Her answer merely referred to the headstrong ways of the young, noting, "Each generation must learn by walking in their own moccasins" (which just happen to be quintessentially American shoes).

Central to Ann's advice about marriage are her assumptions about male and female roles. In 1957, as previously described, Ann discouraged Celia from leaving her unfaithful husband for another man 'who looked better to her' when her husband decided to come back into the picture. This was at a time when Ann felt that keeping the marriage together was of paramount importance, that the responsibility for preserving it rested primarily with the woman, and that the one to be catered to as part of the effort was the man. This is not to say that the man was granted special status by virtue of his masculinity but rather because of his childishness within the bosom of a nearly national matriarchy. In 1956, The Bride complained about a husband who "never picks up after himself." Ann told The Bride to pick up after him and asked, "Didn't you know that a woman's first child is her husband?" Even in the delicate matter of religion, Ann was pretty sure of the woman's sway. Stymied, who said in 1955, "I am serious about my religion," but could not get her unaffiliated boyfriend to embrace it, was told confidently, "The odds are good that one day he'll choose yours."

Ann's anti-intellectual suspicions, which never allowed her to suffer gladly the highbrow, made her quick to spot the woman who might be lording it over her lowbrow husband. In 1956, Mrs. G.K. deplored the fact that her "husband is a slob . . . and his manners are atrocious." Granting that the tone of the letter was less than self-effacing (and that writers with a feeling of superiority should have a Groucho-like wisdom that would avoid any columnist whose confirmation they might be tempted to seek), Mrs. G.K. aggravated her case by adding, "I'm a college graduate and he didn't even finish high school, yet he disagrees with me on matters about which I know a great deal more. When I tell him he's ignorant and uninformed, he just yawns." Ann shot back: "Don't deny the poor fellow the privilege of yawning. It's probably the only chance he gets to open his mouth."

The self-indulgence of men was allowed a fairly wide scope in those days. When P.M. wrote in 1956 that her seventy-five-year-old husband was "such a flirt I can't trust him out of my sight" and asked Ann for suggestions, she was told "I suggest you congratulate the old boy." The dismissal is reminiscent of the one Ann repeated over the years to women who complained about their husbands' wandering eyes: "When he stops looking at others, he'll stop looking at you."

The Ann Landers of the fifties seemed to accept, for example, that most males suffered from an extended Oedipal fixation. Insulted Wife, her husband, and another couple went to a movie in 1957 whose "heroine was a buxom siren who had an abundance of everything. . . . The men started a long-winded discussion of the female in the picture and then began to compare their wives. . . . My husband said, and I quote, 'When a guy sees that Sophia Loren on the screen he wants to go home and throw rocks at his wife.' " Ann did not perceive anything worse in that crudeness than an attempt to be funny: "Laugh at the bum jokes (smart wives have been doing this for years) and let it go at that. It takes more than super dimensions to make a marriage work."

Even when men went beyond looking, it was still up to the woman to take charge. V.L.S. outlined her husband's misdeeds that same year: He "talks in his sleep. He mentions girls by their full names and speaks in clear, distinct tones. . . . I've found long blond hairs on my husband's suit, and I'm a brunette. He often comes home with lipstick on his collar and says a girl fell against him in the bus. I can't keep him in handkerchiefs because he throws so many away." Ann responded, "It's safe to assume you have some real live competition somewhere. The next time he gives out with the nocturnal orations, listen carefully for hints and how YOU can be his dream girl—and get in there and pitch."

But if a mere romantic wistfulness descended on the other sex, the woman was told in no uncertain terms that such daydreaming was not for her. At the same time as V.L.S.'s husband was either fantasizing or actually philandering, Mrs. F. was confiding in Ann that her mind kept going "back to the sweetheart I knew before marriage." Ann wasted few words on her: "Lift yourself out of this fantasy. . . . Your lovely family should be enough to keep life interesting."

In Ann's view, the sanctity of the family unit required the wife to achieve a remarkably tolerant understanding of her childish mate. In December 1955, D.V.S.'s husband confessed that he was in love with an eighteen-year-old. (D.V.S. was twenty-eight and her husband was thirty.) Ann told her, "Your husband is an adolescent fool. . . . The girl obviously is chasing him—and that's pretty flattering for the father of three! Try a little flattery yourself." The following month, Sad Wife said she felt like going home to her mother because she discovered her husband had been unfaithful during her confinement. Ann admitted, "Your husband rates zero for his miserable behavior." But having commiserated, she went on, "What is to be gained by harboring resentment and shedding tears? . . . To be able to forgive is a great virtue." Sad Wife was told, "Handle this in an adult way."

Husbands' escapades were supposed to be little more

than that—the act of breaking loose from a structure that the male was not mature enough to sustain. There were all kinds of ways to bring him back. In her first column, Ann Landers confronted Troubled Wife, who had been married four years and was expecting her third child while her husband was "chasing around town with women." Troubled Wife was told to go with her errant mate to a marriage counselor to "see if, together, you can't find out what's wrong with your marriage."

In January of the following year, Sad (equally depressed, but not the same person as Sad Wife) discovered that the mileage on the family car indicated her husband was logging twenty miles a week instead of the mile he claimed to be going to town. Against what might have been legitimate suspicion, Ann counseled trust: "Keep the bloodhounds off his trail." Two months later it was J.J. who discovered that her husband was flying around the country without her, but with another woman. For her pains, J.J. was the beneficiary of one of Ann's favorite dicta: "Didn't your mother ever tell you that 'husbands and fires go out when unattended?' "

Other wifely complaints of the fifties appeared to have equally simple solutions. Reader's husband "after a few beers [would] pour out his troubles to anyone." The answer: "Give the poor fellow your ear, which is probably what he needs most." Three months later, it's Snowman's Wife who "never shows any sign of affection." The answer: "Continue to be warm and affectionate and in time he may respond." In January 1957, Disgusted Wife tells of her husband who spends all his money "on his friends." The answer: "Try to build up his ego and make home a pleasant place to be." Seven months later, Deserted feels she deserves the pen name: "Almost every evening, if we're sitting around, he'll say, 'I'm going over to Mickey's [the husband's bachelor friend who lived across the street] for a few minutes.' Then he leaves and spends two hours there." Ann answered, "Make things more interesting on your side of the street."

But there were women who felt somehow dissatisfied

and unfulfilled even though their husbands had none of the vices (regularly listed nearly verbatim) that seemed to define the worst sinners for Middle America's wives: "He doesn't drink, gamble or run around and he brings home his paycheck regularly." Details of the advice varied but typically stressed reaffirmation of original bonds. For example, in 1962 the advice to Daphne was: "You [two] were married . . . for some reason. What was it?" The repetitiveness of the advice matched the repetition of the complaint.

The man was the breadwinner in the traditional family, and during the postwar years, a man's hard work at his job was still one of the American virtues. Time at work was thought to strengthen the family rather than undermine it. Worried Wife's husband was a workaholic in 1956: "He gets up in the middle of the night to write notes and smoke cigarettes. He's only 42 and too young to die." Either Ann's aversion to nicotine was not yet as pronounced as it would be one day, or her belief in the work ethic overrode her dislike of cigarettes. It certainly overrode her sense that when a man came home in the evening, the door he closed was supposed to shut out his job. She assured Worried Wife, "Stop worrying—he's not dying, he's LIVING!" The woman's place was with her man, and the man's place was with his job. M.A. wrote in 1956, "My baby is the only grandchild and my parents get so much pleasure from him. My husband wants me to move 2,000 miles away." This presented no problem for Ann: "Your place is with your husband even if it means taking the baby 10,000 miles away from your parents." The possibility of a discussion was not even suggested.

But during the war years, women had discovered that they too had a place in the job market. As the euphoria of postwar reunions and economic health began to subside, the job market began once again to tempt married women. *This* Ann saw as jeopardy to the home. Under optimal conditions, the married woman was not expected to work—even if her decision went against the desires of her husband. In 1956, Ann Landers told J.Y.,

"I'm with you. If you prefer to stay at home, he has no right to ask you to go to work." As times changed, women like J.Y. would be less able, and eventually less willing, to stay home.

Between 1955, when the consumer price index actually dropped by a fraction of a percentage point over the previous year, and 1974, when after steady increases it recorded double-digit inflation, Middle America began experiencing what would be the inescapable realization of the midseventies: The good economic times of the war and postwar years were at an end. By 1978, New Orleans Reader was writing about "two sweet little old ladies who are fighting inflation and inadequate social security by a little petty larceny and shoplifting." In July 1982, Ann had to eat "a double order of crow" for having said that it was "tacky" to order one dinner in a restaurant and then split it. "Hundreds of irate readers" persuaded her she was wrong, and she turned over her column to the letters of those who said that the present state of the economy allowed few luxuries and no waste. In November 1983, she acknowledged that the problem of jobs had "gotten to be a nightmare."

But in the midfifties, when Ann began writing, circumstances still favored J.Y., who preferred not to work. At the time, Mrs. B.J.F. had a husband in the service who did not appear to be particularly desirable: "Every month when I get his allotment check I have to send back at least half of it so he can pay fines for getting drunk. . . . He's begged me to quit my job and come down and work near his base but I'm making good money and living in an ideal place." Ann said, "Quit your job, no matter how good it is—and join your husband which is where you belong." It is not inconceivable that Mrs. B.J.F. was being selfish, and that her husband was drinking their finances away as a result. But it is worth noting that in cases like hers, where two readings of the situation were possible, the ideal of the family unit dictated the answer.

Through the fifties, the wife's job was essentially the home—her husband and her children. Just as Mrs. F. had been told that her family should be enough to keep life more interesting than any romantic daydream, the family was supposed to interest a woman more than any job outside the home. In January 1956, Mrs. B.R. had written that she and her husband "quarrel the whole time and have nothing in common." Her description sounded like the accumulation of a year and a half of boredom since marriage. A job for Mrs. B.R. might have been a possible solution, but the Ann of those days had other ideas: "You are dying of boredom. . . . Make life interesting. Ever hear of children?"

Like the abstract ideal of the home, the abstract ideal of children was absolute. In fact, it was also boundless. Three months after Mrs. B.R.'s complaints, Crazy Mixed-Up Daddy gasped, "My wife and I have been married 10 years and . . . we've been blessed (?) with eight children. . . . I work two jobs. . . . I haven't been to a baseball game in two years. There's no extra money for anything. . . . My wife insists on more children. Her mother had 13 and she's determined to beat her. . . . I wanted to call the last one 'Quits' but she named him Robert, and said, 'There'll be more!' " Ann cheerfully disregarded Daddy's objections and said, "If she's willing to have the babies and raise them, you shouldn't complain about bringing home the bacon." As we have seen, Ann expected the wife who was a victim to come out from under and take charge of her home. But if she was in charge already, she grew into a force that brooked no resistance: "Throw in the sponge, Daddy: you've had it. If your wife is determined to outdo her mother she'll have 14 if it kills you."

Such had been the fifties, but for many they were receding rapidly, and along with them, whole worlds of values and beliefs. During the war, even with the need for women in the work force, a Gallup poll had found that 55 percent of all married men were unwilling to have their wives take a full-time job. But by the midsixties, more men favored having their wives working than did not: 40 percent for, and 34 percent against. But when women were asked the question, nearly half were for women working, and a scant 20 percent opposed it. Even accepting that a deteriorating economy accounted for a good part of the change in men's attitudes, the figures appear to show that the majority of women were now able to envisage themselves managing at least materially without the support of men. And the relation between a job and a woman's independence was becoming apparent in letters to Ann Landers.

In 1965, Dixie, who was "32, unmarried and . . . with no particular desire to rush into a fifth-rate marriage," wanted a "squelcher" for people who asked her why she wasn't married. Ann obliged with, "I'm not married because I haven't met the man who deserves to be as happy as I can make him." That one preserved the woman's ability to center the matrimonial structure, but it also allowed questioners to be squelched—and with Ann Landers's blessing. Dixie had written, "I'm what some people call a career girl. Others might call me an old maid." The distinction may not yet have been altogether clear, but what was clear was the fact that things were changing.

Dixie's letter resonated among readers sensitive to an issue that concerned more and more of them. Two months after it appeared, Career Girl (a signature intended to stress the point) answered:

> Here's a word to Dixie. . . . I am also 32, single and amazed that so many clods have the guts to ask such a personal question.
>
> In my mid-20's it dawned on me that I might never meet a man I wanted to marry, so I began to plan for my future. I started at the bottom in this organization and I've worked my way up to an executive position.
>
> What gets me is that so many rockheads are concerned about my love life. "What do you do for a man?" they inquire solicitously. "It's not normal." (Can you imagine such crust?)

And Career Girl swept right past Ann in her conclusion: "So, Dixie, when the slobs ask you why you aren't married, look 'em in the eye and say, 'Just lucky, I guess.' " This was 1965, and Ann had learned the new tune. She confined herself to a two-line answer: "I like your spirit, Toots. I've said it before, and I'll say it again: Marriage is not for everyone." If she had said it before, it had neither been for very long nor very loud. But she was going to receive many occasions to say it again.

In 1970, and again in 1977, an international survey asked about changing perceptions of marriage. American respondents were asked whether they preferred, among others, the present form of marriage, marriage with greater extramarital freedom, or free union. In 1970, 69 percent favored the present form of marriage, while 13 percent favored greater extramarital freedom, and a mere 7 percent liked the idea of free union. Seven years later, most people still preferred the present form of marriage but their number had dropped to 57 percent (an identical 11 percent now favored extramarital freedom and free union). Americans were not ready for an alternative lifestyle in marriage, but only a little over half of them thought that marriage as they knew it represented the best kind of arrangement.

One of the indications of the changes affecting the institution of marriage after the midsixties is reflected in the changing status of the "Other Woman." This threatening shadow that was always in danger of falling across the sanctified bond is dismissed throughout the fifties. As previously noted, infidelity was usually little more than evidence of the man's immaturity—an occasion for the woman to roll up her sleeves (or whatever) and, according to Ann's expression, "start pitching in."

In 1960, the Other Woman was still considerably ahead of Ann. When Normal Nellie wrote, "For once in your life give some practical advice and don't be so doggone stuffy"—what she wanted from Ann was permission to give the married man she was seeing the down payment for a car. ("He's given me far more than 800 dollars worth of happiness.") What Normal Nellie got instead was a stuffy answer: "Love on the lend-lease plan is not love. It isn't even a reasonable facsimile, particularly when you are negotiating with a married man. . . . My old-fashioned, moth-eaten (and stuffy) advice is to quit trying to justify your immoral behavior by telling yourself you're normal."

But it was now only a matter of time before the Other Woman would stop asking Ann for approval, and the simple imputation of abnormality would no longer be sufficient. The Other Woman was starting to find a voice, and it was becoming an argumentative one that called for counter-argument. Two years after Normal Nellie's letter, enough others had changed the shadow into a reality, evoking an acerbic reaction from Spy Glass to yet another correspondent: "The letter from the Bronxville female presented a fairly solid case for 'The Other Woman.' One of her principal virtues, she boasted, was a keen appreciation for life and the good things it has to offer. . . . I would like to inquire why a woman with so much on the ball would settle for a married man. Surely [she] would be a highly desirable candidate for marriage. Why is she content with a back-alley relationship?" By this time, it was becoming both fashionable and necessary for Ann to delve deeper in the psychology textbooks: "Women who become involved with married men are frequently self-destructive, martyr types. Any gal who finds herself in this spot more than once should face up to this possibility."

Ann's answer yielded considerable ground; it seemed to countenance, at least through indirection, that a woman might not be rushed to judgment for having been *once* "in this spot." And in allowing herself to be engaged in a discussion about a problem once deemed to be transcendable, Ann Landers was investing it with glimmers of a hitherto unheard of legitimacy. Even the public contrition of repentant Other Women fueled spec-

ulation about a subject that formerly had not been
favored with much analysis. In 1970, Horse's Mouth
detailed the plight of those who "dare not be seen in
public. . . . If it's a trip to Europe, the wife goes. If there's
a fur coat, the wife gets it. Christmas, New Year's and
Thanksgiving are reserved for the wife." At the same time
this recital of misery was serving a moral warning, it was
helping delineate the reality of the once invisible Other
Woman.

Horse's Mouth thought she had simply been a fool
("another part of the [horse's] anatomy would be more
appropriate"). Tears in the Pillow broadcast the same
message a few months later ("It's a lousy life and a lonely
one. The road is a rough one and it leads nowhere"). But
her misery did not cancel her love: "Today is my birthday.
I'm alone. My love just phoned to say his wife is ill and he
can't leave her. This isn't the first time he has canceled
plans at the last minute. Of course, there's nothing I can
say or do. My evenings are spent sitting by the phone.
Sometimes it rings. Sometimes it doesn't. I'm afraid to
leave the apartment for fear he'll call and I'll miss him. I
hesitate to invite friends over because he might drop by
when someone is here." The Other Woman was acquiring
not only visibility, she was acquiring dimension as well.

And as if that weren't bad enough, the Other Woman
was also becoming aggressive. The following year, Patience had the nerve to warn The Wife to shape up
because "I know quality when I see it—and lady, he's got
it." This time the battle was joined; in 1972, Ann Landers
told her readers she had received "thousands of superb
letters from women who offered to reply to Patience"—
which demonstrated that by now the Other Woman had
become a recognized participant in the debate.

By an interesting extension, some of the errant men
were also granted a voice. In 1975, Happy at Last was
allowed to write, "As a man who has walked in those
moccasins, I can tell her The Other Woman didn't steal
my affections. My wife lost them and The Other Woman

found them." And Ann's answer showed the extent to which she too was changing: "Your story is one I've heard hundreds of times. But the one I've heard THOUSANDS of times is from the wife whose husband is too tired, too busy or not in the mood." And then she allowed herself this philosophical afterthought: "Too bad there's no way to reshuffle the deck so everybody could be happy." Of course, by 1975, there was nearly one divorce for every two marriages. And on July 1 of that year, Ann herself had been divorced.

What had once been a mere sign of immaturity, a bad joke, was now a problem that required sensitivity and understanding: Even the Other Woman could afford such tact. In 1976, Brown Eyes wrote, "I am eager to marry this beautiful man but I don't want people to think I broke up his marriage. My reputation is important to me and I need to protect it." And through the back door, Ann herself was grudgingly enticed into giving advice: "If the marriage is dead and you don't want people to think you killed it, don't hang around the corpse. Ask George to call you when he's free."

By the 1980s, the Other Woman was quite likely to be as matter-of-fact about her status as she might be about any other part of her existence. A Savvy Other Woman even drew up a number of rules, in order that the married man and his mistress might "both benefit" from the relation: Don't lie about family obligations. Don't insult her intelligence by giving her false encouragement about the future. Be kind and generous. Don't tell her your wife has no interest in sex. And don't be a fool: "The Smart Other Woman sees other men. . . . The scene is more crowded than you think." The scene was not only more crowded, it was evidently also far more open and casual. And Ann Landers, who had by now swallowed most of that unpalatable mouthful, merely commented, "Your sign-off was quite a blockbuster, lady. Thanks for a lively contribution to this space."

A Savvy Other Woman's temperament and articulate-ness suggest that she most likely had means and education. The fact that she sent the code to Ann Landers indicates a change in the column's respondents—a change in the way a number of women were beginning to view marriage and themselves. Four days later, the entire column was taken up with letters by Other Women. Alone on Christmas Eve noted, "If we met by chance, under different circumstances, we would both be friends. I am a lot like you. And after all, he fell in love with both of us—and we both love him." And Ann conceded: "What an eloquent spokeswoman for heaven knows how many! Thanks for writing."

In 1950, about two-thirds of all females between the ages of twenty and twenty-four had been married. By 1960, that figure had climbed to over 70 percent. Since then, it has been declining steadily. By 1984, it had fallen to 43.1 percent. And where most women once considered being thirty and single to be a point of no return, in 1984 less than two-thirds felt there was a point just under the wire at which a woman avoided spinsterhood. Young women were less eager for the bonds of matrimony than they once had been. Greater possibilities in the job market, relaxation of sexual mores, and a more assured sense of self are likely among the primary causes of this new outlook.

In the eighties, people shifted their attention from the ways in which a marriage might be patched up and kept together to questions about the institution itself. In February 1980, Sinking Fast in Georgia asked, "Is marriage all that important, Ann?" Ann read in the question that marriage was what Sinking really wanted, and advised her accordingly on the kind of strategy that would bring it about. But even if Sinking already knew what she wanted, the question was genuine for increasing numbers of other women.

The fairytale notion that marriage and love were necessarily linked could now give way to a more realistic, if somewhat sadder, analysis. In 1982, Wish It Could Have Been for Me wrote:

I was divorced at 23, widowed at 48 and am now married again to a fine man. I have been in love and I have been loved, but never have I been loved by the man I was in love with.

I settled for home and family, security and companionship because there was nothing else. Love just never worked out for me. I know what I have and I am satisfied. I also know how much more I might have had if love had existed on both sides at the same time.

To love and be loved is the richest of all blessings. Deep down I will always feel I missed out on the most magical experience of human-kind.

Ann allowed that the letter writer was, by now, far from being the only one of her kind: "I wonder how many married people (men as well as women) will see themselves in my column today? Millions, you can be sure." The romantic daydream that had been forbidden in the fifties was now permissible in its modern form—the sober speculation about what might have been.

There were other signs that Ann had come to view marriage as a less rigid and, perhaps as a result, less permanent structure. Age differences that had been so taboo when Ann was new in the job remained that way through the sixties. But in 1971, she began to refine her objection. In response to Younger than Springtime (a divorced grandmother who wanted to remarry a man ten years her junior), Ann specified, "If you are 68 and Mr. Wonderful is 58, the light is green. If you are 39 and he is 29—better take a detour."

But Ann was getting more and more mail from those who didn't see age as a limitation, and she was starting to take heed. By 1973, she told Love My Neighbor (the neighbor was twenty and dating a widower with grown children), "Did she ask for your opinion? If not, keep quiet. . . . Maybe in 10 or 15 years he will still be lusty and SHE'LL have lumbago." A year later, the whole question of May-December marriages was buried for good under what Ann called "an unexpected avalanche of letters from women" who thought they should be allowed to mate with any man of their choice—even, as in the case of An Exception, one twice their age.

Children, once the absolutely compelling reason to enter into marriage or to keep the marriage together, became in the seventies an argument more relative than relevant. The biggest shocker of all came in 1976—one that would still be drawing comments in the next decade. Ann Landers decided to take a poll: "Parenthood—if you had a choice, would you do it again?" She expected the results would provide hope for the doubting Thomases— the increasing number of those who thought that having children in the wake of the sixties was a serious mistake and—heresy of heresies—the ones who thought that having a child under any circumstances was not worth the trouble. Ann was caught off base on this one as she had never been before. The outpouring of mail was huge, and 70 percent of the respondents indicated they were sorry they had become parents.

For years, Ann tried to reinterpret the results of her survey, but by the end of 1980 she accepted the verdict. Suspicious in Palo Alto had written, "Bring up your survey again. . . . I ask you, Ann, when did you survey this 70 percent? When the children were babies? One year old? Six years old? Teen-agers? College graduates? Or after they had children of their own?" Ann replied, "That 70 percent represented parents from every group you mentioned. The majority of 'No' responses came from (1) young parents with babies and (2) parents of teen-agers."

In retrospect, one might wonder whether Ann Landers wasn't more correct in her intuitions than she herself allowed. It is quite possible that most people still felt about family life as she did—that she was hearing from an admittedly large segment of her readership, but still a minority. Attempting a first explanation of the shocking results in 1976, she said to Among the 70 Percent Who Are Sorry, "I believe the logical explanation for this phenomenon is (a) the hurt, angry and disenchanted tend to write more readily than the contented, and (b) people tell me things they wouldn't dare tell anyone else."

That first guess sounds right. In the case of a privately troubling question like this one, Ann Landers does not conduct a representative poll but serves as a conduit for the discharge of emotions that may be difficult to express otherwise. In such cases, even though readers might respond in large numbers, a distinction must be made between the unaffected majority of her readers and the fraction that is moved by specific grievance to write.

Although there is no absolute equivalence, one might mention a somewhat different response at about the same time. In 1975, the American Institute of Public Opinion (Gallup) asked women what they would consider to be the ideal life from a list of possibilities: to be married and to have children, to be married but without children, to be unmarried. The greatest number by far— about three-quarters—answered that the ideal life included marriage and children; only 9 percent chose "married without children," and 9 percent chose "unmarried." Since the sample was not otherwise specified, one assumes that a representative portion of the majority was not simply anticipating family life but had already experienced it. (In 1980, four years after Ann Landers's survey, that poll found the majority choice was still the same and had dropped by only 2 percent.)

Another poll, taken by Yankelovich, Skelly and White in 1975 from an unspecified sample, showed that 80 percent of those surveyed felt a happy family life was most important for them (as opposed to the 13 percent who chose the opportunity to develop as an individual, the 7 percent who chose a fulfilling career, and the 4 percent who chose making a lot of money). Two years after Ann Landers's survey, the majority opinion remained the same, though it had dropped to 74 percent. *

---

* *Connie De Boer, "Marriage: A Decaying Institution?"* Public Opinion Quarterly, *Summer 1981, pp. 265–75.*

However one might choose to interpret those figures, there is little doubt that the image of the child-centered family was less compelling than it once had been. A long-term decline in the number of married couples with children was clearly evident by the mideighties. In 1985, there were more married couples without children than with them. Aware of this change, psychologists, who now had a statistical warrant to say so, started allowing that a child might be better off in the peace of a broken home than amid the warfare of an unhappy one. Living together (which Ann continued to resist) did not require children. Adult companionship was no longer equated automatically with the need for a family. Toward the end of the seventies, vasectomies were an accepted topic for Ann Landers, while, at the same time, she expressed her strong advocacy of family planning.

Conversely, some women were starting to think that even the pleasure of having children did not necessarily require them to pay the price of marriage. In 1955, unmarried women accounted for 4.5 percent of all births. By 1982, that figure more than quadrupled (19.4 percent). Much of that increase reflected changes in sexual mores and in the attitudes of youth. But considering the more widespread acceptance of contraception during those years, the figures seem to indicate that fewer women who wanted children necessarily wanted all the rest of the family as once defined by marriage.

Once questioned, marriage could no longer remain the stable ground upon which wives, husbands, and children had once defined themselves. If wives and husbands could no longer find as much of their definition in marriage as they had previously, it was in fact because many of them no longer wished to. But the consequences of these changes affected the ways in which people felt about each other and about roles that had helped define those feelings. As a result, the social weave of American society was being altered.

3
Divorce:
The Last Resort

The year after the conclusion of World War II saw the crest of what had been a steady and ultimately a dramatic rise in the number of this country's divorces. That figure, which had stood at around a quarter of a million pre-war went beyond six hundred thousand in 1946. The following year, the numbers dropped as dramatically to approximately what they were in the last year of the war (just under half a million). As people settled into their post-war lives, the figures remained fairly constant until the late fifties, when the rise began again. From 1963, the rise is annual and steady, topping a million in 1975 (only a small fraction of which is attributable to population increase: Between 1955, when Eppie begins writing, and 1963, the portion represented by population growth equals 47 percent; for the period between 1963 and 1975, that portion declined to 12 percent).

Liberalized laws reflecting a looser attitude toward marriage were enacted and contributed in turn to a further increase in divorces. In 1967, New York added to adultery (until then the sole legal ground for divorce) cruelty, desertion, and two years of separation. After that, the number of divorces granted in New York grew nearly eight times between 1967 and 1975. Subsequently, the trend appears to be irreversible, at least in the long run. In 1981, the number of divorces hits its peak: one hundred thousand couples a month split. Thereafter, there was a slow, three-year decline, but in 1985 the figures began climbing again at an accelerated rate.

Much of the Ann Landers column in the fifties was taken up with marital problems. Ann and a substantial portion of her readers seemed to share a basic assumption: However seriously a marriage might deteriorate, it could remain fixable. That is why so many of the matrimonial questions during those early years are of the how-to kind. Ann even coined an answering phrase, "This is a strictly do-it-yourself project." Over the years, the institution changed, and so did readers' perceptions of it. Although large numbers still want to know about the possibilities of specific marital patchwork, many others have been losing faith in the possibility of patchwork or have moved to a greater, more philosophical distance from the institution.

Increasingly, questions address the "why" of matrimonial dilemmas rather than how to resolve them. Starting in the midsixties, there is a steady decrease in the number of letters asking for marital remedy. Readers became less ready to seek help for a faltering marriage. Today's unsatisfactory marriage is twice as likely to be scrapped as when Ann first began writing.

Still, even the 1955 figure of one divorce for every four marriages suggests considerable use of a drastic solution to matrimonial difficulties. Divorce was never far from the minds of many of Ann's readers during all the years she was writing, although, for a very long time, she refused to look at it as an acceptable answer to nearly any kind of matrimonial wreckage. But, as with marriage, divorce was being modified. And neither least nor last among these changing viewpoints was Ann's own.

Considering marriage to be indissoluble meant that for

even the least promising of matrimonial attempts, couples should try just about any remedy short of divorce. Until the seventies, that was precisely the nature of Ann Landers's advice. During her first month at the column, she received a letter from F.B., a man of forty-six who had been married nineteen years. He said, "My wife claims I go out with other women but this is not true. I can't afford them. I may have a 'visit' over a cocktail or a beer but this isn't 'going out.' I have seen my wife in cars with other men at 6 and 7 in the morning but she tells me these men were OK'd by the bartenders so she thinks she is doing no wrong. Last week she told me she didn't love me any more and wants a divorce. Shall I give it to her or what?" Ann responded against what looked like heavy odds, "Divorce is no solution for a pair of rounders like you." She advised, "Try to rekindle the old spark."

The following month, Desperate wrote, "Mine is a good husband, and a good father to the children, which is the one reason I hesitate to seek a separation or divorce. But too late I find we have nothing in common. His routine (no friends, no hobbies, doesn't like to read or hold intelligent conversation) is just not making me happy." This was a dangerous discourse to attempt on the Ann Landers of those early days. Here was a good family man found to be lacking by a woman who sounded rather self-indulgent and, what was worse, intellectually so. Ann's indignation caused her to overlook the part of Desperate's letter that also said, "I was engaged to another man before I married my husband in blind infatuation, but this other man whom I love is not my reason for thinking of divorce. To me, divorce is a dreadful thing."

Ann might have detected in those words the temptation of a former love, a hypothesis worth addressing since it would have undercut the claim of intellectual incompatibility. Instead, she merely responded with scorn, "What do you mean, you have nothing in common? If children are not the most precious and vital thing any

married couple has in common, I leave it to you to tell me
what is. (Books? Hobbies? Intelligent conversation?) If
your husband (obviously for the sake of the children) is
willing to live with a woman as full of self-pity and
martyrdom as you are, you are luckier than you deserve."

Having repositioned the slighted man on the pedestal
from which Ann thought he had been unjustly toppled
(in her eyes, *he* was obviously the martyr staying on "for
the sake of the children"), she then dismissed the intellectual grievance without further thought, as if anyone
who was married could possibly be "Desperate" for want
of intelligent conversation or a good book to share. She
slammed shut the door that Desperate had tentatively
opened: "Stick to your job as wife and mother and find
out what marriage is all about."

Ann's steadfastness in refusing to countenance divorce
when she was starting out in her job is evidence of the
constant presence of those who felt that divorce was a
reasonable alternative to certain kinds of marriage. Sometimes, the arguments for divorce arose from what seemed
like compelling situations. In April 1957, The Widow
wrote:

> The manner in which I messed up three lives
> is proof of how wrong your advice in triangle
> affairs can be. My husband and I were married
> for 30 years. . . . For the last 10 years we had
> separate bedrooms and drifted apart. One day,
> out of the blue, he asked for a divorce, saying he
> was in love with another woman. I refused,
> thinking he'd get over it. . . . This went on for six
> years. Four months ago he became ill and died.
> The doctor said he had no will to live . . . He
> loved her, Ann. I look back now and realize if it
> weren't for my blind stubbornness at least two
> people might have been very happy.

Ann flatly refused to think that divorce might have
averted the tragedy: "Quit beating yourself over the head

because you refused to turn your husband over to another woman after 24 years of marriage." True to the views she held at the time, Ann placed the blame for what had happened where she usually did—on the woman's failure to keep the matrimonial bond as tight as it should have been: "The real mistake was resigning yourself to 'separate bedrooms' and 'drifting apart.' "

Those of her readers who allowed divorce to enter their lives nevertheless, and who found themselves subsequently having to turn to her for help or solace, could count on little sympathy. Early in 1960, L.A. wrote that she wasn't speaking to her husband that morning because, her entreaties notwithstanding, he had gone the night before to his former household in order to assist his daughter whose drunken mother had met with an accident. Ann's response was typical of the gruff handling such letter writers could expect: "When you married a divorced man you bought the total package. In answer to your question—yes, you do have to put up with it forever. This woman is no longer his wife, but she's the mother of his children and nothing will change that. These are rough lines for you, and you must learn to live with them." The Ann of the fifties and sixties thought that instead of curing marital woes, divorce was likely to become a source of subsequent infection. Until the following decade, she remained convinced that the radiant energy of marriage could endure long after the marriage itself had been extinguished.

Ann was never able to dispel completely her feelings about the centrality of marriage. Even as late as 1981, when Ann could commiserate with the second wife whose husband was a victim of unfair divorce courts, she could not forbear going back to an old pun of hers that still retained some of its harshness: "I am assuming that you are 'The Other Woman,' in which case this is known as the high cost of leaving."

But in the fifties and sixties, she had not yet reached that level of detachment. The persistence of marriage after divorce that seemed so evident to Ann Landers in its interpersonal consequences, was apparent in broader social consequences as well. Name Problems wrote in 1965, "I am getting a divorce from a miserable heel, and I'd like my maiden name back. I don't want anything around to remind me of the man who brought me so much agony." Those were the days when Ann believed· that the woman remained subordinate to the family, whether or not she divorced: "Even if you don't want anything around to remind you of the heel, you're going to have two constant reminders—Johnny and Susie. Children deserve to have a mother with a Mrs. in front of her name. Unload your anger in some other way and keep your husband's name for the children's sake." Ten years later, the emblem for the erosion of that idea would be the erosion of the very designation "Mrs."

Name Problems still belonged to the generation that wrote for approval, and this sign of timidity might have contributed to the starch in Ann Landers's answer. But in the fifties, more than starch informed the answer to similar questions about the protocol of divorce. Polly wrote in 1957, "I want both my parents to attend [my wedding] and I'd particularly like to have my dad give me in marriage. He has agreed, but is hinting strongly that he expects his present wife to be invited to the ceremony. My mother says if this woman is invited, she will not attend." Ann's answer was more interesting for its language than its predictability: "If your father's new wife is a woman of judgment she wouldn't attend the wedding even if she were invited. Your dad should do whatever is in his power to make it a pleasant and memorable day for you. This includes leaving the second Mrs. Zilch at home if she happens to be a clod who hasn't sense enough to stay away." The aura of a marriage that had been terminated three years ago, as had Polly's parents', was still strong enough to reduce one of the present marriage partners to a "zilch."

During the first fifteen years of Ann's column, marriage

derived its strength from an acceptance of social conventions that were still widespread. In 1961, Newark Newt tried to speculate on the disparity in the legal handling of male and female victims of divorce: "I just read the column about the GI who came home from overseas and found his wife six months pregnant. I liked the way you praised him for forgiving her. Now, let's turn the tables. If a wife catches her husband at such shenanigans, she can haul him into court, take him for all he's worth, obligate him forever and make him support the kids until they're of legal age. . . . A husband can't sue for alimony no matter how much in the wrong the wife may be."

Newark Newt's point was, "Before you walk down that aisle, see a lawyer." While this had nothing to do with changing the law in order to allow men to claim support in divorce courts, Ann chose to misread the letter just enough to reaffirm her belief in the conventional family structure, with its attendant responsibilities and privileges: "The traditional role of a husband in our society is to support his wife and family. I do not agree that a caught wife should have to pay alimony."

As we have seen, even a fairly horrendous situation was unlikely to move the early Ann Landers to advise divorce. If she was able to read doubt in the mind of the complainant, Ann would routinely advise, "Ask yourself whether you are better off with him or without him"—but "without him" did not mean divorce. If the situation was clearly dreadful, Ann would specify that "without him" meant separation.

As late as 1965, Half and Half provided Ann with a case in point by telling her about her ex who was tiring of the ubiquitous Other Woman, allowing tender feelings once again to bloom between them: "It sounds crazy I know, but I still love him and I would remarry him in a minute if he asked." Ann's answer is worth quoting in full: "Welcome to the club. Another foolish wife who handed a divorce to her husband just because he asked for it. If you had agreed to a separation and insisted that Ted live elsewhere he probably would have crawled back on all fours. Now you are living with a divorced man who didn't want a divorce at all. Tell Ted to move out and come back only if he wants to live in a respectable, legal manner. And this means marriage."

Ann spelled out her position time and again. In 1957, she did so for Woman of Experience: "You are as wrong as you can be, madame. If you can produce a single column in which I suggested divorce I will buy you a new hat. Separation and divorce are not the same. Buy new glasses." Once divorce was clearly understood to be out of the question, separation (if you were sure it was that) could even be put to tactical use, as Half and Half had been advised. Similarly, Married to a Boy told Ann that were it not for the children, she would have ended her ten-year marriage to her immature husband because he could never hang on to a job and allowed his mother to bail them out. In this letter, the sacredness of the work ethic collided squarely with the sacredness of the marriage vows. Ann advised Married to a Boy to tell her husband that she had self-respect "even if he hasn't. Refuse flatly to live on his mother's hand-outs. Invite him to go to work and stay at it or move out. Then insist on child-support. I'm not suggesting a divorce, but a separation may grow him up."

However, alongside the swingers and others yearning for freedom through divorce, Ann Landers had to reckon with conservative readers as well—and the most carefully spelled-out distinction between separation and divorce was never sufficient to allay the suspicions of those who thought they were able to smell sulfur even on the high ground where Ann believed she was guarding virtue and traditional morality. The following month, A Four-Year Observer told her, "You frequently say in your column that a married woman need not put up with a man she no longer cares for. . . . In other words, you encourage divorce as the easy way out." This forced Ann to up the ante: "If you can show me a single column that

I wrote which advocates divorce I will buy you a new car. (Your choice.)" For the Ann Landers of the fifties and sixties, separation was the middle way between those who were indeed seeing divorce as "the easy way out" in increasing numbers, and those who simply refused to recognize the economic, social, and educational pressures accelerating change during a time of transition.

Signs of that transition could be read in letters like those of Newark Newt or of KO'd, who had written five years before him, "Since you're such a 'crusader,' Landers, why not plug for a change in the divorce laws?" (For this he had been rewarded with one of the earliest forms of "Alimony is the high cost of leaving, Buster.")

There may have been hints of a coming change even in Ann Landers during the midsixties; in January 1965, Ben Thar confessed, "My wife became involved with another man. What she really wanted was more attention from me. But I was too busy. Instead of dealing with the problem intelligently, I decided to get even with her by chasing a young girl. . . . So, who's sorry now? My ex-wife, my three children, the young girl I married and most of all me, because it's all my fault."

There was something different in the tone and language of Ann's answer: "Your fault? Not 100 percent. Your wife should not have handed you a divorce so fast. A trial separation would have made much more sense." A part of the answer conforms to previous ones—the burden of responsibility for keeping the family together is still on the woman's shoulders, and she must therefore not agree to anything more than separation. But what is new is the word *trial*, as if, for the first time, separation might be envisaged as more than a tactical ploy or a kind of respectable limbo—as if one of its outcomes might be divorce.

It is true that the answer to Ben Thar could be read two ways. The justification for reading a change in Ann's tone is suggested by other answers. Earlier that year, she had written in response to No Name, "There is a vast difference between being separated and being divorced. A divorced person, of course, is free to enjoy a social life which includes dates. . . . A separated person, however, is still married, and married people should not become 'emotionally involved' with members of the opposite sex." Not only did the answer forbear excoriating divorce, but its moral affirmation was mitigated by a new acceptance: "If such an involvement does occur, it is best if the children are not aware of it."

Pressure on Ann Landers to change her point of view was evident daily in the letters of those who had already done so. Criticism of automatic divorce judgments was now coming from children and fathers, as well as from second wives. A typical letter was written in 1962: "The letter from the 13-year-old girl who missed her divorced dad could have been written by my own daughter. . . . You are right, Ann, the children are the big losers in a divorce. For the second biggest losers I'd like to nominate the fathers." At this point, Ann was still more intent on the objectionable fact of divorce than on the thrust of the letter: "The amazing thing about the divorce game is that so many people are losers yet it becomes increasingly popular." But she was learning every day.

Ann learned, for example, that statistics evidenced at least one benefit of divorce, which she passed on with muted enthusiasm to Dim View at the end of 1963: "When both parties have been once divorced, the chances for a successful marriage are slightly better than two rookies." But, she hastened to add, "A two-time loser, however, has a lesser chance for a successful marriage." Still, by April 1970, she was willing to concede to Trapped in Georgia, "The divorce laws in some states . . . are grossly unfair to husbands."

Two months later, her response to Ph.D. SOS at last unlocked the door hiding that skeleton. He had written, "When will you stop kidding your readers and tell them that basic human problems are insoluble? At best, one can only learn to live with them." He then went on to explain his signature. He had a Ph.D. and married a woman "who barely made it out of high school." (Remember that the writer of this kind of letter to Ann Landers might be asking for a sharp retort.) But he went on to detail the consequences of his unsatisfactory relationship: "three major illnesses (emotionally created) and finally major surgery to correct internal bleeding." This led him to ask for divorce; she refused. He then proceeded to destroy most of Ann Landers's safety valves: "Don't tell me to consult a marriage counselor, psychiatrist or minister. I have already done so."

Ph.D. SOS may have removed the possibility of psychiatric therapy from Ann Landers's answer, but by this time she had begun analyzing such letters. "A man who has had three emotionally created illnesses and an ulcer operation and remains under the same roof with a woman he gives as the cause for his illness needs to examine his need for punishment. She could not have done all this without your cooperation." And she allowed at least contemplation of what was hitherto not to be contemplated: "Perhaps she can make it difficult for you to get a divorce, but she cannot force you to live with her."

Three months later, Garden City brought to Ann's attention the existence of a group called O.W.L. (Other Women Ltd.): "The purpose of this group is to rehabilitate ex-wives. They help the 'Alimony Junkie' shape up instead of sitting around watching TV, drinking martinis, overeating, and making life miserable for her former husband. . . . The O.W.L. are not against child support. They insist that a father has a moral obligation to take care of his children until they are of legal age. . . . They claim it is unfair for an ex-wife to sit on her backside and collect alimony to 'get even with the louse.' " Asked to express her view, Ann gave the group a grudging endorsement, "The goals of the group, as outlined in your letter, make sense for some ex-wives, but not for all. An exception is the woman who, after 25 or 30 years, gets dumped for a younger model. . . . Ditto the ex-wife who is in poor health, or the discarded mate of a rich man— especially if she helped him get rich." But Ann also allowed, "I do agree that a childless divorcee who puts in fewer than five years should not be allowed to hug the alimony Teddy Bear for the rest of her natural life." It was not much of a concession, but the existence of such a group and the fact that Ann Landers had given it visibility in her column were evidence of changing times.

In 1972, the Reverend Barcley Brown took note of Ann's changing views: "I was sorry to hear you say on your NBC radio show that you've changed your views on divorce. Granted, divorce no longer bears the stigma it once did, but such logic could be extended to other wrongs and brutalities. . . . 'What God has joined together let no man put asunder' is a moral precept to which we are still answerable." Ann responded,

> Thank you for your good letter. I am sorry you and I are having a serious disagreement in principle, but the world is changing and those who refuse to reassess the issues will be sadly out of tune with the times.
>
> I no longer believe that marriage means forever no matter how lousy it is—or "for the sake of the children." I see too many people who had a rotten first marriage and are truly happy with a second husband or wife.
>
> Our basic disagreement (yours and mine) lies in the interpretation of "what God has joined together." If God made the selections, it would be simple. But unfortunately, the selections are made by humans. And humans make mistakes.

Five years earlier, Ann would have considered her own argument to be specious; she would have disallowed it, as she had disallowed the similar arguments of others, by pointing out that errors should be righted, not evaded— and that divorce was an evasion rather than a righting. But by the early seventies, the argument had run its futile course, and Ann Landers was no longer willing to be "out of tune with the times." Three years later, when Eye of the Cyclone asked her, "If divorce isn't the biggest 'copout,' what is? Why should the young be taught to run away from, instead of living up to, what may be the greatest emotional challenge of all," she responded with an equanimity born of the kind of distance she had never allowed. "No outsider is qualified to judge the true character of someone else's marriage," she wrote, going on to say that even "[children's] lives might be far more difficult if they continued to live in a home with parents who abused each other verbally and physically and hated each other."

As a matter of fact, children were becoming articulate witnesses for divorce. I Understand, aged twelve, wrote in March 1974, "This might not be nice to say, but I'm glad my folks got a divorce. When Dad was home, he and Mom fought all the time and it made us kids very nervous. Mom had headaches and Dad had ulcers. Now they both feel fine and treat each other like friends instead of enemies. Us kids feel better too." And the following year, Better for It asked, "Why is it that because a child has divorced parents he is referred to as a 'victim' for the rest of his life? I am one of those so-called victims and I don't feel victimized at all. . . . Would it have been better if my parents had stayed together under false pretenses? Many of my friends' parents fight constantly, cheat on each other right out in the open and live phony lives to 'protect the children.' " Ann concurred, "especially after having seen some of those children whose parents stayed together 'for their sake.' "

Once the possibility of divorce was entertained, all interpersonal relations had to be reexamined in the light of that possibility. Ann proceeded to do so, though with caution and circumspection. In September 1973, Climbing the Walls in Southern California disclosed that her thirty-year-old husband "has absolutely no interest in sex—and I mean none whatsoever," even though he was "successful, considerate and generous with hugs and

kisses on the cheek." The new, hip Ann Landers considered all the possibilities: a psychological problem;
another woman; another man; a physical problem. All of
those being ruled out, and if no counseling were possible, she was prepared to allow Climbing the Walls to
divorce in order to start a new life (even a sexual one) of
a kind previously denied (see Chapter 2): "You must
decide whether or not, at the age of 28, you are willing to
settle for affectionate hugs and kisses on the cheek."

Ann's reference to "another man" pointed to another
reason why, in the craziness of the times, trying to
preserve even once-sacred structures was proving to be
increasingly difficult. By the midseventies, homosexuality, like divorce itself, was an acknowledged fact of adult
life and contributing to the destabilization of matrimonial attempts. Women with experiences similar to that of
Alone a Lot were starting to ask whether bisexuality was
grounds for divorce: Used in Appleton responded, "Tell
her yes, it is. I obtained a divorce a year ago from a
bisexual, and it is considered the same as adultery. . . . It's
a rotten thing to do to a woman." By this time, Ann could
acknowledge the prescription without comment: "Here's
your letter and I hope it helps. I agree—it is a rotten thing
to do to a woman."

In 1956, Worried Wife, whose workaholic husband
took his job home, had been told by Ann *not* to worry:
"He's not dying, he's LIVING!" In the days before divorce,
the breadwinner did not necessarily have to be a nurtur-
ing presence as well; roles were simpler, more defining,
and submission to them was an ethical assertion. Divorce,
weakening the matrimonial structure, allowed the sort of
questioning that traditional roles had inhibited. In October 1975, R.L. asked Ann Landers to publish two letters
she had written to her husband at an interval of fifteen
years. Ann acquiesced, and in so doing reversed the
position she had taken in answer to Worried Wife:

August 1, 1960
Dear Jack: For what seems like the millionth

time, I walked into the house tonight and you are not here. You aren't out fooling around. You are at work on the night shift.

I never wanted you to take that shift and we argued about it. You thought it was well worth the extra money. I told you I didn't care about the money, that I'd rather have a normal family life. But I lost the battle. . . . I realize you are doing what you think is best for me and the children, but you're wrong. Will you please reconsider? I love you.

Your wife

1975
Dear Jack: When the judge said "Divorce granted," you vaguely resembled a man I used to know—but you looked about 40 years older. There is no point in going into the whys and wherefores, but I wonder now, if you could have gazed into a crystal ball and seen what the future held, would you have done things differently?

Our children view you as a stranger. You missed out on all the fun when they were growing up. . . . So now our marriage is over and we must both make new lives for ourselves. If it had been another woman I would have felt better.

Your Ex-Wife

Ann Landers's acceptance of the letters, and of this kind of marital difficulty, was informed by the same, sad wisdom: "Here are both your letters. I print them for the value they might have to others who may be struggling with the same problem. Thanks for sharing your sad story. Perhaps someone, somewhere, will learn from it."

That particular problem was no longer caused by exclusively masculine derelictions. In 1980, A Concerned Mother blasted her own daughter who "wouldn't think of spending an evening bowling with her husband, but she is out night after night attending business meetings or working late to impress her boss." She felt, "if young couples would put half the effort into making their marriages work as they do their careers, the divorce lawyers would have to close up shop." Ann, the career woman par excellence, agreed with Concerned Mother's conclusion, contenting herself with a small caveat: "The gung-ho, super-achieving male more often is guilty of neglecting his family than the female. I'd say the ratio is 50 to 1."

However dramatically times had changed since the days of Worried Wife, they were going to change still more. In 1985, answering Suffering from Culture Shock in Colorado (a woman who had been unable to get either her own mother or her husband's to help out when her child was born), Ann summarized recent American history and took it beyond the times of Concerned Mother:

> The nuclear family began to fall apart when Rosie the Riveter went to work in the defense plant to replace the men who had gone to war. She liked the money and the independence. She also found it stimulating and chose to keep on working. Women decided they wanted to become executives, physicians, lawyers, architects, truck drivers, police officers and fire fighters. . . . They began to sell real estate, get divorced, sit on commercial boards and run for public office.
>
> Lifestyles have changed. . . . We are paying a big price for the demise of the nuclear family. Long-cherished values are becoming a rarity because no one is at home to teach them. Fifty percent of the work force is female. Two-paycheck families are the rule rather than the exception. The altered status of women and the high cost of living have changed everything.

Ann's advice had once been, "Decide if you are better off with him or without him." The woman who was asked to make that decision either had to accept life on the unhappy terms that had prompted her to write for guidance, or, if she was unwilling to do so, she had to continue somehow the same existence with only the excision of the unsatisfactory husband. The advice that Ann now gave sounded similar but had a different thrust: "If you can't learn to live with him, then learn to live without him" (this to someone consulting a marriage counselor and who signed herself Intent to Make a Go of It—Regardless).

"Living without him" was the postdivorce version of "being without him." But where "being" anticipated only continuance with no fundamental change, "living" meant just what it said—remaining alive, determining one's own course of action, pursuing a positive, satisfying existence. In 1974, to Wilted Rose, who was dissatisfied with a divorce that would give her merely a 50-50 split of everything, Ann answered, "please remember, while you are doing your arithmetic, that freedom from a loveless marriage is worth plenty—and I am not talking about money."

In keeping with the new legitimacy of divorce, divorce laws and practices were coming under increasingly critical scrutiny. The Newark Newts were now legion. In 1980, In the Know in Greenville told Ann that her reply to Uncertain in Brandon, Manitoba, "was the pits. You clobbered the man because he wanted a premarital agreement stating there would be no settlement or alimony in case of a divorce. . . . I have been divorced twice and was picked clean both times. Most of the time, the court will award her everything of value and make the man pay her attorney's fee." Ann conceded, "Some men do get picked clean, and if it happened to you twice I can understand your attitude. Until recently women had a big advantage in the divorce courts but the pendulum has begun to swing in the other direction."

Men had begun voicing their grievances. At the end of 1983, Skunked in Illinois voiced the belief that those paying child support "should have some evidence that the money is spent on the kids, and not on the ex-wife's back." Ann agreed, "I believe they are entitled to see the receipts for the merchandise that was supposedly purchased for the children."

What the acceptance of divorce appears to have done is to allow a more rational scrutiny of the problems attendant on the break-up of marriage. The man who had been cast, more or less automatically, in the role of a culprit whose rights were forfeited, could now expect to receive in the courts (and certainly in Ann Landers's column) a more analytic examination of his particular circumstances.

In turn, this allowed attention to shift to the purpose and implementation of laws for divorce and child support. In 1980, Discouraged in Virginia Beach, Virginia, voiced that discouragement: "I heard of URESA (Uniform Reciprocal Enforcement of Support Act) in July and petitioned for child support that was due in May. Every time I tried to learn the status of the legal proceedings I was given a different response. . . . Frankly, I've lost faith in the judicial system."

The very fact that URESA had been passed meant that the issue of divorce had now claimed the attention of people at the governmental level. Over and above that official attention was the articulate and combative attitude of a great many others who felt that the law was not working well enough. What had once been a moral issue was now a legal battle. Ann responded to Discouraged, "Your name is legion. If you don't believe me you should see my mail. I am sending all these complaints to the man in Washington who painted a rosy picture of how the government tracks down slow-pay (or NO-pay) husbands who have run out on their children. I will be just as interested as you in his response."

The prevailing acceptance of divorce received its ultimate confirmation once it had begun affecting social customs. It even became a topic for the questions of etiquette that periodically surface in Ann Landers's column. In 1982, Win, Place and Show offered the following puzzle: "I am John's third wife and I need to know what is proper under the circumstances. John's daughter (by his first wife) is getting married in the spring. [She] has asked her father to give her away. [Her] mother (wife No. 1) will also be attending. [The Daughter] has asked her father's second wife (wife No. 2) to be her matron of honor. My question is about the seating arrangements for the dinner."

Ann addressed the problem philosophically, but with mathematical precision: "People ask me if my mail has changed in the last 26 years. Your letter is an excellent example of one of the major changes. Wife No. 2 (the matron of honor) should be seated with the wedding party, next to the best man. You, wife No. 3, should sit with the guests. If wife No. 1 or wife No. 2 has remarried, you could sit with one of the husbands or between the two."

Where once the Mrs. Zilches of this world had been consigned to the Siberia of unsanctified ground, there now existed new and elaborate rules of decorum for their inclusion. And when in 1984 Trouble in the Family wrote to Ann to ask how her sister should handle wedding invitations complicated by a divorce and two remarriages (Trouble's own wedding "was a disaster"), Ann responded, "Your sister has the right to invite whoever she pleases." She added, "If your sister wishes to include her father's second wife, she should feel free to do so."

On July 1, 1975, Ann announced through her column the news of her own divorce, one day shy of what would have been her thirty-sixth anniversary. "That we are going our separate ways is one of life's strangest ironies. How did it happen that something so good for so long didn't last forever? The lady with all the answers does not know the answer to this one."

These were the midseventies, and the abstract idea of divorce, with its instant villains and victims, was starting to fade, allowing divorce to become more real—a painful

human experience, and one that was perhaps less suscep-
tible to the solace of blame or the balm of recrimination.
Thirty thousand readers wrote to express their sympathy.

And Ann Landers continued to be the expert on
interpersonal problems with a readership that would
soon reach eighty-five million.

4
Our Children: Innocents Lost

In 1946, Dr. Benjamin Spock published *The Common Sense Book of Baby and Child Care*. It was to become the bible of child rearing for middle-class parents of the postwar years. Spock considered the child as an individual, one deserving the same respect presumably owed to his or her parents. Given a culture apt to assume that a book of instruction can furnish the correct formula for success (and ready to believe that if the book is widely accepted the formula must be normative), it was inevitable that Spock's definition of respect—an attentiveness born of affection—would evolve into something more like polite consideration. At first, the child so distanced was seen above all else as fragile and easily scarred. Later, that child appeared to be a curious and alienated entity. Eventually, it would become someone the parents found incomprehensible and even hostile.

Dr. Spock believed that if a child was found in a potentially dangerous situation, such as climbing a tree, it was better to chance that child's breaking an arm than to chance breaking his or her spirit by putting a stop to the activity. After reading Dr. Spock in such large

81

numbers and with such deference, few self-conscious parents were ready to risk damaging their children's spirit.

In 1955, when Esther Pauline Lederer became Ann Landers, the Spock gospel had been around for less than ten years. Although many had been converted already, there remained substantial pockets of people who were unaware that the familiar boundaries of child rearing were being eliminated. Changes were occurring at a pace that would soon leave them out of step with the times, bereft of standards once thought to be immutable. Eventually, others might view their ideas as obsolete (and sometimes even pernicious) parts of the cultural landscape.

The voices of both the old-fashioned disciplinarians and the proponents of new and looser times are heard in the early columns of Ann Landers. Eventually the voice of the first group becomes progressively more bewildered and less assertive (at least until the late seventies). As this occurs, new voices emerge: young people whose relationships, rituals, and problems are less innocent, harder to deal with, and more dangerous. The young climb up perilous trees from which many parents fear removing them.

But first come the fifties. As reflected in Ann Landers's letters, the teens of those days are already centerstage— in fact, her earliest columns are largely theirs—but the teens writing to her then seem surprisingly different from their counterparts in the next decade. In the fifties, most of their dilemmas derive from the problems of dating and young love. Although the graver note of unwanted pregnancies is heard with fair regularity, it is neither the main melody, nor is that melody yet affected by it.

The number of teens writing to Ann Landers is noteworthy for several reasons. First, it reflects their trust in her (she and they frequently think of her as their spokeswoman). Second, it reflects their trust in an authority figure. Their writing is prima facie evidence of the possibility that they will listen, a fact that Ann has always been able to take into account (but perhaps never as consistently as in the fifties and with this age group). Lastly, it reflects their belief that, however desperate they sign or see themselves, they assume there is a way out of their dilemma.

A lot of the early problems are of the boy-meets-girl variety, couched in the quaint language and euphemisms of the times. During Ann's first month at her desk, M.B., fourteen, got interested in her "best girl friend's steady. Now she is heartbroken and I find I don't care for the boy. . . . Please tell me what to do." That was two days after Mixed-up Gal, eighteen, who had "gone steady for three years," discovered after returning from vacation that *her* "best friend" was "going around with" her "steady." Negotiation evidently got her nowhere: "They just laughed and said I was a foolish kid carrying a torch."

Ann Landers countered such dime-store distress with common-sense tactics. To Sincerely Yours, she advised, if "he wants to date others, [you] do some looking around yourself." To Mixed-up (evidently a fairly common state of mind in such situations), she writes, "Why be 'mad' if he dates your girl friend? . . . The minute he detects signs of jealousy and insecurity he'll head for the exit." To Hopeless, who had her eye on her best friend's guy after the couple split up, she writes, "If you value the gal's friendship, don't hop in before the body's cold. Give the deceased romance time for a decent burial."

The advice was to be played out according to traditional roles: Too Old (age fourteen) was told that her thirteen-year-old boyfriend was not necessarily too young for her, "but don't be smarter than he is! Men cannot forgive this!"

Those roles and rituals could even provide insights into the metaphysics of dating and high school love: "He likes you if he's taking you out. If he goes on taking you out, if eventually you are the only one he dates, if one day he even asks you to wear his class ring or pin, it's probably love."

Sometimes, these metaphysics extended into larger areas, such as those involving the realities of the job market or of parental authority. In 1955, Undecided (a high school senior) was told that she should indeed postpone marriage for three years in order to "grab off that nurse's training now . . . one of the most rewarding fields a woman can go into." (Nurses' complaints twenty years later muted that particular paean.) Teen-age girls in clusters would write, "I am 15, have been going with a boy 21, and have been getting really serious about him"; "I am 16, in love with a boy 17, and know that it is not just kid love"; "I am 17. . . . I like one of the boys and I am sure he likes me." Most of them wrote in order to tell of their parents' disapproval, to ask what they should do, and, presumably, to get the answer they expected: "Your mom and dad love you and want what is best in their mature judgment."

The stories of puppy love did not last into the sixties, but provide insights into the kinds of letters that would follow. To return for a moment to M.B.'s letter: "I am 14, attractive and two months ago got interested in my best girl friend's steady. He is 17 and was crazy about her, but I got him anyway." Like all the letters quoted so far, this one came from a young girl—as did indeed the bulk of such letters in the fifties (in a column that has been fed over the years by a fairly even distribution of male and female correspondents, according to Ann Landers—an estimate she has repeated on more than one occasion). In the fifties, women felt themselves to be nubile earlier than men and appear to have been far more active in attempting to tie down a marital partner. A good part of this activity was due undoubtedly to social pressures. Marriage was the approved channel for the sexual energies of women (see Chapter 2).

Ever since the very first columns, an intriguing aggressiveness was evident in many young girls. In December

1955, Old Maids to Be wrote, "We are a group of 14-year-old girls looking for a group of 14-year-old boys or better yet, 16 or 17. We've looked high and low, but all the boys are taken. Please help us trap some fellows—we're desperate." It is perhaps of peripheral interest to note that the collective parting shot and signature, for all their irony, may have betrayed some of the anxiety women in the fifties felt about being able to hook a mate in time. One might note also that Ann demurred only slightly: "Fourteen is a bit too young for 'trapping' fellows. I'd say open season on males is at least a year off." But strategic advice followed nevertheless, "Get rid of that lean and hungry look and don't travel in packs."

The fact that Old Maids preferred older teens seems to indicate that sexual intent or bravado was not exempt from their quest. In 1960, these aggressive tendencies become more noticeable. A typical letter is signed Tired-of-Her-Pestiness: "I'm 15. My best fella is 16. Rod and I aren't going steady but neither of us dates anyone else. A certain girl Rod used to go with calls him on the phone every night. He thinks she's a positive creep and has told her so to her face but she won't give up."

In December 1966, Timid told Ann, "A 17-year-old girl has fallen hard for our son Ben who is the same age. She began by telephoning Ben a couple of times each weekend. Now she calls him at least three times every evening. Ben is a nervous wreck. Yesterday he showed me some notes she had written to him, and he told me the girl must be out of her mind to write such things." This kind of aggressive activity, one of the many forces speeding the momentum of the sexual revolution, is evidence of the extent to which the youth culture was growing, and of the teens' desire to appropriate the social patterns of adults at an ever younger age. After 1970, such letters just about disappeared. There was no longer any reason to write them.

In fact, as the problems of teen-agers became more serious, the younger ones stopped writing in such numbers, and the column began to sound more adult than it had. This is something that would have happened in any event when the teens claimed their right to the adult world. Part of the adult legacy was genuine despair; solutions to adolescent dilemmas could no longer be guaranteed.

Unhappy at Seventeen had written: "I . . . have been going with a group of boys and girls of whom my parents do not approve. They say these friends are too wild and they are 'not my type.' . . . I don't know if I should obey my parents' wishes and quit seeing everyone in the crowd or use my own judgment." Unhappy's letter neither denigrated her parents nor tried to undercut their argument. She seems to have presented it fairly—fairly enough at any rate for one to assume that she anticipated Ann Landers would side with them. But writing to Ann Landers in such a neutral way, even against the anticipation of failure, sounds as if arbitration was being attempted in an impartial court with at least the possibility that parental authority might be questioned.

Public opinion polls taken at an interval of half a century (1924 and 1977) show a loosening of parental influence. In 1924 nearly a third of male adolescents and two-thirds of female adolescents got their sexual education from their parents. In 1977 those figures had been nearly halved for both sexes. In this intimate area, parents seem not to have heeded Dr. Spock's invitation to a dialogue between the generations. In 1924, about one-third of the male adolescents thought it desirable that a father show respect for his children's opinions. Of the young women, 42 percent expected it, presumably because of earlier role training. By 1977, these figures had jumped to 62 percent for males, and a whopping 76 percent for females. *

The fifties were a midpoint. Parental authority was still

_____
* Howard H. Bahr, "Changes in Family Life in Middletown," Public Opinion Quarterly, 44, No. 1, 1980, pp. 35–52.

real enough to encourage the young who were aware of their position on centerstage to begin questioning that authority (conversely, authoritarian parents felt justified by the evidence of more and more teens moving center-stage). During the first month of her column, Ann Landers received a letter from Miss E.F. saying, "In a few months I will be 17 and my father treats me as if I were 10. I can go out only on Sunday and then to the movies with the girls. Once in a while, I am permitted to go to a dance, but I must be in by 12. Father reads in the newspapers about teen-agers who get into all sorts of trouble, and he treats me as if I were one of them." The paradox of E.F.'s letter is that she both bowed to and resented her father's discipline. Knowing already that his treatment was becoming obsolete ("my father treats me as if I were 10"), her rebellion did not go beyond writing, but her intuition was correct. Ann confirmed the obsolescence of the father's discipline: "C'mon, Pop, give a little. You are doing what you think is best for your precious daughter, but she has outgrown the old rules and regulations." Ann would always pull toward the center—away from domineering parents during their time of assertion, away from the children during theirs.

Two months later, Judy (the same age as E.F.) was less lucky: "I'm 16 and have a few boy friends. I'm permitted to go to the movies, but mother always comes along or sends a younger sister. The 'chaperone' sits between me and my date." Ann called this "gestapo tactics," but suggested a subversion of those tactics whose effect, even if successful, must have been minimal: "The seating arrangement is your fault. Haven't you discovered the first one down the aisle is the first one seated? . . . Be 'courteous' and allow mother or sis to go down the aisle first."

Ann may have called the mother's discipline gestapo-like, but in the matter of cinema ethics, the best a sixteen-year-old couple could hope for from Ann Landers in the fifties was to sit side by side in the darkened

theater. Two years later, the discipline was still the same
when Rene wrote, "My boy friend and I went to the
movies the other night. He had his arm around the seat I
was sitting in. We weren't necking or anything like
that. . . . The next day my girl friend's mother called my
mom. She was sitting behind us and we didn't know it.
The story was we necked during the whole show."
Although, as she often did, Ann spoke up for trust by
parents, she was unrelenting on the subject of decorum:
"Your boy friend should not endanger your reputation by
putting his arm around the chair."

Given such norms, the discipline of some parents was
understandably rigid. Another sixteen-year-old, Debbie,
wrote in November 1955 that her "father is trying to
break us up, even though he says he likes the boy. . . . P.S.
My father also thinks I'm too young to go out with boys.
I'm the baby (as my father calls me) of the family." (Ann's
advice: "Just show him patience, understanding and love.
He'll come around.") The following year, D.V. moaned,
"I'm 19 and have a steady boy friend. My mother won't let
me stay out later than 11 on Saturday night. How can I
make her understand I'm old enough to be out until 2
A.M.?" (Ann advised her, "Do this thing in stages. Aim at
midnight for now and in three months get it up to
12:30.")

Besides those teens who sought Ann's assistance to
either confirm or deny their parents' rules, others
showed clearer signs of rebellion. The evidence came
from both the parents and their children. Early in 1956,
M.I.B. wrote, "I'm at the end of my rope. I can't take any
more abuse and foul language from my 18-year-old
daughter." M.I.B.'s daughter was to be something of an
unfortunate trendsetter, as Ann herself acknowledged a
few months later in a moment of weakness. R.M.P.
wanted to know what she could do about her twenty-
two-year-old son in the clutches of a sixteen-year-old
virago. Ann condoled, "Unfortunately, you can't control
someone else's daughter . . . These days you do well to
control your own!"

The rebels of the early sixties sometimes spoke with a halting voice; their letters often blend brass and ingenuousness. An example is Stalag 17's, written toward the end of 1961:

> My father is like a dictator. He thinks a girl 15 is an infant.
> Two weeks ago the kids had a beer-bust. . . . When I told Ike I couldn't go to the beer bust, he said he'd come over to see me. I knew my old man wouldn't let him in the house because I was supposed to be in solitary, so I told Ike to climb in through my bedroom window.
> At about 10:30 P.M. we heard my Dad coming down the hall so Ike got under my bed. Our dog was under the bed and Ike must have stepped on him. Anyway the dog yelped and my dad found Ike.
> Now I'm grounded for a month. Do you realize this is four miserable weeks? I'll crack up. How can I get my Dad to trust me?

The demands of the teens may have been strident and absolute, but they were mitigated, frequently to the point of self-destruction, by the necessity they felt to write and the naïveté that still seeped through their words. Ardis wrote in January 1960, "I'm a junior, 17 years of age, and everyone says I'm the most mature girl in our school. . . . The man I love is 30 years old. (He acts a lot younger.) . . . Don't tell me to stop seeing him. You might as well tell the sun not to set tomorrow. All I want from you is advice on how to get officially engaged. We have been very friendly if you get what I mean." Ardis may have felt herself to be "the most mature girl in our school" (very likely a euphemism), but had to explain her plight to Ann through indirection ("if you get what I mean").

In 1967, maturity came even younger—This Time It's Real was only thirteen but definitely out of sorts: "Ann Landers: I am not calling you dear. You are a mean old woman with a heart of stone. I just read the letter from the 13-year-old girl who wanted to be in love and you told her that a 13-year-old could no more be in love than an oak tree could reach its full growth in three weeks. I am writing to tell you that you are wrong. I am 13 years old and I have been in love three times."

This was the sixties form of the puppy-love letter—etched with generational anger and claims to the social patterns of the adult world. And This Time It's Real was by no means an isolated case—a fact that Ann acknowledged with some sourness: "Every week I receive hundreds of letters from youngsters like you who are in a big fat hurry to rush through life—waiting for absolutely nothing." It was those youngsters, rushing through their young lives, who would soon cause Ann Landers to take a long look at how the "steadies" of a former time now conceived of their world and to advise strongly against what had once been known as steady dating.

This Time It's Real may have been a child of the sixties, but she grew out of the days of change and paradox during which Eppie Lederer first took over the column—when enough fragments of former codes remained to suggest the pattern of what had been. A Worried Friend might thus fret in 1957 about a sixteen-year-old who "stays out all night" because "people will not think she is a nice girl," while Ann found support for her answer in a law now rapidly becoming anachronistic: "If there's a curfew in your town, the girl could be picked up by the police."

It was a time when someone like J.C. still worried that the boy she loved was "always trying to make improper love to me," and Ann told Girl of 14 (in 1955) and Ashamed (in 1956) that kissing games were "so darned dull" or "for the birds." This even though such games had become big among teens, as Worried Girl explained in 1956, reporting on "a party where there was nothing but kissing for five hours." And parents like M.M.M. found themselves awash amid the moral flotsam: "Our daughter is just entering her teens. We made the mistake of keeping the facts of life from her and now we don't know how to change over from the stork story" (1956).

The answer Ann gave M.M.M. held a clue to the future: "If your daughter is entering her teens and you think she is still buying that stork story—I suggest you sit down with her at once. You'll learn plenty." What these middle-class parents would learn was that the freedom that made their children prematurely knowledgeable would leave those children unprotected in areas of their former ignorance. Those middle-class children would soon be as vulnerable as had been the children of the poor and the uneducated. Out-of-wedlock pregnancies, venereal disease, and drugs were about to break out of the confines of the ghetto and find their way into the suburbs.

Shortly after the publication of the Kinsey report in 1948, Princeton students were asked about their reactions to the book. It was generally favorable; they showed Ivy League sophistication in their belief that this controversial inquiry would be liberating, resulting in greater tolerance of other people's behavior and more open discussion about sex. However, about one-quarter percent were "very surprised" at what they discovered in Kinsey; half were "moderately surprised." Only 14 percent claimed worldly wisdom sufficient not to have been surprised at all. (And 12 percent don't seem to have known what their reactions were.) The relative innocence of the young at the end of the Second World War appears to confirm Dorothy Thompson's perception of a national innocence: "[The Kinsey report is] shocking to the ideal picture of how Americans are supposed to behave sexually."

In the midfifties, sexual experimentation (somewhat like pregnancy out of wedlock) usually helped define the kind of person who had indulged. The fall was somehow never quite unexpected, and Ann's advice could be proportionally short. For example, Troubled was nineteen and engaged in January 1956 but haunted by the memory of past lapses ("I made mistakes—if you know what I mean") and wanted to know whether or not to confess. Ann was short and to the point: "Don't dwell on past mistakes. Congratulate yourself on raising your standards." In April of the following year, Carmen wrote, "I'm a girl 19, and almost out of my mind with worry. . . . Like a fool, I gave in to his pleading to 'prove my love.' When I told him I was pregnant, he admitted he was married and had been giving me a line, plus a phony name. I became so hysterical and ill I lost the baby. . . . I know it's crazy but I'm still in love with him in spite of what he's done. Is my life finished at 19? Please help me. I'm desperate." Unwilling to let Carmen turn into Anna Karenina, Ann told her, "If you have anything more to do with this lying fake you deserve whatever you get. Leave town."

In the sixties, sexual encounters among the young were becoming open enough for a teen like Dill Emma to worry (in 1961), "He has never tried to kiss me, except in a brotherly way, on the cheek or the forehead. Once in a while, if the movie is especially romantic he'll hold my hand. I had many boy friends before I started to go with Bill and no fellow ever acted like this. How can I tell if he's alive?" Ann advised her to "feel his wrist and see if you can get a pulse," but as sexual experimentation spread, she was driven to more reflective advice.

In March 1960, G.'s Mom discovered that G. "who is 19 was intimate with her 21-year-old boy friend." Ann told her not to let on, but to "talk with her and speak in generalities. But get across to her the emotional, physical and moral booby-traps of premarital experimentation as best you can." Spock-age parents like G.'s Mom spoke as rationally as they had been taught, but found rational talk could not dispose of post-Spock problems.

The following month, Pat, eighteen, engaged, virginal, but "getting pretty close to the line," wrote, "Everyone says it's wrong, but no one says why. . . . If I had a daughter and she asked me why it's wrong to give yourself before marriage I couldn't tell her why." Ann's reply invoked the moral code, children (as the primary purpose of physical love), respect, and consideration. She also said, "My desk is always piled high with letters from heartbroken girls who were left flat because they had no more to give. They never thought it could happen to them—but it did." We don't know whether Ann's answer satisfied Pat, but it was not going to be enough for the Pats of the future.

With the new morality, euphemisms were fading into quaint obsolescence, with a significant push from Ann Landers. In 1961, "if you know what I mean"—the young readers' usual disguise and designation of sexual matters when thrust into the glare of the family newspaper—was overwhelmed by her bold statement that ours had become a "sex-oriented culture." In this particular area, her ability to assess what was happening moved her linguistically ahead of her readers. More and more of the teens may have been sexually active, but few called it by its proper name until Ann did.

In February 1964, Cupid's Plato, in his "late teens," still expressed it this way: "The girls I take out tell me I'm a great kid, a terrific date and lots of fun, but nobody wants to get serious." Ann thought that it was time for the language of even the family newspaper to catch up with the times: "Young romance is beautiful, healthy and normal. I'm heartily in favor of it. But your letter leaves me with the impression it's not romance you're after, Buddy Boy—it's sex."

No-nonsense language paved the way for no-nonsense advice. A month after Cupid's Plato had been told in the public press what he really had on his mind, Sick at Heart Mother wrote, "Last night our 14-year-old daughter came home from her first date. . . . It was apparent that she had been doing some heavy necking." The moral generalities Ann Landers had dispensed for Pat four years earlier were now replaced by hard-boiled common sense. "Your daughter should be made to understand the serious hazards of heavy necking. The loss of reputation is the least of it. Tell her about pregnancy, VD and the loss of self-respect."

A 1965 polling of adults and teen-agers conducted for *Look* magazine by Gallup found that almost half of them considered syphilis to be the most serious disease. (Cancer came in second place with only 29 percent.) Halfway through the sixties, venereal disease was indeed one of the realities of the new world young people had won for themselves. In 1965, a high school senior told Ann, "Most kids . . . are worried" (and signed the letter Chicken). Ann informed Chicken that reported cases of VD in this country had tripled in the last ten years (since Ann first started handling the column), and that almost 70 percent of the cases were among those aged thirteen to nineteen. Something had been happening since the earlier days of moon and croon. Ann Landers's booklets for young people had previously concerned such topics as *How to Live with Your Parents, Teen-Age Smoking, Teen-Age Drinking, How to Be Well-Liked, The Key to Popularity*, and *Dating Do's and Don'ts*. Soon they began to evidence new urgency in their titles: *Teen-Age Sex: Ten Ways to Cool It*; and *Sex and the Teen-Ager*.

The same dime store dilemmas still informed emotional relationships of teen-agers, but they were now edged with the hard truth of physical jeopardy. In September 1965, a high school junior, Between Heaven and Hell, told a familiar story of young love and parental opposition. But, symptomatic of the times, the flimsy tale was weighted with the unvarnished words of the new age: "My dad says Ron will never amount to anything. Maybe he won't, but I don't care. He's the only fellow who ever gave me a thrill. In other words Ron turns me on. It's getting harder and harder to keep from going all the way. Ron says if two people love each other it's O.K. I think he's right, but the big question is how can I tell if it's really love or just plain sex?"

Between Heaven and Hell felt sufficiently involved and aroused to dismiss parental judgment, but what would have been romantic "love" a few years before was now caught up in the reality of sex—sex being both an accepted fact and the evidence turning an earlier romanticism into something that seemed curiously abstract and yet somehow desirable. Ann tried to distinguish for the high school junior between "the instinctive response to a biological urge" and something bigger—love—that also "contains the magical element of physical excitement." By 1965, even Ann Landers could no longer remain within the abstractions of romance that had been adequate ten years before for Mixed-up Gal or Unhappy at Seventeen.

But "the magical element of physical excitement" itself was in danger of sounding as obsolete as an operetta in a world filled with blunt truths that even adults had shied away from not so many years before. The same *Look* poll taken in the midsixties confirmed general agreement (84 percent) on one point at least: This generation was far more "liberal" about sexual matters than the previous one had been. A majority felt that adolescents were now less moral and modest than those of a former generation.

Toward the end of 1967, Shook Up (sixteen years old) wrote, "I don't know quite how to say this so I will come right out in plain English and tell you that my best friend is a lesbian." In 1970, Tulsa was sixteen and had a seven-month-old daughter: "I've been 'laid off' (fired) twice in the last six months. Everyone is great until they find out I have a child. Then they treat me like I have smallpox. I have never been married so I go by [the designation] Miss Smith." Ann's answer bespoke the awareness of the times: "For openers you can call yourself Mrs. Smith. . . . If someone asked about your husband simply say, 'I am not married.' " In 1976, F.M., a high school junior, asked about contraceptives, "Why is the law so unrealistic? Keeping contraceptives out of the hands of 16- and 17-year-olds does not discourage sexual intercourse. . . . Can you explain from an adult's viewpoint the logic behind such legislation?" And Ann Landers, jettisoning loftier generalities dispensed to Between Heaven and Hell ten years earlier, answered, "There is no logic behind such legislation. The law is a bummer."

It is true that in the sixties, you could still find an occasional stray from a former time, like Shy Guy (a teen-age boy) who confessed in March 1965, "I have never kissed a girl. This chick has gone with fellows who have had a lot of experience in this line and I want to do it right so she won't think I'm a dumb dope." Or like Dizz-gusted ("not a Bible-waving crank [but] an average American teen-ager"), who complained the following May, "Too many times I have taken a date to a movie which was advertised as 'a rollicking comedy' or a 'delightfully gay and witty musical,' and instead we saw a vulgar display of half nude morons chasing each other around the bedroom. . . . What can be done to elevate the standards of films and clean up the movies?" And in the midsixties, even Ann occasionally found herself midway between two different moral tides and two different ways of advising the young.

Two months after Dizzgusted's letter, Miss Overdid It, a sixteen-year-old, wrote to the seventeen-year-old she had "fallen head over heels" in love with that summer and signed off with "Oceans of love with a kiss on each wave." She explained, "His answer arrived today, and I felt like a sap. He started his letter, 'Hi there' and ended with 'So long for now, old Buddy.' " Such a letter should have appeared as the welcome relic of a former time; it seemed to conform to the "healthy and normal" standards that Ann had suggested to Cupid's Plato the year before, and it certainly subscribed to one of the ten ways to cool teen-age sex. A part of Ann recognized Overdid It's virtuous boyfriend, but another part recognized the strong new tides that would soon sweep over the small island of morality on which he still stood, and Ann appropriately turned into Janus: "Finish the next letter with 'Sincerely,' and sign yourself 'Old Buddy.' " But she added, "If he continues to treat you like one of the boys, I suggest you save your stamps."

If one could still hear an occasional Shy Guy or Dizz-gusted in 1965, it was an anachronistic note drowned out by the greater and louder number of those who repre-sented the new—and it was these Ann had to address. A year before Overdid It, Sensible Parents had written about a daughter who wanted "a formal all-white wed-ding. . . . I know very well that when Mary Elizabeth went with this young man they did things that would make her ineligible for a white wedding, if you get what I mean." Ann got what Sensible Parents meant, but she had also gotten too many messages of a different kind: "If Mary Elizabeth wants a white wedding, let her have it. Girls [in her situation] do not forfeit the privilege of a white wedding."

The young felt they were entitled to their desires—for the trappings of purity, as in the case of Mary Elizabeth, or for the opposite, as itemized in 1967 by Wish They'd Get Off My Back, whose message was in his signature: "I'm a teen-ager who is sick and tired of my parents. What I need is less criticism and more sympathy. My grades aren't so hot because I am a nervous wreck from getting yelled at all the time. All I hear from morning till night is 'Take a bath. Stop smoking. Get rid of that beard. Get off the phone. Hang up your clothes. Stand up straight. Get a haircut. Don't be mouthy. Apply yourself.' " This list of what Off My Back now considered to be parental sins is a fair indication of the emancipation expected by teen-agers of the sixties—teen-agers who were more repre-sentative than Shy Guy or Dizzgusted.

By 1969, the voice of these young people increased in volume as it echoed across the nation's campuses, as well as in other places—including Ann Landers's column. Early in 1970, Generation Gapped's Yalie son was think-ing of bringing his girlfriend home for an extended weekend. He wrote to his mother, "Since we are living together here at school, I think it would be very mature and honest of you and Dad if you would permit us to share my room." Confronted with the shocked refusal of his mother, he called her "a hypocrite and cited [her] 'phoniness' as a good example of what the college kids are protesting." The mother added, "We have discussed this problem with other parents who are having the same arguments with their college progeny. Some of the parents are losing the battle. My sister-in-law, for example, allowed her daughter's boyfriend to stay in their home over the holidays. . . . What are your views, Ann?" Ann's views were what they had always been, and pretty much remained, on that particular subject: "Parents who collapse to such outrageous demands are abdicating their responsibilities, encouraging premarital sex and letting their sons and daughters down badly. College kids are still kids. They are testing, probing, pushing, trying to see how far they can go. They don't want everything they ask for. In fact, often they're relieved when they are told 'no.' "

Her firmness notwithstanding, Ann knew she was talking about the defense of a relatively narrow perimeter. She expected parents, in their defense of that perimeter, to be equally clear-sighted. She recommended the following reply: "If you are sleeping together at school, that's your business. A kid who is old enough to go away to school can decide for himself matters of this nature. But don't think you're going to turn our home into a free-love passion pit. We may be square, but these are the rules of the house and you can like it or lump it."

But even as parents received from Ann Landers the support they requested for their moral battles, they were contributing to the change in the moral climate. It was now acceptable for these middle-class parents to discuss with a columnist in the family newspaper the matter of their children "sleeping together." However much Generation Gapped's son might have taxed his mother with "hypocrisy," she articulated realities formerly left unspoken; her language, and that of the family newspaper, were all becoming pretty clear. So clear, in fact, that the new awareness of parents like Generation Gapped sometimes combined with Ann's own awareness—and the old Margaret Sanger liberal in her—to produce amusing markers of that period in American history. In 1970, Another Mother made light of parents who mourned the way children dropped out of their lives in times of generational antagonisms. She, for one, was not going to waste time brooding over their flight from the nest: "I intend to have a ball. I'll work in my garden, take piano lessons, knit an afghan, paint a picture. I'll have extra money to get my hair done and have lunch with the girls. I'll have time and energy to exercise, to take long walks and discover my own sexuality."

Grim though the times may have been for many, for some the times were adding new dimensions to a pragmatic culture, often addicted to the belief that almost any personal achievement was possible. After having had at least three children (her letter was vague as to the precise number), it was now time for Another Mother to discover, along with a new sense of sisterhood ("lunch with the girls"), her "own sexuality." And Ann applauded this seventies updating of Voltaire (*"Il faut cultiver notre jardin"*): "I'll bet my bottom dollar you won't have to call [your children]. They'll call you. Thanks for a great letter."

In the seventies, the baby boomers in their huge numbers had pretty much altered the world they came into. If that altered world was not exactly the one they had envisaged, it was at any rate not the same one to which their parents had grown accustomed. As the shock waves began to subside, adults were able to take a clearer look at the kind of world it was. And Ann Landers, whose advocacy of the young had been restrained during a time of social turmoil by the need to assert what she considered to be fundamental moral standards, could now sort out with finer discrimination the wheat from the chaff.

In 1972, Establishment Square (the signature indicating the writer's assertiveness) visited "12 institutions of higher learning in the East" and complained, "We found the same story everywhere—beautiful campuses, impressive buildings, lovely landscaping—and crummy looking students. Dirty unisex clothing; unshaven, mop-haired males; slobby, braless girls in shawls, jeans, sandals and faded hip-huggers. . . . Manners and decent language appear to be a thing of the past." Ann allowed, "There is no rational defense for personal neglect, dirt, bad manners or foul language," but added, "there is also less hypocrisy, and a stronger commitment to higher ideals. A generation that is against the Vietnam war, outspoken in behalf of equal opportunities for minority groups, dedicated to fighting pollution and saving our environment can't be all bad."

Still, Ann's advocacy came up against evidences of a rebellion whose excesses she was not about to condone. Looking for her support, Fur Is Flying in Austin, Texas, asked the following year, "Is there anything wrong with correcting your dad or mother if they say something fake in front of company?" and was told about the importance of tact and consideration. In 1975, Mom's sixteen-year-old daughter was drinking, having sexual relations, and shoplifting, but rejected counseling: "She says nobody can tell her anything she doesn't already know." She was told to get counseling anyway. In 1977, a sixteen-year-old girl wrote to say she was "sick of this house, sick of this town, sick of being under my parents' thumb, sick of being treated like a baby. Sick of being lonely even though I have lots of friends, sick of this lump in my throat, sick of almost running away but losing courage at the last minute." Ann made the mistake of telling her she was sick all right and suggesting she get some help. This time her response "unleashed an unexpected torrent of letters"—almost exclusively from teens—surprising her with the heat of the many who agreed with the letter writer.

That same sixteen-year-old had also written that she was "sick of the authorities who don't know the wonders of pot but keep screaming about how harmful it is." Drugs were, of course, a significant manifestation of the youth culture and of youthful rebellion. To be sure, teens had gone in for other addictions before. Their drug in the fifties was alcohol (and Ann Landers's list of booklets included *Teen-Age Drinking, Help for the Alcoholic,* and *Booze and You: For Teen-Agers Only*). But smoking cigarettes was the symbolic addiction of the earliest rebels.

Interestingly, a surprising number of those early rebels were asking for recognition of a right rather than an indulgence in the act. In May 1956, Leah H. addressed a mannerly note to Ann Landers: "I'm a girl 13 and will be 14 on July 1. The other day a girl five months younger than I came to our home with her mother and father. They let her smoke in front of them. My parents won't let me smoke even though I want to very much. Will you please tell my parents that it is better for them to give me permission to smoke in front of them than to have me do it behind their backs? I promise I'll quit after a little while. Thank you." Ann Landers told Leah, "Don't criticize your parents because they have enough sense to say no." However, at the end of the year, she received a nearly identical letter from U.C.: "I'm a girl 16 and a high school junior. Do you think I should smoke in front of my mother or behind her back? She's old-fashioned and does not approve of smoking. All the girls in my crowd have been smoking for quite a while. Please say something. Maybe my mother will get hep."

The symbolic cigarette (soon to be replaced by the joint) lost its appeal with the start of the sixties, and toward the end of the decade the more destructive problem of drugs had found its way into the column. In May 1969, Ann Landers ran a letter by Gapped. The telltale signature, similar to so many others, was more evidence that parents now recognized in the misdeeds of their children the intentional digging of a trench meant to separate them—an assertion of rights and a gesture of defiance toward those who might try to abrogate those rights. Gapped wrote, "Our 17-year-old son has admitted he smokes marijuana 'socially' on week-ends but insists he is not a habitual smoker and can quit any time he wants to. . . . I was shocked but tried not to show it. R. is a fine young man, a good student, and as thousands of mothers have said before me, 'I never dreamed I would hear such words from my son's lips.' I know my boy needs professional help but when I suggest it he says he has no problem—that he is just adding enjoyment to his life." In 1969, not too much was known about the effects of marijuana, so Ann Landers suggested the usual carrot-and-stick approach: "Keep the channels of communication open. . . . Remind the son or daughter that marijuana is an illicit drug and anyone caught with the drug can be charged with a felony. And the penalties are stiff."

By the following year, drugs had become so much a part of the youth scene that teens tried candidly to avail themselves of Ann's expertise: "My friend and I are both 17. We have been experimenting with pills and we need some advice. We want to get high but we don't want to do anything crazy like kill ourselves. . . . Just answer our questions and skip the sermon. Thanks."

The situation had become serious enough for Ann to heed the letter, skipping the sermon completely: "I wish I could answer your questions but I can't because I don't know your threshold of tolerance, which depends on many factors such as the condition of your general health, your nervous system, and your level of emotional stability. Nor do I know the strength of the pills you describe. Are they 50 milligrams, 100 or 200?" She ended this irony with only a glancing threat: "If you insist on 'experimenting' I hope you'll have one person present who will stay straight. Someone in the crowd should be on hand to call a doctor or an ambulance or a coroner, whichever is needed."

Parents likewise would soon be skipping the sermon in order to find out how to cope with this new reality. A typical letter in May 1975 was that of C.M.: "Maybe you've given the answer to my question dozens of times, and I never paid any attention to it because I thought it could never affect me. But now I'm having sleepless nights and I need to know something. When a mother suspects her son is 'on something' how can she tell for sure if her hunch is right? If it is right, how can she help him?" The advice at the time was to get a check-up, since personality changes could have other causes. Ann added, "If he tunes you out, you can do nothing but let him know you're here if he needs you. Good luck, dear." The moral battle was lost; true to a cultural instinct that transcended her, Ann Landers had known for some time (at least since the midsixties when she responded to letters like Sick at Heart Mother's) that it was more important now to work within existing circumstances than to try changing them.

As the seventies came to an end, that sense seems to have been shared by a large number of parents. In 1980, Afraid and Heartbroken's letter began, "A year and a half ago, when my son was 17, he took an overdose. Thank God, I found him in time and got him to the hospital." But it was not the overdose that caused the writer to be afraid and heartbroken. She was concerned because her son had once again taken up with the girl who had previously dropped him. The shock of the drug nightmare had attenuated into dull acceptance. Other nightmares could now be lived within its shadows.

Still, Afraid and Heartbroken's letter did provide an interesting clue to a possible consequence of youthful rebellion—the temptation of suicide. The misery of the adult world to which the young had laid claim was now theirs, along with its quotient of pain and disillusionment. In October 1983, Ann noted that the suicide rate in the United States had tripled in the last ten years.

But in 1980, there is also an occasional letter that sounds different. In November, Fed Up in St. Louis writes: "I am writing for all teen-age girls who have had it with one-night stands from guys who use them and toss them aside. . . . I am mad. I want to fight back. It's rotten the way guys abuse girls and get away with it." Two months before, Mixed Up in Florida had written, "I hope you will print this letter and help not only me but other girls. I am 15 years old and I have been dating this guy for one month. Already he wants to have sex. I have said 'no way' every time he has tried something, and we end up in an argument. He says it's natural for people in love to want to share their bodies with one another. The problem is I don't think I am ready for such a move, and I am not in love."

Mixed Up spoke a matter-of-fact language that would have shocked her sisters in the fifties and early sixties, but that matter-of-factness was also free of the conflicting emotions that had informed many such letters during the intervening decades. Mixed Up in Florida did not sound as confused as her signature, and Ann's response matched her language and coolness: "My advice is to give Mr. Hot Pants the deep six."

The following year, Undeclared War in New England sounded a similar note, an intimation that having won their battles, the young were beginning to tire of the spoils: "I am a 13-year-old and live in a rather small town in Vermont. My mother is a well-known psychologist. Recently I started to smoke pot with a girl I hang out with. My mother knows about it, but she won't tell me to quit. . . . I don't feel secure enough to be in complete charge of my own life. Please print this letter so my mother will see it. I feel afraid and alone." Ann Landers sensed a shift in the times and obliged: "Sounds as if your mother has read too many outdated books on how to raise children. Someone should tell her that the permissive approach of the '50s was a dismal failure."

A year later, a letter from Yours Gratefully, D.M., referred to Ann Landers's article in *Family Circle* and her advocacy of Tough Love, an organization to help parents get rid of their guilt feelings and stand up to their overbearing children. Meanwhile, others were stiffening their spines without the benefit of support groups, and just as the Spock revolution had left many pre-Spock parents stranded, it was now the turn of Spock-trained parents to be stuck out on a limb.

In February 1982, Alexandria, La., Complaint fumed, "You must hate children. Several weeks ago you printed a letter and agreed with the writer that youngsters do not belong in beauty shops. A few days later you ran a letter about what a nuisance children are in restaurants. Just last week I heard the manager of a supermarket say he wished he could keep all children under 12 out of his store. . . . Nobody wants kids." In response, Ann ran a letter from For the Record in Arkansas saying, "If your child is boss in the house, he is sure to be a terror in a restaurant, and it's not fair to other patrons who pay for a quiet and restful dinner." For the Record noted parenthetically, "Honestly, some of your readers are exasperating! How do you stand it?"

For the Record's exasperation was something new. It would have been both wrong and strange for the older generation to defend itself a few years earlier. Now, however, it was becoming fashionable for even some of the young to be what the previous decade would have termed square. In June 1981, a whole column reflected the "hundreds" of letters rebutting Ann's statement that most eighteen-year-old males will take advantage of a willing girl. A typical letter from eighteen-year-old Ben Around said, "Your comment that most teen-age boys will 'take anything they can get plus whatever they can talk a girl out of' is from the Middle Ages." These latest Middle Ages were the seventies, but Ben's letter did show the speed at which they were receding in the minds of some.

Ben's letter was especially interesting because it no longer echoed the clamorous rights of the young to sexual freedom, and because it demonstrated a resistance to female aggressiveness. Speaking of the difference between high school and college moralities, Ben noted "My most severe culture shock was getting used to the way the chicks came on to the guys." Sexual freedom may have been an emblem of emancipation during the seventies, but after a decade it seemed to have lost some of its emblematic and actual attraction.

Martha in an Eastern Town confided in February 1983, "I am 13 years old and have been a virgin all my life. I want to stay that way so I can have a big wedding in the same church I was baptized." The naïveté of the fifties was returning for some—though with the face of the eighties. Martha actually seems to have thought it remarkable that at thirteen she should still be a virgin; what sounded a different note was her looking forward to the ritual of wedding.

The voice of Dizzgusted, which had not been heard much since the midsixties, was now reasserting itself in others, like A Canadian Friend, who had written in January 1983, "I have a message for the movie makers that could mean bigger box-office receipts and more enjoyment for the public . . . : I am 17. Most of my friends are somewhere near my age. We do not wish to see raw sex and listen to obscene language." As examples of the films they enjoyed, he cited such hits as *On Golden Pond, Raiders of the Lost Ark, Chariots of Fire*, and *E.T.*

Letters like these may have reflected a change that was starting to occur because of surfeit rather than through critical awareness. But in 1983 one also finds, and with some persistence, letters like Awake in Waco's:

> May I say a word to that 16-year-old dopehead who signed herself Truth Will Win? I am also a teen-ager. This is my country, too. I am well aware that hatred, conflict and violence are tearing our nation apart. We have paid a terrible price for becoming involved in a war we had no business getting into. I, too, have grown up amidst riots, pollution, racial strife and drug addiction.
>
> Our generation will inherit the problem of taking care of the kids with fried brains. What plans do these spaced-out vegetables have for

themselves? People like me, who kept it all together, will have to provide hospitals for the sick ones.

This is not to say that the omelet that had been scrambled during the seventies had been, or could be, unscrambled. In 1984, Fan in Richmond, Va., had "just read a news story that made me feel good. A recent survey showed that marijuana use among teen-agers is on the decline." Ann answered, "That's the good news. The bad news is that teens are turning to alcohol. And the percentage of students who drink regularly would knock your socks off."

The fifties were returning in many different ways, but through doors that had been opened wide during the intervening years. As Waco's letter showed, the drug problem was by no means over. Toward the end of the year, Plenty Worried in Arizona quoted a study published in *USA Today* which reported that one-quarter of the eighth-graders in the Tampa-St. Petersburg area had tried marijuana. Of these, 5.4 percent said they smoked pot about three times a month, and 3 percent said they had tried heroin. These were thirteen-year-olds, and Worried wanted to know whether the situation was as bad outside Florida. Ann assured Worried it was—even though she herself was not always as savvy as the culture warranted.

In August, Maw-Maw in Ohio wrote about her granddaughter who had spent the weekend with her—"a lovely 16-year-old high school sophomore. . . . Yesterday she dumped the contents of her shoulder-strap bag on the floor, in search of the house keys. Out tumbled a pair of pliers. I asked her what on earth she carried those for. She replied, 'To pull up my jeans.' . . . I am only 57 years old, not exactly an antique, but I am unable to relate to this sort of thing. Will you please explain."

Ann volunteered: "There seems to be a contest under way for the tightest-fitting jeans known to humankind. . . . I am not surprised that your granddaughter needs pliers."

That answer tripped her up on the subject of pliers, jeans, and the drug culture. She was promptly brought up to date by the many letters informing her about the use of pliers as joint holders.

That Martha in an Eastern Town could congratulate herself on being a virgin at thirteen was evidence that the problems of sex had not yet quite disappeared either. Aware of this, Ann Landers took a strong stand in 1983 against what she called "the squeal rule"—the proposed regulation by the Department of Health and Human Services mandating any federally funded clinic dispensing birth control devices to a girl under eighteen to send a registered letter to her parents informing them of the fact. Two years before, she had written what amounted to an open letter on the need for the sexual education of teens:

> Recently on the Phil Donahue show there were two teen-aged mothers—one who had become pregnant at 13, the other at 14. These girls were not morons or gutter types. They were attractive, articulate young people—15 and 19 years of age. The 19-year-old (her child is now 4) said she did not know that what she was doing could result in having a baby. No one had talked to her about sex.
>
> The 15-year-old (her child is now almost 2) said [it] never occurred to her that she could get pregnant because "I was so young."
>
> There were more than 1 million teen-age pregnancies last year. Something is not working. . . . Sex education in schools has NOT failed. It hasn't been given a chance. . . . Children mature physically three years earlier than they did 40 years ago. Advertising, the media, rock music (ever listen to the lyrics?) and films push sex like crazy. [Sex] can be extremely damaging to their health.

Children continued to be a focus of adult attention in

the eighties, but as the adults' fear of their children began to dissipate, the nature of the concern for the rights of the young changed. A typical letter was written in February 1982 by A Woman Who Cares about a subject that had been claiming increasing space in Ann Landers's columns: "Child abuse is a hideous thing. . . . Every child should be aware that he or she is protected by law. . . . Urge every young girl whose father is abusing her not to be afraid to go to the police station and ask for help." Ann noted that the subject had netted her "hundreds of letters from social workers and counselors from every state in the union, as well as Canada."

After the generational confrontations of the seventies, it was time to look at deeper and perhaps atavistic divisions. The harsh realities of the times afforded a harsher, more realistic look at what had been left unspoken during a period of euphemisms and greater innocence. Alongside those harsh realities, the kind of analysis that would have been previously too distasteful for probing—and not only in the family newspaper—no longer seemed particularly out of place.

The family was permanently affected, too, failing to survive as the hallowed abstraction it was thought to be in the fifties. The confrontation between generations may have lost the ritualistic bitterness that had been nearly mandatory during the sixties and seventies, but the gap was evidently not bridged. Another subject surfacing with great regularity (especially in 1983 and 1984) was that of runaways. In June 1984, Caring in D.C. noted, "Nearly a million and a half children run away from home every year. Some of them never return." Ann Landers commented, "Almost always the runaway is running FROM something, not TO something."

Those of the young who wished to do so could now run away. It was one of the freedoms they had won during the last two decades. But, as Ann's answer implied, there was nothing much left for them to run to. Apparently, they were driven away by the consequences of a poor bargain—the happiness that was supposed to have been purchased at the price of innocence just failed to materialize.

And so, to a certain extent, the naïveté of the fifties returned, but without the innocence. Equally immature, equally vulnerable young people looked at a world that had lost its appeal. What they saw was simply frightening because of the unshielded eyes with which they saw it. In April 1982, End of Conversation in Cleveland reported the exchange she had heard between an eight-year-old girl and her third-grade teacher:

> Mary: Was George Washington president when you were in college?
> Teacher: No. John F. Kennedy was.
> Mary: Who was president when your mother was in college?
> Teacher: Calvin Coolidge.
> Mary: Is he still alive?
> Teacher: No, he died a long time ago.
> Mary: Who shot him?

Those chilling final words disclose a part of what the world may have become for even someone as young as Mary—in view of which, Ann's comment ("I wonder how many people will see the link between Mary's last question and over 55 million handguns that are loose in this country") seems to have been especially reductive.

5
Weakened Families, Worried Parents

The year 1955 was not a bad time to become Ann Landers. When Eppie Lederer did so, she could still refer to a generally accepted social structure. Ann Landers and her readers lived in about the same social and ethical world. Even contentions between definable groups occurred within an arena familiar to each. This helped Ann Landers maintain a large and interested readership. Since everybody spoke approximately the same language, her words and those of her readers were likely to interest a large audience.

When those constituencies were parents and children, the climate of the Spock years was particularly conducive to letter writing. That climate helped foster a more assertive voice in the young and was starting to confuse some of their parents. As a result, parents became increasingly dependent correspondents.

In the first columns, which belonged largely to teenagers, Ann lent a sympathetic ear. Parents in the fifties were not beyond feeling occasionally that discipline might have greater virtue than Dr. Spock allowed. (As a rule, Ann Landers did not feel any more than he did that general truths or moralistic principles offered satisfactory ground for modern upbringing. Like him, she favored a more pragmatic approach to allay interpersonal tensions.)

But the next two decades were going to be especially hard on parents. Many would find themselves confronting children seemingly determined, as a matter of personal privilege, to flaunt those very aspects of life their parents had confined to shadowy secrecy—and, as a matter of personal affront, to flout those who would prevent them from doing so.

Sexual activity had been an adult privilege protected by the marital bedroom or, less licitly, by euphemism. Beginning in the sixties, however, the privilege would be indulged or claimed as an overt celebration by the younger generation. This open sexuality led to further embarrassment when such open sexuality revealed hitherto unmentionable deviance. The genteel alcoholism and self-indulgent but legitimized overmedication of suburbia would find an ugly reflection in the blatancy of the youth's drug scene.

The young were starting to practice a form of activism. Parents who could afford for their offspring the leisure to enjoy rites of passage through left-wing beliefs discovered that here, too, the young wanted enactment. They were not necessarily content to be, as was more or less customary, a mainly verbal annoyance to be put up with for a time.

To top it all off, preserving decorum, which had been considered to be a nearly sacred middle-class duty, was about to be profaned and subverted at nearly every level. It is little wonder that after a time, parents began to crowd out their children seeking advice and support from Ann Landers. In the ensuing struggle over whether or not children would be able to assume traditionally adult rights, the adults' claim to the column would evidence one of the few times parents pushed more than they were pushed.

This reappropriation of the column is a reminder that the fact of writing is an important part of the letter's message. In the case of parents, this fact is particularly important. As one might expect, there are few letters from parents expressing satisfaction with their off-spring—since, presumably, such parents would have no reason to communicate with Ann Landers.

In the case of parents, those who were having no particular difficulties with their children thus left the field to those wishing to express steadfastness or simple bewilderment during times of rapid change. The alterations in the composition of these two groups (the "strong" and the "weak"), their relative proportions, the fluctuating nature of their concerns and reactions, compose the evolution of parenting during the turbulent third of a century ushered in by the fifties.

Of the two groups, the bewildered parents are likely to be the most frequent correspondents. Their numbers grew during the sixties and seventies as they absorbed members of the other group. But both are represented at all times, and in the midfifties, there is interesting evidence of the kind of "strong" parenting that still surfaced, some of which was noted in the previous chapter.

In December 1955, Bee Bee complained, "I'm a girl 16. Mother says I'm too young to date, too young to drive, too young to be out after 12, too young to smoke, drink or work. I'm writing to ask what a girl my age can do?" (Ann didn't even concede the dating—even though two weeks earlier she had told fifteen-year-old Miss No Name that she could date, "if you're a responsible chick"—and simply responded, "She can go to school and work hard to make good grades.")

A year later, M.C.M. wrote, "I'm 17 and for two years have gone with a fine boy who is studying for the ministry. We plan to marry when I graduate. My mother is so suspicious of us she has just about wrecked our romance. She knows where we are every minute, has set up curfews, doesn't allow us to go to drive-ins and so on.

We abide by her rules. Yet when I return from a date she scolds me because my clothes are wrinkled and makes insulting remarks. My boy friend becomes embarrassed and leaves." Ann wasn't moved by the religious calling of the young man and evidently did not feel, in 1956, that M.C.M.'s mother was a crank—she conceded only the wrinkles ("because they indicate nothing") and counseled obedience. "Young people in love are supposed to respect experience and wisdom. Mother has been around the track and she knows where the detours and dangerous curves are."

The following year, I.M. Gypped, just about to turn seventeen, said he felt he was suffering for his older brother's mistakes. That older brother "abused privileges something awful and went through six cars in two years." Gypped, who had his license, was not allowed to drive the family car unaccompanied. Ann told him, "Your folks aren't punishing you for your brother's mistakes, they're just smart enough not to make the same mistake twice." Before 1970, it was still possible (though at distant intervals) to find this kind of teen-age letter complaining about a firm parental hand that does not appear to be unreasonably heavy. At the start of 1969, No Infant lamented, "I'm a 13-year-old girl with a 38-year-old problem. My mother. Whenever I am invited to spend the night at a girl's house, she has to know the name, address and phone number of the girl. I don't mind this, but I DO mind when she calls the mother of the girl and gives her the third degree."

The considerable difference between M.C.M.'s mother and No Infant's reflects the difference between the kind of authority some parents felt they could impose in the midfifties, and the more rational (if harder to impose) discipline of the following decade, when the young had effectively loosened parental grips. Evidence of this kind of quiet parental authority is actually rare in the sixties and seldom seen in the seventies. Instead, as we noted in the previous chapter, complainants in the next two

decades become suspect as witnesses of parental dereliction, since they are apt to show indignation seemingly
out of proportion to the "dereliction" that triggered it
(and because, as No Infant's letter shows, they are able to
identify it even at a very young age).

But alongside the stern or firm parents of the fifties,
one notes already a good many others wavering between
former notions of discipline and the new principles
influencing (and confusing) child rearing. In May 1956,
Old-Fashioned Mom wrote:

> I have three daughters, 13, 14 and 16. They
> stick together like glue. No matter what their
> father and I decide, they have a list of logical
> reasons why it should be done another way.
> They're smart girls, Ann, and have made me
> wonder if my methods for child-rearing have
> been wrong. They tell us the modern approach
> is to allow the child to develop as an individ-
> ual—to be given the freedom to learn from his
> own mistakes. They resent discipline and say we
> are thwarting their natural instincts and damag-
> ing their personalities. They say we should take
> a child guidance course. What's your opinion?

This was an early instance of smart children using Dr.
Spock against their parents. In time, the strategy would
become an overused ploy. Although it was still relatively
new in 1956, it was already powerful. Old-Fashioned
Mom may have signed herself thus, but her signature was
just about the only assertive part of her letter—uncer-
tainty seeped through the rest of it. However, Ann was
still a rock. Availing herself of a pun she would make
famous, she responded, " 'Child guidance' is what a lot of
people are getting lately," and she went on without any
word mincing: "You wouldn't let your daughters fall off a
cliff to 'learn by experience,' would you? An undisci-
plined child is a nuisance to himself and everybody else."
She conceded to the times only minimally: "It's all right

to let a child stub his toe—but don't stand by and allow him to fracture his skull."

Although parents like Old-Fashioned Mom were already showing signs of waffling, the Ann Landers of the fifties could be the teens' champion at small expense thanks to other parents who were still overstrict or out of step. (Notable examples were those who had to be told not to read their children's mail or diaries—advice Ann found necessary to repeat even during the crisis years. Its updated and upscaled counterpart was, "Stay out of your children's business"—MYOB becoming a frequent and symbolic injunction.)

Ann's endorsement of teens was based largely on stylistic analyses—if the teen's letter seemed to show the kind of "responsibility" Miss No Name had evidently been able to demonstrate, the teen-ager was likely to get a friendly boost from Ann. If, on the other hand, the teen showed, even under similar circumstances, the kind of unwarranted rebellion that Ann read in Bee Bee's epistle, her advice was "listen to your parents." Here, too, she favored a pragmatic case-by-case approach rather than the imposition of uniform rules.

But this does not mean that there were *no* rules; there were, and they derived tautologically from her belief in an indwelling sense of right and wrong shared by all— parents as well as children. It was simply a question of whether or not the individual was willing to heed this knowledge. Children who did this would find themselves in compliance with parents acting likewise. However, if Ann thought parents were the ones being lax or remiss in their observance of the rules, they could count on getting their knuckles rapped. Parents were expected to be fair, generous, and loving. But they were also expected to uphold the law—a part of the test some of them appear to have been failing already in the midfifties.

In 1956, Distraught Dad wrote:

I'm the father of a girl 13. She's well developed physically and mentally—is sassy, fresh, carefree

and lazy like most girls her age. She's hopelessly
in love with a boy 17 who is not her type. He's an
accomplished pianist and cares for nothing but
music. Constantly he medicates himself, sneez-
ing, wheezing, coughing and disinfecting—the
worst hypochondriac I ever saw.

This summer I took them on a two-week
vacation in a trailer hoping to open the girl's
eyes. She didn't leave his side for 10 minutes. He
complained endlessly about the altitude, mos-
quitoes, heat, cold and dirt. Now she does nothing but moon around the house and wait for the
phone to ring. We're beside ourselves. What
shall we do about this girl?

That letter evidenced some interesting confusions. The
father seemed to be aware of his daughter's shortcomings
and of her incipient sexuality. Yet he appeared resigned
to those shortcomings, as if by now they defined thirteen-
year-old girls. As for his daughter's sexual persona, the
father demonstrated a curious ambivalence. He evidently
felt that a healthily "developed" creature like her could
only be turned off by a thoroughgoing hypochondriac—
even one four years her senior. But one cannot help
reading in his action a certain amount of aggression, as if
he were not only trying to teach his daughter about the
mediocrity of the asexual male, but also showing that
male how inadequate he was when contrasted to the
girl's vitality.

Ann Landers took due note of this pedagogic fiasco
already tinged with the permissiveness and futility of the
next decade, and upbraided Distraught Dad by zeroing in
on the sexual jeopardy (having perhaps sensed the father's ambiguous impulses): "Why did you take these two
kids on a vacation (and in a trailer yet!) and expose them
to constant companionship for two weeks? If this is your
idea of discouraging young romance, you had better open
your eyes. Your daughter is only 13 and her social life
should be limited to two evenings a week."

That same year, a just plain "Dad" wrote, "My wife is

very much upset over our 17-year-old son and insisted I write to you for advice. He's a good boy but has been suspended twice from school for being involved in minor car accidents during lunch period. He had liquor on his breath but neither time was he intoxicated." In later years, when the weakness of parents would take the form of soul-searching and questing for reasons, such naïve trust in an errant son might have made the letter sound like a Yalie joke. In 1956, however, permissiveness manifested itself differently. Parents tacitly acknowledged the derelictions of their offspring but tried to excuse them. It was a simpler way of seeing things, and Ann Landers could afford to be equally simple. Dad was advised to shape up in order not to "fail" his son.

Other parents were just weak, without regard to the times or anything else. Those were the ones who found it easier to write Ann Landers than to confront their progeny, and there were many of them. In October 1956, A Blue Mother wrote, "I have a daughter 17 who has gotten completely out of hand. . . . Last night at the supper table she told me to 'shut up.' This cut me like a knife. I have three married kids and not one of them ever caused me a minute's trouble. Please tell me what to do about this girl." The following day, it was a letter from Upset Mom, sounding a little like Dad: "Our 18-year-old son graduated in June. He won't work and stays in bed until noon every day. The only thing he's interested in is bowling. . . . He doesn't drink or smoke and is not what you'd call a 'bad boy.' We'd send him to college but he isn't interested. My husband says he should go into the service."

Dad's letter and Upset Mom's sounded another common note. In each, one detects the father's weakness or indifference—a desire on his part to eliminate the problem by either excusing it or getting rid of it ("he should go into the service"). In a surprisingly large number of cases, it is indeed the father who appears to be the less forceful or more fearful of the two parents. In September 1957, Bewildered wrote, "My husband and I are having trouble with our 11-year-old son. He was born late in our lives (we are both 53) and we were so thrilled . . . that the boy is a little spoiled. My husband says he's just a normal spirited kid and when I try to discipline him he claims I'm too tough. Last night when our son told me to 'get lost' I decided that was the limit, so I gave him a good swat. . . . My husband became angry and scolded me in the presence of the child." (Ann told Bewildered her real problem was her husband and advised her to "educate" him.)

In 1960, there is a letter from Old Fogey of 35. It is worth noting how often children must have used the generational argument against their parents, and how often the parents felt older than their years. She described "a small scale civil war" in her family because she wouldn't let her thirteen-year-old wear her boyfriend's ring on a chain around her neck. The mother told her to give the ring back and that "going steady" was out of the question: "She went into a tantrum and the rafters shook. . . . My husband says I'm handling it all wrong. He thinks we should let her go [to the movies with her boyfriend] and in a month she'll be tired of Bill and break up with him. . . . How can a mother stand up to this sort of pressure?" Ann, describing herself as an "Ancient Ruin of 41," repeated her usual advice: "Children need and want guidance. Don't be afraid to say no."

In 1962, F.D. wrote, "The problem centers around our 8-year-old, Sue. When I ask her to do something she just sits there. Ed invariably jumps to her defense. . . . Ed says I yell at her too much. I know he's right, but I think he's partly to blame too." Again, Ann identified the husband as the problem (assuming, as she might have in the case of Bewildered, that the husband was "waging a cold war against" the wife).

Fathers like Distraught Dad and F.D.'s husband may have shown an interesting ambivalence toward their daughters, but throughout the years, the weakness of fathers transcends even sexual ties. In 1975, when some parents were trying to reassert control, Helpless asked, "What do you think of a father who sits like a bump on a log and pretends he is deaf when you are reprimanding one of the children?" Four months later, in November, All's Quiet on the Western Front responded to yet another "mother who was miserable because her husband . . . forced her to handle everything. Of course the kids viewed her as the heavy and their father looked like a saint," suggesting that fathers should step in, as he had, with far greater authority.

But even fathers with a complaint and an idea about what should be done were frequently less apt to act on it than to discharge their frustration by writing, like One Against Three in May 1965: "Our children are 7 and 9. They love to watch TV. My wife thinks this is great, because it keeps them out of her hair for hours. . . . When I tell my wife to put the kids to bed, she says 'They will go when they are tired.' . . . This goes on night after night." Apparently unable to face his wife any more than he could his children or his responsibilities ("When I tell *my wife* to put the kids to bed"), One Against Three is indicative of a weakness in the weld of parental authority—the lax father—which may have contributed to the disarray of many families by the end of the decade, but which certainly predated it.

The weakness of lax parents is instanced and magnified by the letters they write. Most of them are variations of One Against Three's, dissipating in their statement to Ann Landers the energy that might have been directed to the situation they complain about. The Folks sent Ann a typical list of grievances in 1960: "Our 16-year-old daughter is driving us berserk. She just skims by in her studies, yet every evening her steady boyfriend shows up here before we leave the supper table and stays as late as he feels like it. They sit in the living room and turn the TV on to what they want to watch and then we get the fish eye because they think we are hanging around policing them. The boy bums cigarettes off me and to tell you the truth I can't stand the kid. He quit school last year and I think he's trying to get Nellie to do the same thing. What can we do?" Not a word in the letter suggests even remotely an attempt by The Folks to assert control or, for that matter, even to communicate their feelings to the culprits. Still, these were only intimations of the crisis to come, and Ann could still tell The Folks patiently, "Kids need controls and limits set for them. Put the shoe on the other foot, then put the foot down."

Ann's forbearance may have stemmed in part from many parents' confusion about their disciplinary rights. (This wavering was already exploited in 1956 by Old-Fashioned Mom's three smart daughters.) Even institutions such as dish washing, which had been long sacred to the American family, were being questioned, and by increasingly young rebels. Censored asked at the end of 1965 about her son Donald who didn't want to take turns with his sister doing the dishes: "Donald says a 13-year-old should not be asked to do sissy stuff around the house." Parents who may have been less than firm to begin with were now starting to think their 13-year-olds were legitimate participants in the debate on child rearing. "My husband and I want to be fair. Will you give us your opinion?" Ann censored Censored one more time by telling her that "Chores should be done by both boys and girls without resentment or complaint."

The times were also right for bringing back the "Dads" of the fifties, now lustered with a new legitimacy. In August 1970, Proud of Our Boy wrote, "Our 16-year-old son and his friend are in serious trouble because some stupid person put temptation in front of them. . . . Juddy and a 15-year-old pal were walking along the street last evening and they saw a 1970 Chevrolet with the key in the ignition. On a moment's impulse they decided to go for a little ride. . . . The police treated them as if they were murderers. Please say something about irresponsible adults who tempt kids and expect them to be superhuman." That particular problem had become so common

by then that the police and certain state laws acknowledged it, forcing Ann to concede that keys should not be
left in cars. But Ann could evidence moments of precrisis
toughness in the second half of 1970. Proud of Our Boy
was told, "Your letter is a beautiful example of what is
wrong with many of today's youth. Parents like you have
been making excuses for your children for so long it is
pitiful."

As the sixties were progressing, parents who might still
have been tempted to hold the line would be getting less
and less support from their peers. Early in 1961, Ann
Landers acknowledged having struck a raw nerve among
a large number of readers: "Dear Readers: Remember
'Bitter 15,' the lad who was paying his own school tuition
and buying his own clothes? I thought his parents had
done a superb job of teaching him self-reliance and I said
so. . . . Many readers agreed with me. Many did not."
Among those that did not were letters like those of Mad:
"You're nuts. Did you say the parents were raising a
wonderful boy? It sounds to me as if the boy is raising
himself. What are they doing besides letting him live in
the house and take his meals with them?" Likewise,
Furious wrote, "Your reply to 'Bitter 15' was shocking. I
think the parents should be reported to the juvenile
authorities in their city."

Parents losing the generational battle felt curiously
defensive ("mad" and "furious") when shown instances
of those who hadn't. However, this was less and less likely
to happen. In August 1965, Behind the Times? wrote:

> Last weekend I took my sons (aged 10 and 12)
> to the hardware store. The neighbor boy (he's
> 13) asked if he could ride along.
>
> I noticed the boys handling some combination
> locks which were out on the counter but I didn't
> pay any attention. Last night I saw my younger

son playing with one of the locks. I asked him
where he got it. He answered "Jimmie (the
neighbor boy) took some locks and gave one to
Bob and one to me."

I asked if Jimmie had paid for the locks and he
replied "No." I then asked if he knew that was
stealing. He said, "Bob and I didn't steal them,
Jimmie did."

I called Bob in and announced that I was
taking them both down to the hardware
store. . . . I telephoned Jimmie's mother and
asked if she'd like to bring her son along. She
said, "No. It would damage him psychologically." She then gave me a lecture on "Traumas
in children" and added, "Apparently you are not
up on the latest."

The letter's signature (Behind the Times?) acknowledges and condemns a velocity of change that was a bit
much even for Ann. She was moved to one of her very
occasional flights of moral rhetoric: "The decline of
morals in today's society is due to the failure of parents to
teach their children respect for truth, integrity, decency
and other so-called 'old-fashioned' virtues."

But by 1970, the "traumas" that Behind the Times? had
been warned about were in the public domain, and even
Ann had to acknowledge them for a while: "Pass the
humble pie. . . . Every now and then I reverse my advice,
usually because the readers have persuaded me I was
wrong. And so it was in the case of the mother who found
a collection of nude pictures in a box under her son's
bed. She wrote to say she had cured her 17-year-old son
by pasting the nudes on the living room wall. . . . I thought
it was ingenious and amusing, and I said so. Hundreds of
readers let me know it wasn't funny."

Even granting that the woman's cure was as childish as
the son's behavior, the tone and content of the reaction

to Ann's advice is still interesting to note: "Hundreds more said it was a destructive thing to do to a 17-year-old boy. They said the lad's behavior was normal and Mom should have kept her hot little hands off the pictures and said nothing." By 1970, the young had proved strong enough to loose the weak grip of faltering parents, while convincing them at the same time of the frailty of their own egos—"saying nothing" was now the enlightened approach. And at the crest of the tide, Ann went along. It was now Mom who had the "hot little hands."

Parental confusion in the sixties and seventies seems to have taken different forms, according to whether it occurred in cities or in rural areas. To the extent indicated, "weak" parents appear to be urban in the majority, and among the better educated of Ann's letter writers, while the "strong" ones are found more frequently in farm families and small towns. The confusion of parents who felt it was important to be in the vanguard of changing times extends into a period of what might be called "enlightenment," during which they try reacting to the crisis in the same spirit as they might to a fad.

In 1960, Standing Alone wrote, "We know a couple we consider close friends. They are intelligent, good company and well-respected in the community. . . . This couple considers themselves ultra modern and highly sophisticated. They have two teen-age children, a boy 15 and a girl 17. The parents tell risqué jokes and use profanity (and worse) in the presence of their children. . . . When the kids left, I told Mrs. ——— I thought her joke was unsuitable for the kids. She replied, 'Don't be so naïve. The kids know as much as we do. I believe in treating them as adults.' "

Ten years later, Just Me (an adult of the seventies who could no longer feel safe using any other kind of self-description) suggested, "Today's youth has different goals and different values [from their "upper-middle-class parents"], and those differences are what created the gap we've been hearing about"—an instance among many of adults, burying themselves with the shovel the young had handed them.

The following year, an unwittingly funny letter appeared. Mixed Mates were in search of "a new set of etiquette guidelines" to help "confused parents": "Our two daughters have been living with their boyfriends for over a year. Neither has plans for marriage at the present time because 'it isn't necessary.' . . . When children marry, an announcement appears in the papers, but we seem to have acquired a couple of sons-in-law by virtue of the fact that they are shacked up with our daughters." The parents, already caught up in the crude idioms of the times, were now trying to swing with the new conventions by grafting bits of more familiar ones onto them. But this was 1971, and Ann Landers (in any event never kindly disposed toward cohabitation that wasn't marital) had begun to swing back toward the status quo ante. She asked Mixed Mates, "Where did you get the idea these two jokers are sons-in-law?" and told the parents they were under no obligation to explain anything.

In the eighties, when some previously beaten parents were attempting comebacks, one notices their occasional attempt to appropriate the kind of sophistry that had been used against them for so long. It Happened to Me, who was contemplating the prospect of being a parent, discovered in 1980 that the best defense was an offense with the enemy's weapons: "I have read so many letters in your column from children and adults who blame their parents for raising them 'wrong,' . . . Why don't these people understand that their parents had parents too? If a person is going to lay all his problems on his parents' backs, he must also blame his grandparents and his great-grandparents."

We noted the defensiveness of parents in the sixties and seventies directed against those who had not yet lost the battle. Small-town anger manifested itself as early, but it lasted longer, had its own voice and targets, and was usually brought on by instances of the new freedom rather than by the presence of those who opposed it. In January 1960, Concerned Parents noticed their seventeen-year-old son "bringing home books from the library on sex, also French novels and that certain book which I shall not name but it's one the postmaster said was 'filthy.' My husband and I were at a loss so we phoned his English teacher who said, 'The boy is doing well in school. . . . Leave him alone.' We peeked at that certain book and we were shocked. Do you think the teacher gave us good advice?" Ann did indeed, and in so doing made many more like-minded parents suspicious of her.

Six months later, it was Fool Yourself Not who was mad at another of Ann's standard admonitions to parents: "What do you mean by telling mothers they have no right to look at their daughters' diaries and read their mail? How can mothers find out what is going on in this age of crazy mixed-up kids, high school beer drunks, rock 'n' roll maniacs and overcrowded homes for unwed mothers?"

And occasionally Ann heard from the Bible Belt, as in 1966 when Square and Proud of It shared his insights with her: "I have determined what is wrong with the world. The Bible teaches us that the father should be the head of the house. But is he? . . . Both parents are afraid of their children. . . . I've seen 15-year-old punks smoking cigarettes. I have two nieces aged 13 and 14, and they both look like tramps. If I can see it, why can't their parents?" Ann counseled against generalizing, but was confronting sufficient evidence of cave-in fathers and other parental derelictions to agree with the letter's thrust.

For once, she wasn't overly put off by the letter's fundamentalist prejudices—even though they usually pricked her liberalism. For example, in 1960, Mrs. K. wrote about her sixteen-year-old daughter, an honor student who now wanted to wear lipstick and date, "I say the reason she makes good grades and stays out of trouble is because we are strict. I hate the way the young girls of today paint up. I say keep them away from temptation and the devil. What do you say?" What Ann said was predictable under the circumstances—though the advice might not have been quite as trenchant if Mrs. K.'s nose had not been so sensitive to satanic sulphur: "A 16-year-old should be wearing lipstick and dating, if she wants to. Too much discipline can make a teen-ager feel caged." And, for good measure, Ann warned Mrs. K. that the caged ones were the worst.

Meanwhile, the more sophisticated parents were trying to respond to kids who were sowing oats that were wilder than any they could remember from their own youth. The generation that had grown up after the Depression and lived through the austerity of the war was suddenly faced with the joint consequences of freedom and economic ease.

In 1966, Adrift Without Answers wanted to know what to do about her daughter Lois, who had "hemmed up all her dresses so that they hit her about four inches above the knees. She wants everything tight around the hips, and the louder the colors and patterns the better. She goes around both day and night wearing sunglasses as large as coffee cups. Her hair (which she irons on a board) hangs in her eyes and looks ghastly." Then, Adrift provided the key to what was really amiss: "My husband and I have had some serious talks about what to do, but we just don't know where to draw the line." Adrift promptly hid behind her peers: "Will you please print this letter not only for us but for other parents who must be equally baffled?"

This was a measure of Ann Landers's power and influence: She was now in a position to fill the vacuum in parents who felt "adrift without answers" with her own. And she rose to the task with precision: "Styles DO change—and they will continue to change because it's good for morale and good for business. But some of the stuff I've seen lately—not only on teen-agers, but on their mothers—may be considered fashionable, but it strikes me as positively indecent. The op look and the pop look and the ironed hair and the kooky glasses—O.K., if a girl keeps herself clean. But those skin-tight, thigh-high skirts are vulgar. There's nothing left for a girl to do to attract attention except to set her hair on fire."

Interestingly, Ann granted Lois all she wanted (except the skirt); the point of her letter was elsewhere, and had to do with parents resisting peer pressure: "Parents not only have the right but they have an obligation to say, 'This far—and NO further!' There comes a point at which respectability must take precedence over 'trend'—and, so help me, over 'what everybody else in the crowd is doing.' " The definition of "respectability" was left to the inborn sense that, Ann believed, was given to all—even though that is where Adrift Without Answers and her spouse had come in.

The peer pressure that Ann was trying to resist was affecting parents as much as kids. (Adrift had given evidence of this kind of comfort in numbers with her reference to "other parents who must be equally baffled.") As early as 1957, Somebody's Mom wanted to know what to do about her thirteen-year-old: "She's a darling girl with high ideals. Her little social club, comprised of fifteen girls, is planning a pajama party. These young ladies range in age from 13 to 15 years of age and the party is to be held at a downtown hotel. . . . All the girls have permission from their parents, but I'm reluctant to approve the idea. I somehow feel a girl 13 should not be spending the night in a hotel with girl friends." And then came the admission of doubt, apparent in so many of these letters—and the reason for their being written: "Of course my daughter is upset with me and thinks I'm being very stuffy. Am I?"

This provided Ann with one of her earlier attempts to stiffen a correspondent's spine: "You are sensible to refuse to permit a girl of 13 to spend the night whooping it up with her club sisters in a downtown hotel." One might contrast this gentle support of Somebody's Mom with the kind of brusqueness Ann felt she had to resort to in 1975 while advising Sad Father, a widower whose shrewish daughter objected to the presence of his cousin [a woman] in what had been her mother's home: "The trouble is you aren't standing—you're lying down and letting your bossy daughter walk all over you. Tell her in plain language that YOU will decide who comes into your home—and to keep her oar out of your water."

The sixties soon made it apparent that crazy fashions and pajama parties were the least of parents' difficulties with their children. In 1960, Can't Sleep said, "I'm so nervous I can hardly write this letter. I just found out for certain that my 18-year-old son is intimately involved with a girl 17. . . . I'm a widow and my son's education is all planned and provided for by a trust which his father set aside. I don't want anything to interfere with his college education. I'm afraid if this girl continues to go with my son she may insist on an early marriage and spoil his life." It was never easy for a parent alone to bring up a child, but the times were certainly not making it any easier. And, as Ann pointed out, they were preventing people from keeping their priorities straight: "You are so preoccupied with your son's future that you ignore the fact that he shares the blame—and the responsibility." Ann may have sensed that the claims of a new freedom strengthened in someone like Can't Sleep an older prejudice condoning the male's sexual irresponsibility.

Fifteen years later, the times had procured that kind of freedom for both sexes, and some "enlightened" parents were showing total confusion in their responses. At the start of 1975, Another Mother wrote, "I read with interest your advice to the mother who signed herself 'Numb.' She walked in on her 17-year-old daughter and boyfriend and caught them in the act. As the mother of five beautiful, dimpled blonde girls, I'd be thankful that I caught them and not their dad. Fathers have a thing about daughters, you know."

This introduction notwithstanding, Another Mother went on to specify what she would do if she were in the same situation as Numb. She concluded, "I'd tell them they might decide that sex outside of marriage isn't right, but abstaining would take a lot of self-control and discipline. This means being alone as little as possible, more double-dating with another couple who don't neck and pet. Vow to abstain from kissing in a car or any other place where sex might be possible." For some reason, Ann decided to print this compendium of modern parental noninterference (*"they* might decide that sex outside of marriage isn't right") and futile puritanical strategies. But she felt it necessary to counter that confusion with her own bottom-line sense of the times: "The odds for permanent abstinence are small. Along with the hope, trust and confidence, I'd make sure that daughter had plenty of information."

In July 1980, Worried in Middletown, N.Y., referred to a previous column on "bed-hopping" and said, "My daughter is 19. She is so immature it kills me. The girl doesn't know the first thing about men. After the second date she goes out and buys her current 'love' expensive presents and smothers him with attention. . . . I know she's sick but she won't see a doctor. She says she is very happy with her life and I should not try to impose my standards on her. Maybe she is right and I am wrong. She is in perfect health and I'm a nervous wreck." This letter is another example of a writer with vestigial assertiveness ("She is so immature it kills me," "I know she's sick") finally swept away by doubts common to so many parents incapabable of responding to their children in a world whose rules had been so drastically changed.

That same month, most of the column was devoted to a letter of Baltimore Heartache: "The lovely, intelligent 19-year-old daughter of a dear friend was killed recently in a tragic accident. The parents are inconsolable. To make matters worse, they found birth control pills in the dead girl's purse. . . . What can we say to alleviate the pain? How can we rear our own daughters so they will not go down the same road? Is this something the majority of young people are doing now? . . . Please say something to help our friends who not only must face the loss of their daughter but also their failure to keep her pure for the wedding bed."

The letter struck an incongruous note—that parents who were sorrowing over the death of a daughter should have added to that sorrow because of her sexual life seemed improbable in 1980. But it was perhaps this very reversion by bewildered parents that caused Ann Landers to sound the final knell of the old morality:

> At the onset of any discussion of teen-age behavior, we must accept the fact that this is not the same world we grew up in. . . . Parental guidance and exemplary role models are helpful, but the pill has changed everything. Also there are peer pressure, advertising, movies, TV and highly seductive music. Today, in terms of physical maturation, a 13-year-old is where a 16-year-old was 40 years ago. . . . In my opinion, all this sleeping around is sad. It has very little to do with love and caring. I liked it better the other way. But we cannot turn the clock back. Parents do NOT have the last word. Each individual, in the final analysis, is responsible for himself or herself.

Ann had been a long-time proponent of the old sexual morality, and she remained one, but she knew that the times no longer lent themselves to this kind of moral advocacy. She continued to argue the case for premarital abstinence but put more emphasis on, and trust in, the sexual education of the young.

Anyway, jeopardies greater than sex were threatening the teen-agers of the seventies—among which the most serious was undoubtedly the drug culture. Parents were trying to recognize in their children symptoms that might be either specific or attributable to the strange new scene: "When a mother suspects her son is 'on something,' how can she tell for sure if her hunch is right? . . . I might be mistaken, Ann, but he has undergone such a complete personality change—he isn't the same kid we once knew. Help us, please."

Other equally pathetic parents and grandparents were confused in different ways. Heartsick Gram wrote in 1970, "Today was the saddest day of my life. I took my granddaughter to the police station. I asked the authorities to put her in a home for unruly girls. She is only 15." She recounted her attempts to raise this "sweet, reliable girl" of divorced parents, and the child's gradual dissipation, "running with these strange-looking kids and behaving as if she was drunk or drugged. I knew she was on something but I didn't know what. The final straw was when she was so drowsy I couldn't wake her. I thought she was unconscious. When she finally came to, I decided to turn her in. Did I do the right thing, Ann?"

Toward the end of 1975, Helpless and Miserable wrote, "Our 27-year-old son is a drug addict. He lives at home and refuses to work. . . . My husband is sick and wants to retire. Where are the laws in the country anyway? Why must aged parents be forced to keep a son who is in such terrible shape and makes their life a living hell?" Ann had to inform these parents that the youth culture had not affected the laws of the land: "Nowhere does it say parents must keep a 27-year-old son in their home. You could have kicked him out legally six years ago."

Helpless and Miserable were not the only parents who seemed to have lost their hold on any kind of rudder. A sense of adaptation to defeat occurs in many letters written after 1970. At the beginning of 1975, another Grandma wrote, "This past week my grandson was suspended from school (he's a 10th-grader) because he arrived on Monday morning so drunk he couldn't see straight. He fell out of his seat. . . . When my daughter-in-law was called by the principal to come and take her son home, she said 'Thank God he's not on drugs.' " The indulgent "Dad" of 1956, reincarnated as Proud of Our Boy in 1970, was emerging in yet another and more modern form five years later.

The polls of the early seventies document wide acceptance of drugs among adolescents. An interview of students by Gallup in February 1971 reveals that even though the results of clinical studies were not yet in, 85 percent believed marijuana was not harmful. Nearly half of all students had smoked marijuana, about the same number as had recently experimented with various hallucinogens. Confronted with this widespread evidence, resignation to defeat was one aspect of parental reaction in the seventies; another was something fast approaching self-laceration:

> We have a 17-year-old son whose entire personality changed about three years ago. He has been on drugs, totaled two cars, won't attend regular school, refuses to work, comes in whenever he feels like it (drunk or stoned), has little contact with the other members of the family, doesn't care for girls (says he can't find the "right one"), has seen a psychiatrist three times, went to a mental health clinic, refuses to go back, says they are all crazy there. . . . We are a middle-class, church-going family, have given him plenty of love and done our best. Now I ask you, is this a normal child? (Distraught Parents, October 1985)

The following year, Meant Well Parents wrote, "What wisdom, consolation or advice can you give parents in their 50s who have worked hard to achieve the American dream, loved their kids and tried to give them the best world ever? . . . Many of our children are on drugs, unemployed drop-outs, migrant drifters, angry with the world, hostile toward us. . . . How much and for how long should parents pay in terms of self-recrimination, worry, disappointment and financial support?" Ann took note of the seriousness of the problem in her answer: "To you and the thousands of other parents who are miserable because of 'what you have done' to your children, I say this: Stop beating yourselves. . . . Enough of this 'You damaged me, now take care of me' nonsense. It's a copout."

How much effect Ann's words had on the self-lacerators is difficult to ascertain, but the magnitude of their number can be judged by the fact that when Ann reprinted her words in 1980, she noted, "That particular column has been requested almost more than any other." Ann's advice notwithstanding, signs of breast beating continue, as evidenced in 1984 by Heartsick in Amarillo: "I have a problem that is breaking my heart. Our lovely bright daughter has told me that she is a lesbian. . . . Did we raise her wrong? Is it our fault that she is like this? I must tell you that this girl was very popular in school and had lots of dates." Her own counsel failing, there remained for Ann Landers only to turn over Heartsick in Amarillo to one of the support groups that always seem to spring up in response to a specific social distress (in this case, the Federation of Parents and Friends of Lesbians and Gays).

In the second part of 1970, Ann Landers was starting to think it was time her readers consigned to history the previous year, as well as the turbulence that had led up to it. She felt the reins had to be picked up again and the spotlight turned back on parents. Not that the drumbeat of Ann Landers's admonitions to weak parents had ever relented. In 1956, she told A Blue Mother, whose daughter had suddenly "gotten completely out of hand," that the change was not sudden but had been "in the making a long time. A 17-year-old girl is a minor and you are responsible for her." In 1965, she told S.I.L., "Parents who are unable to handle their children should get outside help. They should not give up and let the kids run wild."

She had always looked first to wavering fathers and mothers for the causes of youthful misbehavior and had seldom minced words in detailing parental shortcomings. But as the 1969 crisis neared, the burden of such analyses shifted to the young and took greater note of other factors influencing their behavior. At the start of 1970, for example, she alluded to what was happening on campuses in speaking to Longview, Washington, who complained about grandparents spoiling her children: "Some of the most destructive and violent students come from affluent homes. Many were raised by permissive parents who smothered them with things, things, and more things. These unhappy kids feel cheated and bought-off and are registering their resentment by rejecting every symbol of authority." Ann Landers's comment still mentioned parental permissiveness, but youthful rebellion had reached such proportions by then that it was necessary to include broader psycho-sociological consideration.

Still, Ann Landers was clearly anxious to make the crisis more manageable by getting back to her identification of root causes—parents—as in the happier days of 1960 when she had gotten "a well-known national organization" into trouble. That year, her advice "don't be a pal to your son" appeared "on the opening day of [the organization's] national drive to encourage a better relationship between fathers and sons," using the slogan "Pals Forever." She then compounded the trouble she had caused by refusing to back down: "If I had been asked for a slogan I would have suggested 'Friends Forever.' The word pal suggests a 'buddy-buddy' tie-up which puts Pa right down there at the 11-year-old level. . . . The dad who tries to be a 'chum' is like the boss who dances and drinks all evening with his secretary at the office party and then expects her to say, 'Yes, sir,' on Monday morning."

In September 1970, Mr. J.P.S., Bureau of Children's
Services, Trenton, N.J., wrote, "I was shocked by your
insensitivity to the feelings of that 13-year-old girl who
didn't want to leave her friends and move to Omaha."
Ann answered, "Sorry, I don't agree. Why should a father
pass up an opportunity for advancement because his
child doesn't want to leave her friends? . . . There has
been too much indulgence, too much catering, too much
'putting the kids first.' There is plenty of evidence that
kids who have been raised this way are hopelessly messed
up."

That same year, Bub No. 2 had written, "I'll bet you've
had a zillion letters from people who are furious with Los
Angeles Bub—the man who wrote to say he doesn't
dislike cats—it was children he hates. Bub went on to say
he is sick of our child-centered society and that most
parents are scared to death of their kids. They cater to
them, bribe them and live in fear of incurring their
disfavor." This was close to the thrust of Square and
Proud of It's letter in 1966. This time, however, Ann
struck a different tone: "You are right, I did get a zillion
angry letters from readers, but I received half a zillion
letters from people who wrote as you did." A zillion is
twice as much as half a zillion, but if one can judge from
her mail through 1975, even half a zillion sounds rather
more optimistic than accurate. What it does show is Ann
Landers trying to cast out in a direction her readers
would be slower to accept.

The fact is that parents were tired. However much they
catered to their kids, most of them were sorry they had
had them in the first place. Ann Landers, who was starting
to stress with renewed emphasis that parents should
reassert control, did not quite realize the extent of the
strain on those same parents brought on by ten years of
increasingly difficult relations with their children. In the
first week of April 1970, a little before one detects those
signs of a toughening in Ann Landers herself, Betrayed
wrote, "Shall I have a child (at age 30) and despise it, or

stick to my position and take a chance on losing the man I love?" Betrayed was haunted by memories of her own difficult childhood, not by what was happening in the world, so it is not her view of children that interests us here—rather, it is Ann Landers's. She replied, "Your feelings about children are grossly immature. I suggest counseling." In April 1970, Ann derived her advice from the assumption that children were a natural and desirable part of family life. As we know, the stress of the decade changed that perception of the family. In 1976, responding to her poll, "Parenthood—if you had a choice, would you do it again?" 70 percent of the huge numbers that answered told her no, they would not.

The change in the attitude of eighties parents had other causes as well. Spoiled children had been, at least in part, children of more affluent times; now the economy was faltering. Some, who had left home, were returning just when many parents were starting to enjoy a taste of the freedom that had so long been denied them. The later seventies and the eighties evidenced an unusually large number of letters like that of Irritated Mother Hen in Stockton: "As the economy slows down I'm sure there are other parents who are facing the same problem we are. A child who left home a few years ago returns 'temporarily'—just until he or she can get back on sound economical footing. Meanwhile, after getting over the trauma of the empty nest, parents have learned to enjoy the freedom of being just a couple again." Likewise, We Made It on Our Own wrote, "Can you stand a letter that disagrees with the conciliatory tone most of your respondents have expressed in regard to adult children who have moved back with the parents because they have lost their jobs?" The last letter shows that even though not all parents were reasserting themselves, Ann's "half a zillion" counterpunchers were beginning to appear.

Also beginning to appear were support groups for parents needing to strengthen each other as they strengthened their grip. Among them were Tough Love and Parents Who Care, whose program was detailed in 1980 by A Midwestern Mom Who Likes the Idea:

1. Teen-agers are required to stay home on school nights except for school or community events. (No running the streets or driving around aimlessly.)
2. Weekend curfews for ninth-graders between 11 and 11:30 P.M. 10th graders, 11:30 and midnight. 11th graders, midnight and 12:30 A.M.
3. Parents should feel free to contact parents who are hosting parties to find out if there will be adult supervision and whether alcohol will be permitted.
4. For their own children's parties, parents should be visible and feel free to ask anyone with drugs or alcohol to leave.
5. Parents should get to know their children's friends and their parents.

Thus it happens that in the eighties, among the self-questioning and guilt-ridden letters, there are occasionally some that are different, detached from a formerly oppressive involvement with children, even to the point of placing some of yesterday's traumas within an ironic distance. An example is Sauce for the Goose in Ashland, Wisc.: "I thought I had heard everything, but that letter in your column about the kid in Denver who is filing suit against his parents because they did a lousy job of raising him did it. Now I think I'll sue my kids because they didn't turn out the way my husband and I hoped they would." Another might be the one written by Happy with the Thought:

It is a common occurrence, these days, to divorce a spouse. But what do you think of divorcing your children?
My husband and I raised our three to the best

of our ability. We spent time with them, took them to church, encouraged their participation in sports and music. Everything was fine until they hit the mid-teen years. Suddenly peer pressure took over. All the things they were taught as youngsters went out the window. . . .

Last week my wife and I decided to divorce all three of our children. There will be no reconciliation until they agree to behave like responsible adults.

The detachment of irony is most likely healthier than the former agonizing of some, but it is still detachment. In many families, children and parents continue to view each other as separate beings inhabiting mutually exclusive worlds. And parenting remains a hazardous occupation. Early in 1986, joining Oklahoma Reader who had proposed a toast to mothers, Ann expressed the belief that all signs of a return to parental authority notwithstanding, the damage of two previous decades remained: "Never was there a more difficult time to raise children."

6
The Changing Woman

On the question of women, Ann Landers demonstrates a familiar, but perhaps more visible, pattern of response: an attentiveness to the prevalent mood of her readers, that anticipates it at times and resists it at others. Because her earlier judgments were influenced by a conviction that family life was at the center of our society and that women were the center of that center, she tended to view women primarily as homemakers and husbands' helpers. This was the case even though she herself was the prime instance of a career woman who combined home and office, who demonstrated to what dizzying heights careerism could lead, and who would eventually divorce.

If we are to believe Margo Howard's recollections in *Eppie: The Story of Ann Landers*, Esther Pauline Lederer was a loving mother and a devoted wife—but a driving and driven woman as well:

> We moved in the summer of 1954. It was sure
> a different Chicago than the one we had lived in
> before. . . . Now there were doormen and taxis

and traffic and elegance. . . . After weeks of
sifting offers, [Father] accepted the presidency
of the Autopoint Corporation, an advertising-
specialty firm dealing mainly in ball-point pens
and pencils. . . .

With Father and me squared away, Mother
could now resume her hobby-career. Since she
had been about to be named Democratic national committeewoman from Wisconsin, she
figured she could just change her base and
continue in Chicago. She figured wrong.

Going to her old friend Colonel Arvey, she
asked for guidance about how to proceed. Jack
Arvey was the top Democrat in Chicago politics
then, even counting Mayor Daley. He didn't miss
a beat in response to her question. She couldn't
just pick up where she left off, he explained,
because Illinois was not Wisconsin. The Chicago
machine was not manned by La Follette Demo-
crats, let alone women. "If you persist," he told
her, "I will worry that you might wind up in Lake
Michigan wearing a cement ankle bracelet." . . .
Mother was surprised—and a little bit stuck. She
would spend months figuring out what to do
with herself. But she did know one thing: she
would do something.

Mother knew she had a calling, she just didn't
know what it was. Being shut out of politics put
the kibosh on the thing she knew how to do best,
but there had to be something else. The mystery
occupation had no delineation in her mind, but
she knew she would know it when she saw it.

She saw it one morning in August of 1955.
Reading the *Sun-Times*, Will Munnecke's paper.

What Eppie saw was the Ann Landers column, and what
she decided was that poor Ann Landers must be swamped
with letters seeking her wise counsel. She would help the
beleaguered columnist. She accordingly called "Uncle
Will" at his office. " 'I've figured out what I want to do,'
she announced. 'I'll help Ann Landers answer the mail.'

There was a lengthy pause on the other end. 'It's odd,' Will mused, 'that you are calling me now. Ruth Crowley, our Ann Landers, died suddenly last week. I'll have to call you back.' " Her daughter added, "Mother's timing was startling, even to her."

By the time Munnecke did call back, Eppie had come up with another idea: She would simply take over the column. Munnecke was a sufficiently good friend to laugh out loud at her, and that, of course, was one of the last times he did.

Margo describes both her parents as workaholics: "They both had enormous drive and energy. . . . If mother had been nudged into a career as a way of coping with Father's immersion in work, she went at it like a born-again zealot. . . . Father's need was to get away from being the boy with no money, Mother's was to outdistance a twin sister with whom she'd always been compared." But Eppie was also a mother—a Jewish mother—who was a part of Ann Landers before even she knew it. Margo Howard recalls her mother's first visit to her in college: "The first time she came to school was when she gave a speech in Boston. She seemed quite like a visiting movie star—with dark glasses and a mink coat, greeting everyone—until we got to my room. Talking with my roommate, she spied my laundry bag hanging on the back of the door. She walked over, got it down, and sorted out what could be washed by hand. Then she went to our little sink and did laundry. My roommate was spellbound, but it was old-hat to me. This was entirely in keeping for Mother, who had always been compulsive about getting things done."

This compulsion about "getting things done" describes a quotient of energy with which more common mortals are rarely endowed. Eppie could not display herself as a role model for her readers, nor did she try. She never expected her women readers to combine a career at home and another away from home. (She was of course assisted in her career by money and connections.

Nevertheless, one has the feeling that her drive was still the most important ingredient in her success.)

On the question of being a wife, she had a much more traditional side. "Mother decided . . . that Herblock, the gifted political cartoonist, should have a nice Jewish wife—and for years she told him she would find him one. She was floored when his brother died in Chicago and was told the wake would be at St. Somebody's. Why, she asked Herb, would his brother have a wake? 'Because we're Catholic,' he told her. Not one to take no for an answer, Mother told him she was still going to find him a nice Jewish girl because they made wonderful wives."

Of her own first and immature marriage, Margo writes, "I decided then that marriage was the next logical step, probably because my parents provided a good model. My image of their marriage had been formed by little things—mostly romantic—things like watching them dance together in the living room to a phonograph record, hearing Father refer to Mother as 'heaven eyes,' and knowing that when he was traveling he would call her every night from wherever he was in the world."

There were also more significant signs: "She was a paradox, of course. The ultimate liberated woman, she played the game—the old-fashioned one—in which she never acknowledged the degree to which her life was her own. It seemed funny and fey that 'Jules's Wife' was sewn into the linings of her furs all the years they were married. It was a remark, however, that she didn't wish to be regarded as off on her own. It was nothing she cared to think about . . . just something she wanted to do."

She finally divorced Jules—even though one might wonder, as Margo seems to, whether a driving, ambitious part of Eppie had not escaped long before, leaving him with only the presence of someone playing the traditional role of a wife. However that may be, her column upheld the wife's role even after she acknowledged divorce. Over the years, she would be advising women whose letters showed increasing signs of restlessness within traditional roles. But even though she would encourage them, as a feminist and an understanding sister, she never encouraged them to the detriment of a marital structure in which the woman was the sexual and working adjunct of the man.

This does not mean, however, that even during the relative innocence of the fifties, the man who took advantage of those roles would escape getting his just desserts at her hands. In 1957, J.H.H. wrote, "My wife and I have been married almost nine years and we have six lovely little ones. We used to have a fairly normal home life but now things are beginning to change. . . . It seems that every night when I come home from work, my wife is washing, ironing or folding things. I maintain that if a woman plans her work properly she should be finished by the time her husband comes home. . . . She's been nagging me to stay home Saturdays and watch the kids so she can go shopping without them." Using the form of address she reserved for those who angered her, Ann replied, "If you wanted sympathy, Buster, you came to the wrong party."

Hard-Boiled Harry, who had written five months earlier, was less innocent. He sensed a change in the offing: "I'm an able-bodied, hard-working man and I don't give my [bus] seat to anybody. Women demand equal pay, the right to vote, they drink in bars, smoke on the street and wear slacks. They want to be treated like man's equal . . . so I say, let's treat 'em equal all the way down the line!" Ann's answer hit Hard-Boiled Harry on two fronts, first telling him about the nearly 20 million women who were in the work force at the time, and then denouncing the cad, "I hope, Harry, someone gives YOUR mother a seat."

But when the innocent was within bounds that still obtained in the fifties, he was likely to get a more favorable reading—even when it was his victim who complained. We have already recorded Ann's 1957 wisdom to Mrs. Thru-the-Mill: "The male is the hunter . . . it's the nature of the beast." The beast enjoyed other privileges as well. That same year, F.M. wrote, "I am 7½ months pregnant and enjoy wearing overalls. When my husband comes home at night and sees me, he raises the rafters." Ann told her, "A woman in overalls 7½ months pregnant must be something less than gorgeous. Pregnancy offers no license to look like a slob. . . . Get out of the farmer outfit at once."

Those were also the days when people like Top Banana wrote in periodically with tales of woe consequent upon beating a boyfriend at sports. (Top Banana was a cracker-jack golfer who had also bested hers at tennis, a game he taught her!) Top Banana wrote, "Now we've started to bowl together. I've never bowled before but I seem to have a knack for it. I see trouble ahead. My girl friend says I should let him do better at this if it kills me. I don't agree. What do you think?" Ann replied, "It's less than smart for a woman to consistently parade her superiority whether it's intellectual or athletic. How important is it to win the game if you lose the guy?" Even in 1960, Top Banana was a step ahead of Ann Landers on that one. Like Hard-Boiled Harry, Top Banana most likely sensed that times had started to change.

Three months after Hard-Boiled Harry, Mrs. Ted E. wrote, "I live in a neighborhood where the majority of women are employed either full or part time. . . . I stick out like a sore thumb because I'm the only full-time housewife in the group. One of my neighbors said to me recently, 'Why don't you work?' When I told her I enjoyed staying at home, that I actually liked cooking, cleaning and being with my children, she looked at me as if I were crazy." Ann commended her, "You are probably one of the sanest people who has written to me in ages. My hat is off to you." Ann's commendation was an attempt to bolster a woman who already had sufficient doubts about her traditional role to write.

But changes set in motion by Rosie the Riveter during the Second World War were not going to be reversed. Good times and bad times would contribute to their

momentum, either affording women better access to the
job market or requiring it. Along with a new economic
outlook, women were getting a new sense of themselves.
Two months after her recommendation to Top Banana,
Long Suffering Top Banana countered her: "Tsk tsk, Ann
Landers—how important is it to win a guy who can't lose
a game?"

It is thus possible that Ann Landers may have started in
the fifties with a somewhat more traditional view of
women than a lot of urban women already had of themselves. Or it may be that Ann Landers was concerned with
maintaining the integrity of the family defined according
to conventional roles at a time when signs of its break-up
were becoming apparent.

Most immediately visible in the conventional role of
the woman were surfaces—the way the woman looked
and the decorum of her actions. Ann Landers may have
laced into Hard-Boiled Harry, but she picked up two of
his points in her advice to Emancipated Ella in 1961. Ella
was "burning with rage" because Ann Landers had said
that a woman alone at a bar is fair game for a proposition;
Ella argued, "Women are no longer household drudges.
We can vote, hold executive positions, and we control
most of the country's wealth. We have equal rights and
deserve equal privileges." Ann said: "You can beat your
gums from here to maternity about the equality of the
sexes, but it's just a phrase, dearie. There are certain
things a man can do that a woman can't—if she wishes to
be considered a lady. Two that occur to me at the
moment are (1) smoke a cigarette on the street and (2)
sit in a bar alone." Given her own set of definitions, Ann
Landers was certainly correct in her appraisal. The question was whether women were going to define a "lady" in
quite the same way for as long as she would—or whether
they would be interested in being so defined at all for
very much longer.

Ann Landers certainly stuck to a traditional definition
of women longer than one might have expected. Ten

years after she started writing the column, Grand Island grumbled, "I'm a middle-aged man who has been dating a middle-aged woman for over a year. . . . Whenever I take Lillian out for an evening, whether it's to the theater, a movie, or a concert, she insists on paying her own way. . . . It makes me uncomfortable to accept money from her. Her reply is, 'I don't want to be indebted to anyone.' " Even though Lillian seemed to be a little more rigid than gracious, Ann's answer sounded equally rigid: "Lillian is attempting to preserve her independence at the expense of your dignity. . . . Explain your feelings and make it clear that from now on you insist on paying her way."

Women were not only supposed to be the eternal guests of men; they were also supposed to keep their husband's name after divorce, not go out wearing curlers, and not wear what displeased their husbands. About names, Ann wrote to Name Problems, in 1965, "Children deserve to have a mother with a Mrs. in front of her name." In 1968, regarding curlers, Ann said, "Apparently I struck some raw nerves around the country. My drop-dead mail tripled this week. . . . My position remains unchanged"—and it was still too early to ask why curlers played such an important role in the lives of so many women. In 1971, to Chomping at the Bit in Bellingham, she wrote, "Since [your husband] has stated such strong opposition against the pantsuit, that should settle the question for you, Petunia." This was advice she had already given F.M. in 1957, and would continue to stand by, even in 1973, when she "received a load of letters from women who accused [her] of being 'anti-female.' "

Most notably, the man displaced the woman as bread winner. In September 1965, Judith wrote that her husband "actually dislikes his job and would prefer to stay home and keep house." They therefore "agreed that if I become the sole wage earner my word would be law and that I'd be 'the head of the house.' Our relatives and friends say it can't work and that eventually he will grow to hate me for robbing him of his manhood."

Ann Landers may have read potential signs of trouble for a presumptive "head of the house" who felt a need for arbitration, but even so, her sarcastic rejection seemed to be out of proportion to the letter's seriousness: "Any husband who would rather keep house than go to work is a pretty queer duck to begin with. And you, Madame (I mean, Sir) selected this weirdie because you are a little kooked up yourself. Since you need someone to keep your pants pressed and he prefers house dresses to trousers, the plan sounds ideal."

The following month, The Outsider, whose children were now grown, told Ann she wanted to get back into the business her father had left her, even though it had been ably managed by her husband while she was tending house. Her husband refused. "Last night I made my last stand. Either I go back in the business or I sell it. Well, I was called everything in the book." Again, granting that it is difficult for someone who felt the need to write to project an image of strength, Ann's answer seemed less analytic than it might have been: "If you insist on shooting your way into the business, you'll create real trouble. According to your own testimony your husband has done well, so keep quiet and stay home."

By 1970, the term *women's liberation* had found its way into the column, but though she used the words, Ann Landers still had reservations about the idea. Once again, she was outdistanced by some of her readers. In May 1970, Boston expressed dismay: "A friend said she read in a wire-service story that you gave a speech at Harvard Medical School to the Community Psychiatrists in which you attacked the Women's Liberation groups. I can't believe it. Please say it isn't so." Although it wasn't quite so, it was very nearly so. Ann explained, "This is what I said, and I was quoted accurately: 'Women should be paid in accordance with their ability to produce. They should not be discriminated against because they are women. I do feel, however, that some of the screamers and picketers are on shaky ground when they try to bust into everything male and demand that they be accepted. This approach turns a lot of men off and makes them anti-female.' " At the time, though she recognized the need for economic parity between the sexes, Ann was not prepared to give up the roles that fitted the sexes into her understanding of an orderly society. Since, like most movements in their inception, feminism tended toward excess, she found more to criticize than to praise in 1970.

The same year, Love That Uniform asked whether she could join the marines immediately if she promised to shed enough of her 240 pounds in due time. Ann, in a splenetic moment, asked, "Which uniform? His or hers? What with Women's Lib trying to muscle in everywhere I'm not taking anything for granted." Three years later, Non Plussed and Still Laughing wrote about what had happened to him: "I went to the men's room of our office building and ran into a dame! So help me, Ann Landers, she was coming out as I opened the door to go in. An attractive, middle-aged woman greeted me with complete composure and said, 'I'm new here and couldn't find the ladies' room. I hope you don't mind.' " With less good humor than her correspondent, Ann replied, "I would not be surprised if one day 'His' and 'Hers' became 'Theirs.' While I'm NOT recommending it, I say brace yourself, Buddy—everything points in that direction." It seems clear that in 1973, Ann saw the women's revolution as more annoying and longer-lasting than the students'.

Time and again, Ann Landers's irritation and advice roused the more advanced of her early-seventies readers to voice retaliation. Besides the "load of letters" she received in 1973 from women who thought she was "antifemale," one writer from Cleveland even said, "You're up to your old tricks of playing to the male readers." A couple of years later, she ran into another angry protest, having turned thumbs down on a white bridal gown for women getting married a second time.

One writer complained, "Does the pastel dress [you recommend] serve as a symbol that the bride is tainted?" Ann Landers kept her cool: "Sorry, dear, but one just doesn't kick centuries of tradition in the teeth."

Seemingly oblivious to certain sensitivities, she roused the ire of Happily Married Libber the following month with another wifely recommendation: "You suggested that she give him a pedicure. Your answer elevated my blood pressure at least 50 points. The thought of a woman down on her knees cutting a man's toenails (which he was obviously too lazy to do) sparked rebellion in me." Addressing her correspondent as Dear Lib, Ann rubbed some more wifely salt into her wounds: "To get down on one's knees can be a very good thing— whether to pray, scrub a floor or cut a husband's toenails. When you stand, you are a little taller for the experience."

During the second half of the seventies, Ann started relenting, falling more into step with the prevalent sensitivities of women—even though she would still commit an occasional goof. In 1980, No Dog Myself but Sympathetic told her, "I was very disappointed in your response to a young man who wondered if he had to take out an overweight, dull, uninteresting girl just because his aunt had asked him to. You said, 'If the girl is a dog . . .' The term 'dog,' in my opinion, is degrading and unworthy of you." In her answer, Ann didn't acknowledge the reproach and merely confined herself to deflating the myth "that good looks guarantee popularity."

The following year, she ran into much bigger trouble for having dismissed Go-Go Machine's complaints about her sexual life ("Count your blessing and kwitcherbeefin") to the extent of having to make a public acknowledgment: "Remember the letter from the woman whose husband was constantly after her for sex? Well, I'll never forget it. I haven't read such angry mail since the first edition of a metropolitan newspaper left out an ingredient in the lemon pie recipe."

Two years later, she had to devote yet another whole column to undo the damage caused by her response to Dog-Gone in Lexington; that poor soul, saddled with the burden of the family dog, had given her husband an ultimatum, "It's me or the dog," and he had chosen the dog. Ann told Dog-Gone the matter wasn't worth a divorce and to take the dog to obedience school. As usual, Ann's advice was common sense. As in other such cases, it was common sense that did not take into account newly articulated sensitivities.

In 1984, Ann confessed to Outraged in Virginia, "You would not believe the volume of angry mail generated by that line"—the line being "When the girl you kiss goodnight after the first date gives you as good a kiss as you gave her, you were not the first there, Mister." And in 1985, she received two thousand letters for having said, "pilots . are husbands, sweethearts, fathers, sons and brothers." She apologized, "I should have said, 'Pilots are husbands, sweethearts, fathers, sons, brothers, mothers, sisters, daughters, aunts, nieces and grandmothers.' Next time I'll be more careful." But there was something in the length of her amended list that cast a small shadow of suspicion over her recantation.

It would be wrong, however, to view Ann Landers as a reactionary with regard to women's concerns. Many of her reactions were brought on by the kind of silliness that often follows in the wake of serious movements. In 1975, Congressman Jonathan Bingham told her how he came to suggest Ms. to designate the New Woman. Ann, who did not particularly feel the need for this kind of consciousness reminder, told him that she still preferred Miss. ("I still think of Ms. as an abbreviation for manuscript or multiple sclerosis.") And two years later, she likewise dismissed P.T. from San Francisco who had asked, "Why don't you create a new pronoun exclusively denoting him or her? May I suggest 'hem' " ("I'm not particularly interested in coining new words. I have enough trouble with the old ones").

As late as 1984, there were still outrages Ann found easy to resist, like Silver Spgs, Md.'s: "Recently a woman wrote to you and described how she held on to her husband by dancing for him in an outfit she made from a sheer curtain. Obviously the major attraction between the two was sexual. I found her letter revolting and was amazed that you let her get away with such cheap exhibitionism. . . . I feel sorry for the wife who has to dance around in a sheer curtain to hold her man. I'll bet you received a ton of mail from women who feel as I do." Ann told Silver Spgs coolly, "Actually you are the only one who complained. Many women wrote to ask if I could get a pattern for the 'harem costume.' " (Throughout her columns, there is constant recognition of the fact that one of the attractions between men and women is indeed sexual—and that women should be aware of that aspect of the male, should enjoy it, and even abet it. In 1982, 20 and Free wrote against diets ["not everybody can be thin, and not everyone wants to be"] and in favor of "jiggles," prompting a prurient rejoinder from Ann, "You and the dozens of Chicago construction workers during lunch hour on Michigan Ave. The jigglers are their dessert. Thanks for the upper.")

One should keep in mind that a part of Ann Landers had been deeply feminist from the start, even though it was easier in the fifties to be breezy about many of the problems that would brook no levity ten or fifteen years later. When N.E.S. wrote in 1956, he was "fed up on reading how the 'weaker' sex gets pushed around by the male. Women want equal rights. Yet they insist we light their cigarettes, hold their coats, open the doors." Ann could be cute about it and dismiss the gripe as a nonproblem: "The battle of the sexes will never be won. There's too much fraternizing with the enemy!" But Ann could also identify and address more serious questions.

Time and again, she confronted letters like that of Fedup (the same year): "I have a problem concerning my job. An older man who does business with the firm insists on flirting and touching me whenever he comes into the office. I simply can't stand him. I told my boss I'd like to ask him to keep his hands to himself but he said the man is a good client and I must put up with him." Ann delivered an "Open letter to secretaries, receptionists and other 'sacrificial lambs' of the outer office," whose message was, "It's part of your job to be friendly, pleasant and congenial—but your person is private property and by tone and manner you can post an oral HANDS OFF sign a yard wide and a mile high."

Although Ann had to repeat the admonition a number of times, as in the case of Andrea in 1960: "[A reception-ist's] person belongs to her and not to the job" or of Mishandled Miss in 1967: "Your body belongs to YOU, dummy" letters like Fed-up's eventually disappeared.

An interesting sidelight concerns Ann's advice about children playing "doctor," which she always assumed to be a normal part of the child's sexual awakening. In 1977, responding to a question from Mother in a Dilemma, she amended her usual answer to suit other aspects of the times: "Such behavior is not abnormal—however, you should alert the little girl's mother, also the boy's. Young children of the opposite sex [sic] ought not to be left to play unsupervised for long periods of time. They should also be told not to touch each other's private parts, NOT because it's bad, but because bodies are personal prop-erty and not playthings." This advice raises the intriguing question of how to distinguish between the child's "nor-mal" sexual curiosity and sexual curiosity that is "abnormal."

It is also worth keeping in mind that the conventions of the fifties were deeply rooted. Male chauvinism had not yet been labeled. Ann Landers herself was an occasional, if unintended, target of cloddish readers—the casual recipient of letters that evidenced not only a limited view of the world but addressed her in the patronizing tone that devolved from such a view. A case in point might be the 1957 letter from Vic, which began, "You're a woman with good sense. Will you please tell my wife to stay home where she belongs?" Vic's wife wanted a job. It may have been this kind of letter repeated over a period of time that helped erode Ann's ability to concur, even though her own earliest feelings were not so different from Vic's.

It was not exceptional for men of the fifties like Vic to assume that their hitherto unquestioned centrality would remain unquestioned, or for them to be dismayed when they encountered postwar women ready to fly on their own wings. That same year, J.D. wrote, "You can't get the Modern Woman to look at you twice unless you can present her with a marriage license which includes a five-year option plus an agreement that she can walk out on you at any time and take with her all your worldly goods, in addition to a healthy cut of your future earnings."

Three years later, it was Knothead Len asking, "Women are so independent it's hard to know when to take the initiative these days. Will you please help us stumbling men by printing the answer to a few simple rules of etiquette?" And he proceeded to ask what he should do in the presence of this new breed when leaving an elevator, going down the aisle of a theater, ordering in a restaurant, and so on.

Considering this largely conservative audience, Ann evidenced in other ways as well a no-nonsense kind of feminist awareness. In 1960, A Good Boss wrote, "Please straighten out my wife. She'll listen to you but not to me. I have a very capable secretary who does many extra favors for me. I try to show my gratitude by being especially considerate of her. Almost every weekend this secretary goes home for the weekend. . . . Saturday I get dressed in the morning, pick her up at her apartment and drive her to the bus station. My wife objects to this." Ann Landers may have been sensitive to matrimonial jeopardy, but her answer had a fine working-class ring to it: "There are other ways to show your secretary you appreciate her loyalty. Try money. A raise in salary is a practical and healthy way to say 'Thank you.' "

Five years later, House Divided wrote about a TV

giveaway show she had attended with a friend: "Several people from the audience volunteered to compete for prizes. I was horrified when a woman who was about 8½ months pregnant got up on the stage. . . . The M.C. kept repeating, 'in your condition' as if he had to point out to the audience what her condition was. My friend thought this was very funny. I was appalled. Don't you think it was tasteless for the host to exploit the woman this way?" Ann's answer was short and to the point: "This type of show lives on exploitation—and she invited it. So save your sympathy."

The following month, Ann showed signs of irritation with those who questioned the right of a woman to live alone. Solo and Happy had asked for "an answer to put these clods in their place." Ann provided her with what seemed like overkill ammunition: "The next time someone asks if you have a roommate, say, 'No. I live alone because I like to do my housework in the nude.' That should clear their sinuses."

Answers like those showed little more than the fact that when scratched, the feminist in Ann Landers reacted. But there were also important feminist issues in the public domain to which she now lent her considerable support. One of these was abortion. The late sixties and the seventies were times of accelerating change. A Gallup poll conducted in 1969 had shown that half of the respondents would oppose a law allowing women to terminate pregnancy during the first three months. (Forty percent said they would favor such a law.) When the question was asked again in 1973, those favoring such a law narrowly outnumbered opponents, 46 to 45 percent. In 1973, the Supreme Court decided that state laws making it illegal for a woman to have an abortion during the first three months of pregnancy were unconstitutional. In 1975, a Harris poll asked people how they felt about this decision. By this time, 54 percent favored it, and only 38 percent were against.

Ann was speaking out for legalized abortion at a time

when those who approved of it were still in the minority. In 1969, Lawrence, Kansas, congratulated her: "I'm glad you had the courage to come out and say the abortion laws are unjust, archaic and should be sharply amended." Ann reiterated her position in strong terms: "At least a dozen states are in the process of trying to liberalize their laws on abortion and I say the revision is long overdue. I believe that no woman, married or single, should be forced by the government to have a child she does not want if her physician decides he can safely terminate the pregnancy."

The following year, M.J.M. asked, "Why must it be the sole responsibility of the female to keep from getting pregnant?" and urged the practice of vasectomy. Ann concurred, "My medical consultants tell me that a vasectomy is a safe, sane operation, and that it in no way reduces a man's virility. . . . Yes, I'm with you."

In 1979, it was the Equal Rights Amendment, and once again Ann had to confront uninformed letter writers, pro and con. That year, Open Ears and Ready to Listen related anti-ERA sentiment often heard before, observing that women who want to be equal deserve "no breaks because of sex." Ann was forced to dot the reader's i's, explaining that her argument had "nothing to do with the Equal Rights Amendment (which I support), but it has a lot to do with common sense."

In the seventies, in spite of her occasional lapses, Ann Landers's credentials were sufficiently well established that women activists recognized her as an ally. In 1970 Betrayed wrote, "The letter from the mother who tore you to pieces because you printed 'dirty' letters and discussed 'filthy' things like V.D., masturbation and illicit sex really ticked me off. . . . What is dirty is to let a girl grow up and not tell her what her body should mean to her, how it responds to the opposite sex, and what can happen if she allows a boy to take liberties with her."

What Betrayed had noted was a steady opposition to women's rights that kept surfacing in letters to the column and was helping define Ann Landers as a feminist through her response. That opposition was widespread and it came from both men and women. As late as 1977, when a CBS News/New York Times Poll asked what impact the women's movement had on family life, the majority of respondents (44 percent) said they felt it had contributed to its breakdown (as opposed to the mere 18 percent who thought it had bettered family structures and the 38 percent who thought it had made no difference). Interestingly, of those who felt negative about women's movements, a larger proportion was female (47 percent—nearly one woman out of every two), as opposed to only 41 percent of the men.

As the consciousness of women became more widely articulated, that opposition became more vocal. Even the threadbare argument enunciated by Open Ears and so many others over the years could find psychotic defenders. In 1968, Ann printed a letter that said "American women want the same privileges that men get, such as smoking cigarettes on the street, sitting on bar stools, lapping up the booze, driving cabs and trucks, working in factories and becoming lawyers, doctors and engineers. Yet they expect men to get up on the bus and give them their seats. During the last war, Germany had the same problems and they solved it very simply. They removed all the seats in the buses and provided the passengers with ceiling straps." The letter was appropriately signed Heil Deutschland. The following year, A Mother in Massachusetts vented her spleen: "I was shocked by your seeming approval of legal abortions. Have you taken leave of your senses? Don't you realize millions of people look to you for moral guidance? Our priest has, on occasion, used your column as a basis for his sermons."

In 1975, Just Askin' brought the weight of the law down on Ann Landers: "Did you read in the newspaper how a court decided in the case of that Connecticut waitress who refused to shave her legs because the men who waited tables weren't required to shave theirs?

Apparently she considered her boss' request 'sexist.'
Well, honeybun, according to law, the owner of an eating
place can fire a hairy-legged lady. . . . Obviously someone
involved in the case wrote to you before it got to court.
You said the woman should not be forced to shave her
legs, and suggested that both men and women who
waited tables should be required to wear opaque stock-
ings. What do you think now?" Ann answered, "The same
as I did before."

The anger that gave rise to the glee of Just Askin'
continued to inform letters even in the eighties. The
women's movement was a convenient pretext for other
discontents. In 1980, a boss who signed himself Fed Up
in Seattle exclaimed, "Women's lib has gone too far" and
then proceeded to detail his secretary's irresponsibili-
ties. Ann had to give him a lesson in logic: "Your first
sentence is a non sequitur. Your secretary's lack of
respect for her job doesn't have a pea-pickin' thing to do
with women's lib."

Three months later, P.J. in Fla. was able to weave
evidence of economic distress, the unfairness of divorce
laws and natural female rapacity into an attack on wom-
en's movements:

> Now that the liberal female movers and shak-
> ers are taking over everywhere, I would like to
> call attention to a new game called "Matinee
> Love-In." Here's how it's played:
> While the hard-working husband is slaving
> away, trying to earn some more 49-cent dollars,
> and the kids are in school, it is not difficult for a
> clever wife to set up a stable of daytime lovers.
> . . . No serious involvements, you understand—
> just fun and games.
> Sooner or later someone discovers her mis-
> conduct—and the story is out. But before the
> poor, innocent husband has a chance to recover
> from the shock, she has hit him with a no-fault
> divorce. When the smoke clears, she ends up

with the house, the children, and alimony, t'boot. This is justice? In a pig's eye!

Three years later, Had Enough and Willing to Admit It concluded, "Because of women's lib, super-aggressive women have turned men off." It was at this juncture that an innocent reply by Ann would bring the roof down. She told Had Enough that "Sexuality is a divine gift from the Almighty. To give it back, unused, would—I am sure—disappoint Him." The following March, she was forced to devote two columns to the "mail that ran 30 to 1 against me" with angry letters "still pouring in." More on this in the next chapter.

Perhaps a fitting conclusion to this evidence of male resistance to dispossession of what they considered to be their world is found in Ann's apology for yet another remark that had grated on sensitive ears. The letter was from Guilty in Bogota: "Your answer to the woman who wanted to know why bankers had more sex appeal than people in any other field showed strong sexist bias. You assumed that all bankers are male. For shame!" Ann meant to respond, "I plead guilty as charged. And now I must pray to God for forgiveness and hope She will be merciful." But in a small upstate New York paper, *The Ithaca Journal*, her response appeared as "And now I must pray to God for forgiveness and hope He will be merciful."

The stubborn reaction of men is matched, if not intensified, by the growing self-assertion of women. As noted, that assertion was evident already in the midfifties—and even strong enough to leave Ann Landers behind on a number of occasions. But with the start of the seventies, the column begins to reflect a steady outpouring of letters from women attentive to, and increasingly indignant over, nearly every kind of female jeopardy. In January 1975, Informed Reader told Ann, "Your advice wasn't tough enough for the girl who sent $10 for something to enlarge her bust and received a plastic male hand. She should have written to the magazine that carried the ad, informed the Better Business Bureau, called the Attorney General of her state and the state where the company is located, written the U.S. postal authorities, notified the Federal Trade Commission and written to the Bureau of Consumer Affairs in Washington, D.C. She would not only have gotten her $10 back, but put the crooks out of business." Ann could only bow to this impressive display of firepower and thank her reader.

Six months later, D.L.K. wrote, "The income-tax deadline has long since passed but I'm still mad enough about those cockeyed forms to write to Ann Landers. I wish the government would get something straight. The 'housewives' of this country are not 'unemployed.' We are pretty damned busy." Again, Ann agreed: "I'm for revising the language on those IRS forms. How about it, Washington?"

But Ann didn't feel compelled to agree with all forms of female assertiveness. In 1979, No Tramp blasted her: "You ought to update your advice or throw in the towel, Sister. I refer to that bit of antiquated counsel: 'Decent girls aren't sitting on bar stools waiting to get picked up.' . . . Working girls who want to meet men have to go where the men are. And they are in bars after 5:00 p.m. So get with it, Grandma." Ann was undeterred by the fact that No Tramp looked at her from a generational distance, intending to show the difference between contemporary mores ("no tramp") and the ways of those who had no modern clue ("grandma"). She replied, "OK, work the bars after 5:00 p.m., and do you know what you'll find? Men who are also working the bars." (Once again, Ann may have accepted the dialogue because No Tramp—however boorish—had initiated it. No Tramp may have been looking at Ann across a generational chasm of her own making, but she was still looking at her.)

Women were claiming an ever greater share of the job market (by 1986, the total of female professionals would surpass the males). It was not surprising that the voice of women was sufficiently pervasive in the eighties to articulate two sides of the same issue and split the sisterhood. Acceptable (or necessary) mores required a new look at some newly solved problems. Among these was the economic legitimacy of housewives, only lately identified by women like D.L.K. In 1980, Full Time Secretary and Housewife from Bowling Green, Ky. wrote, "I read recently that housewives are trying to get Social Security benefits because their husbands work. I'm sick and tired of people leeching off my paycheck. . . . Face it, 'Housewife'—you ARE 'just a housewife.' You are not a nurse, lawyer, secretary, factory worker, doctor, vet, street cleaner, postal worker or anyone who works. What you do all day is what the women listed above have to do when they get home from work." Ann ducked out on that one: "If there ever was a letter for which there are pros and cons, you've written it, sister."

Other working housewives proposed more aggressive solutions. Nine months after Full Time's letter, No Dumbell in Beaumont suggested,

> I'm sick and tired [many of these ladies appear to have been "sick and tired"] of reading about wives who work eight hours a day, and then "have to" come home and do all the housework and take care of the kids. The key phrase is "have to." What kind of nuts are they?
> Very few husbands will volunteer to do anything in the house or help with the children on their own. These women need to memorize the following sentence: "If you want to eat at home this week you can do the marketing, or we'll eat out." Also, a few days without clean underwear will help the most stubborn holdout to learn how to run the washing machine.

Ann agreed: "You're singing my song."

A heightened consciousness of self was also causing women to look in places hitherto undreamed of for signs

of male dereliction. In August 1981, A.W. from Knights-
town, Ind., discovered one such place in the delivery
room: "In my opinion, the present-day practice of allowing fathers to accompany their wives into the delivery
room is a good thing. The man who helped start her
pregnancy should have the guts to help her finish it."
Another was on the bridal path, as pointed out by I
Belong to Me the following month: "Giving the bride
away is a custom that dates back to the Middle Ages,
when a woman was considered nothing more than a
possession—first of her father, then her husband. Today a
woman is her own person." Ann acknowledged meekly
not knowing that modern couples "are dropping the
archaic formality of 'giving away' the bride."

In 1984, N.J. Beef found fault with some of Ann's
counsel: "No kudos for your archaic reply to 'Handcuffed
in N.Y.' The dinner partner with Roman hands and
Russian fingers should have been slapped right across the
face. You copped out when you suggested that she tell
the louse to knock it off or she'd ask her husband to
change places with her and explain the reason. . . .
Anything less than public humiliation is too good for the
skunks." Exhibiting the same short fuse and short sense
of history that allowed other members of embattled
constituencies (teen-agers, for example) likewise to
term "archaic" or from the "Middle Ages" a reply or
custom they did not care for, N.J. Beef felt free to stand
up for downtrodden women through a little racial tread-
ing of her own (unless we assume she was able to define
just what a "Roman hand" was, or "Russian fingers").

The rhetoric and self-indulgence of such letters could
not obscure the very real and important changes that
were occurring. Besides the ERA and birth control,
which Ann Landers championed vigorously, other concerns arose, such as those of battered and abused
women. When Women's Strength, Women's Services, the
Salvation Army, and other groups began organizing to
help women needing protection, Ann Landers's column
functioned as a constant referral service.

In May 1983, Ann Landers ran one of her occasional open letters to her readers:

> I read something recently that really blew me out of the water. In spite of all the back-breaking work of the women's movement and frontline heroines in the vanguard of business and industry, the prejudice against females is still very strong.
>
> In the February issue of *Redbook*, Dr. Alice Baumgartner and her colleagues at the Institute for Equality in Education at the University of Colorado surveyed 2,000 children throughout the state. They asked one question: "If you woke up tomorrow and discovered you were a boy (or a girl), how would your life be different?"
>
> The responses were startling. There was a serious lack of respect for females. In fact, they were held in contempt by both sexes. Many girls said if they were boys, their lives would be better economically and status-wise and they would enjoy more freedom and have a better time with less responsibility. One girl said, "If I were a boy, my father might have loved me more."
>
> Boys felt that if they had to be girls, they must be beautiful and know how to put on makeup and dress well. "No one would be interested in my brain," said one respondent.
>
> When boys considered the possibility that females could marry and work outside the home, the jobs they listed most often were secretaries, nurses, cocktail waitresses, social workers, models, airline stewardesses and prostitutes. "Boys still see women in roles as serving others," Dr. Baumgartner said. . . .

The bottom line seems to be that boys knew they were valued by their parents, but girls were not as sure. They felt their brothers were the favorites.

Why did "children" in Colorado believe that one of the jobs a woman might aspire to is that of "prostitute"? The choice is so outrageous that it compels questioning how they defined the other jobs—"secretaries, nurses, cocktail waitresses, social workers, models, airline stewardesses."

When they thought of cocktail waitresses, did they not select that category knowing it frequently requires women to add to the service they perform (bringing drinks to customers) a sexual dimension through the clothes they are forced to wear or the common association of liquor and sex? (The young respondents of *Redbook* specified "cocktail waitresses" rather than waitresses pure and simple.) In thinking of models, was their choice unaffected by the knowledge that selling clothes often demands that the model exhibit her body as well as the fashions?

Because of their sexual information of these women's roles, one might legitimately infer that when they saw women in jobs that catered to someone else's well-being (their own? a man's?) in a one-on-one situation— whether in the place of business (secretaries and airline stewardesses) or in a moment of physical need (nurses and social workers)—their precocious evaluation of women evidenced Freud's sense of the mother-whore.

According to *Redbook*'s survey, men in 1983 started seeing women as sexual objects at a young age indeed. When asked to imagine themselves as women, those males must have momentarily sensed what it means to be raped.

7
The Forbidden Topic Everyone Discusses: Sex

Sexual concern informs an overwhelmingly large number of the questions put to Ann Landers. This concern never abates; only the points of view and social mores change. Most significant among those changes is a relaxation of certain taboos, allowing statement and analysis of what was once addressed mainly through circumlocution and inference. In fact, the sexual revolution freed us from many constraints—excluding, of course, an obsessive need to talk about sex.

When one looks back at the earliest columns, one is struck by the relative ease with which two of the most enduring problems deriving from sexual activity were treated—extramarital pregnancies and adultery. The column's very first letter concerned adultery. Mr. K., a married auto-racing buff whose wife had no interest in cars, had fallen for a married woman, who was also fond of racing even though her husband was as indifferent as Mr. K.'s wife. Ann responded with a volley of puns, starting with the famous, "Time wounds all heels—and you'll get yours." The same column also ran a letter of Steady Reader, who had met a man who could never call her or take her out and whom she could see "only once a day when he delivers food at my home." Ann disposed of that one by replying that the fellow was mainly delivering baloney.

As we have seen, the libido of the errant male was usually treated as a form of childishness in the early days—something the mothering wife was expected to handle. Later that year, D.V.S. wrote about her husband having fallen in love with a teen-ager after nine years of marriage. Ann said, "The girl obviously is chasing him—and that's pretty flattering for the father of three! Try a little flattery yourself. . . . Then really forget and forgive." Three weeks later, it was the twenty-nine-year-old husband of I.E.M., seventeen, trying to unload his wife on her mother—most likely with malice aforethought. Ann replied to I.E.M., "Tell him you're not moving and you want to make the best of the situation and need his help. Don't mention 'other women'. . . why give him ideas? Your obligation to your children should top the bill."

The woman's responsibility for keeping the home together as the mothering presence on whom the child and husband depended is an Ann Landers notion that would persist through the midseventies, at least inasmuch as the child was concerned. In 1957, Fargo complained about her husband of eleven years: "In spite of his promises he continues to see this worthless girl. I feel cheap welcoming him back time after time. If she'd take him out of my life completely I'd feel better than sharing him with her." Ann put duty staunchly above well-being: "A woman who brought five children into the world doesn't have the right to hand her husband over to a 'worthless tramp.' . . . The children would be the real losers if you threw your husband out on his ear."

Ten years later, Ann was telling Fed Up to Here whose husband was never home, "Marriage is not a 50-50 proposition. It's more like 80-20—with the wife doing 80 percent of the giving and, yes, 80 percent of the FORgiving." And in 1975, Ann told My Turn for Happiness that a woman's job was never done—not even after her husband was in his grave: "Don't tarnish your husband's halo in an attempt to justify your own behavior. It would be a rotten thing to do. You were a noble woman to protect him. Keep that skeleton in the closet where it belongs." This repeated stressing of the woman's need to forgive in order to preserve the home achieves a paradoxical extension in the seventies, when yesterday's forgiveness becomes a timely acceptance of, or contribution to, the disintegration of the family structure.

Since the husband's derelictions were viewed primarily as libidinal (we will have occasion to note further Ann Landers's reduction of many such tendencies to mere sex), the wife's counterattack was supposed to be sexual as well. The advice was usually a variation of "turn on the heat." The prototypical answer was to Jo Ann in 1965, who had attempted unsuccessfully to negotiate with her husband's paramour: "You must carry on as if you were the only female in the world. This means no checking, no third-degree, no accusations. Be pleasant, relaxed, and fight fire with fire. Or, to put it bluntly, turn on the heat." That advice comes after many earlier ones of the same kind. In fact, a Lysistratan example occurs during the first year of the column, when Desperate told of her husband's unfaithfulness and was advised, "If you will stop giving him the rights and privileges of being a husband until he is prepared to grow up and behave like one, this cheap 'romance' of his will fade, pronto."

The woman's primary responsibility to preserve the home was such that, in the early days, her husband's libidinal sins might well pale in comparison with her own sins of commission or omission. In 1955, R.I.G. said, in the quaint idiom of the times, "My husband has been stepping out on me since the second year [of our marriage] and makes no bones about it." Ann replied sternly, "First, stop griping. Second, stop waiting on him hand and foot. Third, take a good long look at yourself. What is there about you that would keep a man at home? Better reacquaint him with your 'virtues.' "

The following year, Frustrated wrote, "I thought I

broke up [my husband's affair] nine years ago but I was mistaken. Shall I divorce him. . . . This woman has money and bought my husband a beautiful car when we couldn't afford to buy one ourselves." Ann replied, quite correctly, "Sorry, madame, when you allowed him to accept the car you gave your silent approval to the whole dirty business." She never hit the husband, saying instead, "Don't divorce him, however. Your children would be the real victims. Pick up the pieces of your battered marriage and show some principle for a change."

In 1965, No Compre asked, "Why would a handsome, successful, respected man leave a beautiful, brilliant, accomplished, generous, loving wife for a cheap, loud, crude, ignorant, gold-digging tramp?" Ann answered, "Maybe he is going through the male menopause and is off his trolley. Or, perhaps, that cheap, loud, crude, ignorant, gold-digging tramp fills an emotional need in the man that his beautiful, brilliant, accomplished, generous, loving wife does not."

Many women were not prepared to remain indefinitely responsible for immature men, and with the seventies, the prospect of divorce and sexual renewal began looking good to a number of them. Ann started shifting her ground, acknowledging that simply turning on the heat might sometimes be more important for a woman than where, or for what reason, it was being turned on.

By the end of 1970, Ann's advice omitted the moralizing. Renee had informed her, "After 18 months of excuses (and getting kissed goodnight on the forehead) I was convinced that I must be the most undesirable woman in the world. It was then that an attractive man at work rescued me from a nervous breakdown by suggesting that we have an affair. I accepted immediately." And so, evidently, did Renee's husband. Paying lip service to counseling, Ann replied, "If he refuses, see a lawyer. You might be eligible for an annulment. I see no reason for a 23-year-old girl to settle for a brother-sister marriage with cheating privileges."

The following year, The Scarlet Letter said, "OK. So a wife is supposed to forgive her husband who cheats in Vietnam. . . . But what about the woman's 'physical needs' as you put it? . . . If she does likewise, is she to be forgiven too?" Ann told her, "The answer is yes." And in 1980, Madison, Wis., Worrier, who was fifty and planning to marry a man of sixty, confessed, "We have been going together for two years. 'C' has never made any physical advances toward me, although he has had many opportunities." Ann said, "If you've been going together for two years and 'C' has made no physical advances, something is out of kilter. I suggest you discuss it with him before you buy that beige lace dress." (The color is a reminder of Ann's vestigial belief in the importance of the primal marriage.)

One can measure the change in the moral climate by comparing Ann's answer to Worrier and the ones she had given in the fifties to some others, at a time when the beige (or, preferably, white) dress was the only way to legitimize sexual relations. In the first month of the column, Mrs. L., a widow, admitted, "I have been going with a very nice widower for two years. We are both 49 and highly respectable people. Somehow we lost our heads six weeks ago and I have not seen him since." The sterner Ann of the fifties answered, "You've made a mistake. . . . Since you have such strong feelings for one another, how come no one thought of getting a ring on your finger and that piece of paper in your hand first?"

And two years later, Miss Jones wrote the kind of letter that few of her sisters would be able to understand in another ten years: "I'm 23 and have been seeing a great deal of a fellow who is 30. He's a most captivating guy. . . . Our romance is reaching the white-heat stage, if you know what I mean. Every time I see him it becomes a little tougher to keep him in line." She concluded, "I think I love this guy and I need some level-headed advice at once." Since Ann Landers was writing for a public that still numbered such euphemistic adults, she speculated (ever keeping a wary eye to the number one priority): "Make it plain you're interested in marriage and see what this does to lover boy's blood pressure. I'll bet it will drop so low you won't be able to get a pulse."

The relative innocence of the fifties is reflected even in the rogues who were trying to bed innocent maidens— but who felt compelled, nevertheless, to write Ann Landers about it. In 1957, Ziggy described "a cashier in a theater and she looks like a jewel in her little glass box. I'm sorry to say she's married. She tells me her husband is a big ox with no manners and she plans to divorce him one of these days. . . . I know you are a broad-minded person and you'll wish me luck. My philosophy is, 'You only live once.' " For which Ziggy was rewarded with, "The way you're doing it, once is enough."

As late as 1970, Color Me Gone tried another approach: "Everything in the world is changing and your column is a faithful reflection of those changes. So why don't you say something about society's unfair criticism of the married man who is forced to seek the warmth and companionship of someone other than his wife." Ann Landers was prepared to accept that point of view only when the wife's trumpet was being blown too loudly, as in the case of No Compre. Color Me Gone was simply dismissed: "No point in trying to reach you since you're gone." But by 1970, Color Me Gone was already something of an anachronism. Most such letters had become scarce, along with other kinds of innocence. Everything in the world was indeed changing, and the column reflected those changes.

Alongside the misguided who looked to Ann Landers for an approval of dalliance (in earlier times when such approval might still have seemed necessary to some), and when Ann's unblinking view of "chemistry" in relationships, especially adolescents', could be misinterpreted as moral leniency, there were also those for whom sexual relationships were fraught with either puzzlement or real pain. And their numbers remained. In 1966, Too Late remembered the last words of her husband just before he died of a heart attack: " 'I love you. Please forgive me. I realize now that you are the only one I have ever wanted.' " Too Late commented, "He loved me, I'm sure, but he wasn't grown up enough to forsake all others. . . . He kept asking me to be patient—that things would work out someday. Well, someday will never come. And I am bitter. . . . Before he slipped away, I held his hand and whispered, 'I love you, dearest, and I always will.' But I lied."

Six years later, there is this cry for help from Saturn: "What is wrong with a woman who has been married six years, has a wonderful husband and two adorable children and feels herself attracted to another man? I didn't want this to happen but it seems beyond my control. . . . Am I crazy? Can the solution be found in self-discipline?" Ann allowed that it might, but added "distance" for safety.

Two years after Saturn, Alone and Waiting wrote, "I've read many times your advice to women who discover their husbands are running around: 'Wait it out.' . . . While I wait, how do I keep from losing my mind? How do I acquire the appetite so I can eat? How can I keep smiling in front of the children and other relatives when my heart is breaking? How do I hold back the tears until I'm alone so I can cry my eyes out? How do I drive thoughts of suicide out of my mind because I cannot face life without him?" Ann told her hastily, "No man is worth killing yourself over," but in the face of such acute distress emphasized counseling.

In the free and easy eighties, A Crazy Lady in Chicago admitted, "My problem is of a strange nature. I have been seeing a married man for several years. I am married also. We really do love each other, but divorce is out for both him and me—so we decided to settle for whatever we can get. I am eaten up by anger whenever I think of him making love to his wife. . . . I make it a rule never to have sex with my husband on the day I know I will be meeting my lover. I think he owes it to me to save himself for me the way I save myself for him. Am I being unfair? Am I nutty? Am I too demanding?" This being 1982, and Ann having given up trying to moralize her readers back to virtue, she replied, "You aren't nutty, but you are stupid (and maybe a bit masochistic) to ask a question for which the answer drives you mahoola." And instead of the sarcastic sermon that would have been expected earlier, she added only, "My advice is stay off that subject or resign yourself to continued torture."

Of course, alongside these sufferers, there were always those who felt no pain. In 1957, The Happy Ex explained why: "My former husband married the 'Other Woman.' They are very happy and I don't begrudge them a thing." She explained that things were better for her, too: "I'm much happier and so is my child. Our house was never a home. It was filled with tension and distrust." In 1957, Ann Landers considered that such equanimity was tantamount to subversion of the family structure. She gave The Happy Ex the back of her hand: "Merely because I print a letter doesn't mean that I agree with it." Toward the end of the sixties, it was adolescents deaf to the thought that any desire of theirs might not be realized: "I am 15 and could pass for 19. I can buy beer in any tavern without showing an ID card. . . . Neil is 23 and I'm sure he'll be a big star some day. He wants me to marry him but we have no money and he isn't working at present. . . . Don't tell me I'm a foolish kid because love is for the young and this is the real thing."

The nonsufferers were in fact those who saw opportunities in the elimination of rules and discipline that would have hampered them before. In seeking those opportunities, they were contributing to a further alteration of social habits that had been relatively stable until shortly after the end of World War II. That stability, rejected as constraint by some, had been the security of others. Many of them started expressing their puzzlement and dismay to Ann Landers.

In 1965, Sweet Adeline informed her, "I am going with a gentleman who is separated but not divorced. Kenny and I are together Monday through Thursday. On Friday he moves right in with his estranged wife and children— suitcase and all." A certain flexibility was evidently giving a new dimension to such concepts as estrangement. Five years later, Monterey was in a hurry: "I'll get right to the point. There is no time to waste. I have a strong hunch that my wife is practicing prostitution.... Prostitution is illegal in California and I would hate for my wife to have a police record." By now the times were such that Ann did not even wonder whether this might be a Yalie joke; she answered with a weary patience born of the times, "The law should be the least of your worries."

And another five years later, it was someone who signed herself, appropriately, Uncertain:

> I am a wife, 26 years old, who is deeply troubled about the place of fidelity in marriage. A few months ago I discovered that my husband was unfaithful. Not a week goes by that I don't hear about another couple in our crowd who is cheating. . . . Since the unfortunate episode occurred in our own marriage, my husband has told me he is very sorry for the hurt he caused but he let me know he doesn't feel he committed such a terrible offense. I am very confused.
>
> I want to be fair and open-minded, yet I cannot accept this new-style design for living. Will you please tell me if, in the year 1975, faithfulness to one's spouse is out of date? . . . How wrong is it if most couples do it?

Ann's answer was both a recognition of the times ("there is unquestionably more cheating in 1975 than there was 40 years ago") and an affirmation of faith: "Nor do I believe that if everyone did it, it would then be 'all right.' " Ann gave as reasons for this new state of affairs "opportunities and modes of travel, women in the business world, an increase in sexual stimulation created by movies, TV and advertising."

One wonders whether this new acceptance was not enlarged by the newly acquired freedom to talk about it, as evidenced by the letters of Monterey and Uncertain. Verbalizing one's extramarital sins seems to have removed some of their stigma, and the verbal classes (students and others sufficiently well-off to acquire this kind of skill) seemed increasingly able to master an articulate kind of speciousness. In 1980, Desperate in Williamsport complained, "My husband and I are swingers. (We meet new couples to have sex with them). My husband kept after me for months until I agreed to go along with it. We've tried it a few times, and I don't like it. I just don't care about having sex with other men." By 1980, for someone like Desperate in Williamsport, the rejection of former codes resulted in a surfeit of freedom.

Before the glare of words brought visibility and a degree of legitimacy to sexual concerns, the encounter between men and women was never discussed much beyond its initial stages. Its sexual development extended into the more shadowy realms of mystery and imagination. These realms were private, frequently illicit, sometimes dangerous, and always profoundly enticing.

Their imaginative extension is most apparent in the fifties. In 1955, we find one of the first of what will be steadily similar letters: "I'm 45 and have been married 24 years. We have four children and nine grandchildren. The man I married is very nice, but I can't say I'm madly in love with him. Lately I've been very blue. My mind goes back to the sweetheart I knew before marriage. I find myself wondering if he wasn't my true love." In those simpler days, Ann Landers's advice was equally simple: "Lift yourself out of this fantasy. . . . Your lovely family should be enough to keep life interesting."

The following year, Distracted Wife worried: "I've been married eleven years and have three darling children. My husband is a fine fellow. . . . For the past six

months one of the girl's bachelor brothers has been
joining the group and I'm scared to death. When I'm
around him I feel like a school girl. . . . He's never made
a pass. If he does I'll just melt." This brought out the
moralist in Ann Landers: "Temptations are bound to
appear in the course of a lifetime. How we meet them
often spells the difference between happiness and misery. Don't abandon your moral principles for the momen-
tary thrill of a sordid romantic escapade."

Four months later, it was Liz: "I suppose I'm being
foolish. . . . I was crazy about a boy I went with in college.
We were never officially engaged, but I kept hoping. To
make a long story short, he married someone else. I got
over it, and met and married a very wonderful guy. . . .
This is the problem. I'm going home for a visit next
month and will see my old crush for the first time in 10
years. He has since been divorced and I understand he's
as handsome as ever. I am ashamed to admit how excited
I get when I think of seeing him again." Ann repeated
once more, "You're living in a state of fantasy, Liz."

The following year, Dimpled Chin was experiencing
the same doubts: "I've been married three years and have
a child. Everything was fine until my old boy friend came
back from the Army and moved across the court. I see
him every day. It's eating me up inside to think that I
could have had him but I was too stupid. . . . My husband
is a swell person but when I see the other guy, whistles
blow and bells ring. . . . Please, Ann, I feel terribly
helpless." Ann told her, "Grow up and make your marriage work."

The wistfulness of these letters at what might have
been acknowledges that there is no recovering the past.
The act of writing Ann Landers confirms it, and Ann
merely delivers what she assumes will be the coup de
grace. The letter writers know they will need a fallback
position in the real world. Most of them acknowledge a
good husband and wonderful children. These women of
the fifties know they are fantasizing in a letter the

romantic interlude that the morality of the times forbids.

One can still find an occasional letter of this sort after the fifties. In 1965, Empty tells about the "mad, ecstatic affair" she had had with the "attractive, intellectually stimulating, physically exciting man" she met after her husband died—and who then walked out of her life. "It has been several months now, and I can't get him out of my mind. . . . Please tell me how can a woman recover from a broken heart?" Ann's words remained pretty much the same over the years: "Substitute another thought— something real and constructive—for the fantasy."

In 1969, Nutty Joyce sends in a replay of so many earlier letters: "I've been married 12 years to a wonderful man and we have a beautiful family. . . . These past few months I've been having these wild daydreams about a former love whom I have not seen in 10 years. . . . These ridiculous daydreams started to haunt me about three months ago when I heard 'our song' on the radio. I began to relive the glorious moments we shared." This resulted in carbon-copy advice: "When you feel a daydream coming on, substitute in its place a real life episode."

But after the seventies such daydreams become rare. The sweeping aside of old codes is more apt to allow realization than to foster imagination. Open talk about sexual dilemmas reduces the darker places in which the dream could previously grow. Starting with the seventies, unhappy wives (and a few unhappy husbands) began taking a harder and more analytic look at their circumstances instead of merely substituting for them the insubstantiality of a romantic image.

Part of the romantic image was made possible by, and fostered, the idea of love that was a mainstay of the fifties. There were many starry-eyed dreamers in those days, but they are not all teen-agers. In August 1957, V.M. related, "Last year I met a wonderful guy and we fell in love. . . . The other night he [told] me how he had become involved with a girl from the wrong side of the tracks. She is expecting his baby and now he has to marry her. He said he doesn't love her and never did. . . . I love him, Ann, and am heartsick over this whole mess. Please give me some advice to go on." That advice was not likely what V.M. wanted to hear: "Put on your track shoes, Sister; and run in the other direction."

Two months earlier, Ann had given the same advice to Babe, even though Babe's letter sounded less naïve: "I'm a girl 28 who has gone with a man four years. I've kept him out of jail by making good his rubber checks. When he needed money to attend his mother's funeral, I gave him $300. Later I found out his mother died 10 years ago. . . . Two weeks ago I found some woman's things in his laundry bag. We had a fight and I threw him out. . . . He hasn't been around since and I'm so lonesome I could die. I know I'm nuts, but I love the guy."

Ann Landers's reading of such letters stressed their foolishness and, in order to do so, ignored their pain. If it was a teen invoking love, Ann was tempted to read the invocation as a cover for sex. Bill wrote in 1955, "I like a girl very much but she doesn't seem to like me. . . . She seems friendly at all times. She invites me to her house a couple of nights a week and we watch television. I don't know what's wrong, but she just doesn't seem to like me." Ann quickly got to the core of that one, "If you mean she won't go in for heavy smooching, she's right—and you know it."

For the same reason, Ann rejected once and for all the idea that love might be possible at first sight. In 1960, she ran the following: "Confidential to the hundreds of women who wrote to tell me I'm off my trolley: I repeat—there is no such thing as love at first sight. You gals who were knocked off your pins at first meeting and are now living happily ever after, please note. It wasn't love that you experienced on the initial glimpse. It was a chemical reaction. The guy just happened to turn out [right]."

In the letters of adults, she saw romantic love mainly as a potential threat to marriage. Within the marriage, it presumably played no significant part. In 1956, Other Woman wrote, "The man I love is with his wife and children. He is a fine, honorable person. When he's away on business, he never cheats on his wife, although he has many opportunities. I am his true love, and we curse the fates that did not bring us together 10 years ago so we could have married. I've tried to stay away, but it's impossible. I'm not a whole person unless I'm in his presence. . . . Shall I go to Europe for a year?"

Admittedly, Other Woman's letter did not have quite the ring one might have wished for, but it is doubtful whether she could ever have found the right voice to move Ann Landers. (One suspects that, under similar circumstances, Camille would have been no more than a woman of ill repute.) Ann told her, "Europe isn't far enough and a year isn't long enough. . . . Shake yourself out of this fantasy and look at this sordid situation minus the Gypsy violins and soft lights. . . . When your entertainment value has expired, he'll make some boring remarks about how . . . he would like nothing better than to marry you [but] just can't give up his children."

Ann's views combined her earliest conviction that the gravitational pull of the family allowed few to escape combined with her suspicion that love was a deceptive abstraction. The combination of these beliefs informed her answers to letters like those of This?—No Sweet Music, who had complained in 1960 that her husband "never once told me he loves me. . . . When I asked him point blank if he really loved me he replied, 'I'm still here.' " Even this kind of oafishness was redeemed for Ann by what she read as honesty subverting the delusory words of love: "[His] actions speak more eloquently than any poetry he might spout."

When Ann Landers attempted to distinguish for her readers between love and "a chemical reaction," she was in fact establishing an order of priorities. As we have seen, she considered sex to be dangerous in many ways if it occurred before or outside marriage. It got teens into all kinds of trouble and confusion, it jeopardized the holy institution of matrimony—and even when only imagined, it sent people off into unhealthy flights of fancy.

Yet once the sacred knot was secured, sex became an important and necessary ingredient in the preservation of a good marriage. For this reason, she repeatedly admonished nonperformers, "if you don't use it, you'll lose it." In 1960, Mrs. Miss wrote, "I married a wonderful guy. He is 23 and told me when we first started to go together a year ago that he thinks a girl is entitled to a pure groom, the same way a fellow is entitled to a pure bride. Well, we had a difficult time keeping our emotions under control but we managed somehow. We were married a month ago and he is still pure." Mrs. Miss then went on to detail the many excuses her husband had used to avoid being one. Since he and his fiancee had found it "difficult" to keep their "emotions under control" before the wedding night, one might be tempted to read shyness or fear of unsatisfactory performance in the groom's reticence—especially as Mrs. Miss still considered him to be "a wonderful guy." But for Ann Landers, in 1960 at least, high principles before marriage could turn into instant dereliction upon signing the marriage contract. This caused Ann to disregard anything as trivial as shyness or fear of unsatisfactory performance. She wasted few words: "You'd better tell him to go to work on his mind, which is sick. . . . If he refuses to see a doctor . . . , I suggest you see your clergyman—and your lawyer—about an annulment."

After 1960, increasing sexual freedom afforded greater possibilities of actual performance and lessened the need for a surrogate imagination. Letters like Bitter's began to appear: "My husband is right when he says I have no interest in sex. Why should I have? Any animal can have a sex life. What I want is a love life." But in spite of Ann's admission, "My mail indicates you've got plenty of company," little attention would be paid to this kind of complaint for the next fifteen years. It surfaces with tidal wave force in the eighties, however. In the meantime, the virtues of open and untrammeled sex were all the rage, causing Ann's readers to ask her for redefinition of former moral codes.

Lonely-hearts questions had been a frequent topic of the fifties. In the sixties, that interest made way for another. The new unbinding of sex was beginning to cause transitional perplexities. Readers who were not yet swinging with the times started asking questions about strange modes of conduct between men and women, while the more avant-garde or militant started questioning the way we had previously handled our intimacies. Letters of star-crossed lovers thus tended to be replaced in the sixties by those of readers interested in the moral and social consequences of sexual behavior that was becoming less secretive.

As usual, there were those for whom the changing times came too quickly. According to their temperament, they responded with bafflement, disbelief, or anger. In 1960, the wife of a couple who had just converted a large colonial home into a wayside inn was worrying about the effect of changing times on her enterprise. Her signature, Against Sin, bespoke righteous indignation, but her letter indicated a certain panic, "How can morally decent hotel keepers protect themselves against such goings on?" At the time, Ann thought that everyone was still steeped in a former innocence and advised her, "Ask for identification at the time of registration. Those who are who they SAY they are, will not mind proving it. Those who become indignant and leave in a huff probably had no business trying to register in the first place."

In 1960, Ann could still be confirmed in her moral conservatism by letters like that of Misunderstood, the spokesman for four college sophomores, two boys and two girls, who had planned to take a weekend trip together and who, having informed their parents, "were shocked to learn that they were all against it." Ann told Misunderstood that it was not really a question of morals but of decorum: "If you want to be considered respectable you must live within the framework of society's conventions."

The following year, it was Kismet, thirty-two, who wanted to know whether it was all right for her to go on a trip with a man of forty whom she had been dating for a little over half a year. Assuming that if Kismet asked, it was because she didn't feel quite right about the trip, Ann again stressed propriety. She then slipped in a plug for the concern that was usually uppermost in her mind at such times, "Incidentally, there's an old-fashioned custom that would make this trip just dandy. I wonder if he's heard of it. It's called marriage." Ann may have read correctly that Kismet was an old-fashioned woman, but old-fasioned women were rapidly going the way of those four college sophomores, and by the end of the sixties Ann would find herself talking to readers who expected to play by another set of rules.

As the decade progressed and the mystery of sex continued to diminish, the mystery of the body did, too. By the midsixties, the body was being displayed with an assertiveness that put some people on edge. In 1966, Rootbound complained, "Everywhere we look we are assaulted by transparent blouses, plunging necklines, thigh-high hems, bare midriffs and naked backs." On that one, Ann held the line gamely: "The vast majority of men I've heard from find the whole topless, bottomless, backless, frontless thing a big fat bore."

But by 1970, complaints about the body too freely displayed had also become somewhat boring for Ann Landers. When Speechless began his letter with "Naked people on stage [attracting] thousands of nuts standing in line to pay $23 for a ticket" and ended by relating the misdeeds of a California sex therapist, Ann confined her criticism to the sex therapist. That same year, after Beaumont patted her on the back for turning thumbs down on nudism, she admitted, "Not all readers agreed with my advice. Some called me a dirty old lady."

And by the seventies, nudism became a matter of moral integrity. In 1973, Augusta, Maine, reproached her,

"Please don't foster the superstition that any part of the body is indecent. I am looking forward to the day when we will be sufficiently mature to accept complete nudity in public." Ann decided to close the argument by agreeing to disagree: "We are all products of our culture, and I was not brought up to accept nudity in public. If this labels me a narrow-minded, backward-looking prude, so be it."

In the early sixties, there were still college students like Misunderstood and adults like Kismet who felt the need to consult Ann Landers before undertaking a course of action that might shock. But there were definite signs already of a change in the prevailing winds. Misunderstood's letter contained such clues. He was evidently surprised at his parents' intransigence, even though his code still required him to consult them. He then assumed, mistakenly, that the change he discerned on the moral landscape would be reflected by Ann Landers. But he was angry as well, his anger evidencing not only his disappointment in the resistance of moral arbiters to those changes, but also his clear understanding of the moral bottom line: "We are all good, clean kids and resent the implication."

That anger at the imposition of a former morality was growing even louder elsewhere—in fact, loud enough for Ann to hear it. Three years after Against Sin, another landlady, Indignant, was told by a young woman in the apartment building she owned, "We are adults. What we do in our apartment is our business." Indignant asked, "As a property owner do I have the right to insist on morality on my premises?" Times had changed—what had not been acceptable in yesterday's wayside inn was acceptable in today's apartment. Ann said, "A landlady is not expected to assume the role of a matron in a house of correction. Tenants are obliged to pay rent, keep the property in good condition and refrain from disturbing the neighbors."

This was the decade when Emancipated Ellas were

starting to ask Ann Landers, "If a man can go to a bar alone for a little relaxation and not be considered a bum, why can't a woman?" We have already noted that Ann was also getting an education on the subject of pajama parties. In 1964, she was forced to devote a whole column to the matter, admitting, "I was told [by thousands] that pajama parties are very much a part of campus life and I must be square as a chair." One of the letters said, "Everyone wears underwear and nobody has ever gotten into trouble at a pajama party—so far as I know. It's the motel parties that are dynamite." And in a graver register, we have seen how, in the seventies, this new sexual outlook was affecting marriages, how many adolescents were claiming it as a symbol of adult freedom, and how some women considered it to be a part of liberation— like Augusta, Maine, whose letter also said, "Within my lifetime we have made tremendous strides in liberating ourselves from the terrible sense of body shame. . . . I remember so well—and it was only 20 years ago—when one of us would lower a bathing suit strap so we might tan evenly, a beach guard would hurry over and ask us to please 'be careful' and not show anything that shouldn't be seen."

As Ann showed in her response to Augusta, Maine, there was not much point after 1970 in fighting to preserve many of the proprieties that had once governed sexual conduct. There were anyway different and serious problems attendant upon a new acceptance of sexuality, as well as an opportunity to put that acceptance to constructive use. One of the problems the column had encountered from the start was that of the unwed mother. In those days, however, the problem was reduced to its simplest terms. In June 1957, N.L.B., 23, had written that she had broken up with the married man who fathered her child, but he had found her and they were living together again. Beyond asking N.L.B. when she would "wake up and smell the coffee," Ann's advice did not venture much beyond no-nonsense admonition:

"Plenty of girls go to work and support themselves. You can too." It would take readers some time to catch up with Ann on this advice—which she stuck to, while integrating it into a more complex structure.

In 1960, Sharp Cookie told her, "Your advice that unmarried pregnant girls should 'go it alone' and not force the skunk into a marriage he doesn't want, gives the American male an open-end ticket to live it up and skip merrily along his way." Ann acknowledged "having received hundreds of letters on this subject" but remained of the same mind: "Even marriages based on mutual love and respect run into snags. What chance has a marriage when at least one of the parties feels as if he's being sent to jail?"

Two months after N.L.B., No Gauguin called his present married life a lie: "Seven years ago while in the Air Force in Japan I made an alliance with a beautiful Japanese girl. Our love brought forth a child. I've never seen such adoration and quiet bliss in this country. . . . I returned to America with every intention of sending for my sweetheart and child and having a Western ceremony. Government red-tape interfered and I became caught in the web of conventional American living." This unfavorable comparison of American culture to an alien one, combined with its criticism of marriage, was too much for Ann Landers. She called her correspondent a phony and then asked him, "If you found life in Japan so blissful why didn't you stay over there?" Questions relating to the victim—the Japanese woman—were swept aside by Ann's indignation.

The moral issue governing out-of-wedlock pregnancy devolved, for the earlier Ann Landers, from her feeling that the woman was, even premaritally, the potential foundation on which the family structure depended. When the consciousness of women began formulating questions, Protesting Injustice asked why her pregnant girlfriend had to leave school while the equally culprit male did not. Ann's response was a synopsis of her tenets on the subject: "Who said life was fair? . . . The girl is the big loser in the game called unmarried love. Kids who want to sample the physical pleasure of marriage would do well to consider all the possibilities. Since the female gets pregnant and her body undergoes the changes, it is her responsibility to call the signals—and to hold that line."

But it had been clear during all the time Eppie wrote the column that this line was not always held. And Ann Landers notwithstanding, the situation was not getting any better; there would be more than a million teen-age pregnancies by 1980. The following year, Fitchburg, Mass., Inquiry—a psychology major at the University of Louisiana—informed her that about one-third of all unwed mothers had willed their situation. He listed the major reasons: rebellion against parental authority, hanging on to a boyfriend, substitution for parental loss in a broken home, low self-esteem, and a need for self-elevation in the eyes of the world. For these, Ann advised counseling, just as she advised, after the fact, marriage (or forgiveness to preserve the marriage) whenever possible, and, as a last resort, giving up the infant for adoption.

A more open discussion of sexual matters had the commensurate effect of starting to bring formerly unacceptable pregnancies out of their once necessary wrap of shame. In 1963, Dunce Cap wrote that, at 27, she was having the baby of a married man. "I know, legally, this man must support my child but I don't want anything from him. All I want is to use his name when I check into the hospital." Ann answered, "You may not use the man's name. It belongs to his wife. Make up another name, or put a Mrs. in front of your own." Other than informing Dunce Cap that "the word 'illegitimate' is no longer stamped on birth certificates," Ann Landers let the advice go at that.

In May 1965, Second Thoughts wrote that she and her cousin had a falling out because the latter, who had become pregnant by a married man, embarrassed her by showing up at work until two weeks before the baby's birth. Ann answered, "Your cousin was trying to hold her head up, and you knocked it down. Please be kind to her from now on."

Six months later, it was possible for Carol's Aunt to stretch adult permissiveness to a degree previously undreamt of. Her niece Carol had just become pregnant at sixteen, though no one seemed quite sure by whom. Yet, "If you met Carol Lee you'd say she is a perfect lady—quiet, reserved and on the shy side. And that brings me to the point of this letter. It's the sweet, innocent girls who get into trouble. The experienced chippies are far too wise. So why is the girl who has a baby out of wedlock branded as 'bad'? The very fact that she gets into trouble is proof of her innocence." Ann dragged her feet on that one: "I don't have any good conduct medals lying around for sweet, innocent young things who get pregnant and don't know who the father is." But the letter of Carol's Aunt did show families starting to demonstrate an unusual amount of resilience when confronted with this kind of crisis.

Two years later, Ann consoled Paid in Full, not quite sixteen, who feared she would always be considered "damaged goods" after having her out-of-wedlock child: "I have received and published many letters from girls who have had out-of-wedlock babies, and I can tell you that some of them DO meet and marry nice men. . . . One mistake does not brand you as worthless."

By 1968, one detects a distinct lessening of the indignation that had moved school authorities to close their doors to Protesting Injustice's friend: Waiting for the Word was concerned about last year's prom queen who was supposed to crown this year's, "None of us objects to her presence, but we don't know if it would be right to let her crown the new queen. She will be in her seventh month when the coronation takes place." That such a question should arise at all proved to be something of a dilemma for Ann Landers: "It's awfully hard—like impossible—for me to believe that the girl would WANT to participate in the coronation under the circumstances. Why don't you ask her. If she says yes, write again."

By the end of the sixties, there were a good many more parents like Carol's Aunt, able to face their child's unsanctioned pregnancy without blinking at it. A year after Waiting for the Word, Parent Trouble said, "My girl and I are both in high school. We are very much in love. Last week Sarah learned she was pregnant. Yesterday we told our parents we want to get married. My folks say it's all right with them. Sarah's parents say no. They want her to go to her aunt's in Wisconsin and have the baby, then put it up for adoption." Ann delegated that one to the family clergyman.

And finally, in the seventies, the concern of those with an acute social consciousness helped change yesterday's aberration into today's normalcy by urging attention to the sensitivities of those formerly considered miscreants— and, by now, to the sensitivity of their innocent offspring. Toward the end of 1971, Tarrytown, N.Y., wrote, "It is my suggestion that these days, when out-of-wedlock children are showing up in school more and more, the [family] tree project should be abolished. Thanks for your help."

Tarrytown, N.Y.'s sense of things was right. Out-of-wedlock pregnancies had become frequent enough by the seventies for familiarity to lessen contempt. Related but different concerns now started to claim space in the column. The problems of the practical seventies would be abortions and contraception rather than the social preoccupation of the moral fifties with the scandal of the unwed mother.

Abortions had always been a live issue in the column, but it is one whose nature changed radically along with other changes in sexual mores. In 1956, for example, it was not always easy to distinguish those who would be later known as prolifers from very early liberals. That year, Ann Landers got into a lengthy tug-of-war with some of her readers for having counseled against giving a baby shower for an unmarried girl of fifteen. Mr. and Mrs. Leon C. wrote, "You have dredged up the blackest mud to dirty the pages of a fine newspaper by referring to the birth of a new human being as an 'unfortunate event.' " Ann didn't budge: "In my opinion this is an unfortunate event and I see very little to celebrate." At the end of the month, the discussion was still raging—and Ann was still holding her ground.

Whatever motivated Mr. and Mrs. Leon C. to write, their enthusiasm for childbirth did not mention abortion, even negatively. It was not a topic for the family newspaper, even though the best estimate is that around a million of them were performed annually at the time. It was not until the midsixties that individual states began decriminalizing the procedure. As we saw in the preceding chapter, it was only in 1973 that two landmark decisions of the Supreme Court struck at most of the restrictive abortion laws. Therefore, few open references to abortion appear in the column until the midsixties. One of the earliest was from Child of the Gods in 1966: "I don't think I've ever seen a letter that began: 'I'm 20 and just had an abortion.' Well I am and I did." As one might expect, the letter was a strong attack against premarital indulgence.

The attack from Child of the Gods must have derived in part from the danger and furtiveness attendant on abortions at the time; but one cannot discount the social stigma that extended beyond the operating table. That stigma was heavy enough for even the poor to try legitimizing premarital sex through common-law marrige. It was an expedient that seemed to satisfy a surprisingly large number of men, though there is little evidence to indicate that it ensured the psychological well-being of women.

Alma wrote in 1956, "I've been living common-law with a man for seven years. We have three kids who think we are married. All our friends and family think so too. . . . He treats me better than most of my married friends get treated by their legal husbands. But I'm becoming very discouraged." What discouraged Alma was not immediately apparent from her letter, but whatever their reasons, she and other women valued marriage very much as Ann Landers did, and Ann regularly obliged them with stiff reprimands for not having legalized their situation. Ann may have derived part of her conviction from other letters, like that written later in the year by C.L.W.: "I've been living with a man for 20 years and carrying his name. I'm 47, he's 54. We were in business together. . . . Recently we decided to sell the business and buy a home. Now he tells me to 'get out.' " C.L.W.'s problem interested the Ann Landers of those days mainly as a moral case in point. She told her, as she told many others in similar words, "You are qualified to write quite a letter to the girls who play house without benefit of clergy."

After the fifties, the column has few references to common-law arrangements. People in greater numbers start living together, and more often because they want to than because they feel they should. Women grow more conscious of their rights, and, as we have seen, concerns shift from morality to the practical consequences of sex more freely practiced.

In 1966, Child of the Gods noted accurately that she couldn't remember a previous letter on the subject of abortion. But at the start of the seventies, the topic had been aired sufficiently to lose much of its dread.

In 1970, a Harris poll asked whether respondents thought abortion was murder. Those who did not think so already outnumbered those who did, 48 percent to 41 percent. (When, with the passing of three more years and a somewhat less incendiary question, the same pollsters asked whether respondents favored legalized abortion up to three months of pregancy, 52 percent answered yes, and only 41 percent opposed it.)

By then, as we have seen, Ann Landers was engaged in

a hot debate with Catholic readers because she had come out unequivocally in support of liberalized abortion laws. Just as proponents of the right to life would challenge the legality of the Supreme Court decisions from the moment they were handed down, so would Ann Landers be challenged periodically for her statement that abortion laws are "archaic, inhuman and discriminatory against the poor." Even long after her fight was legally won, Ann Landers remained entangled in its consequences. On September 7 and 8, 1981, she ran two consecutive columns devoted to Dr. George Ryan's testimony at a Senate Judiciary subcommittee hearing on the Human Life bill. Those two columns in turn generated heavy mail throughout the rest of the year, letters favoring her position running 30 percent ahead of those against.

Abortion in the fifties had been a necessity for the underprivileged that even the underprivileged tended to resist because of the associated stigma and danger. By the end of the seventies, it had become something of a modish cause for many, the grounds of the debate as well as its semantics shifting to Planned Parenthood. Here again, Ann Landers was in the lead. In 1979, she would send someone like Sweet 16 to Planned Parenthood for further information on "the time of the month a girl can have intercourse without getting pregnant." For that she became the target of indignant letters from those who were morally outraged, like Deeply Disappointed in Huntsville, Ala.:

> Have you gone off your rocker? Your answer to the girl who had two abortions by the time she was 18 was the worst yet. The tramp wasn't asking for advice, she was giving it. On and on she went about how foolish she had been, the depressions that followed her abortions—and then, like it was the Holy Grail or something, she finds Planned Parenthood. Hooray, she shouts triumphantly, "I will never be in trouble again!" . . .

People look to you to uphold decent standards. Sending them to Planned Parenthood will
not help young girls hold steadfast against the
ever-mounting pressures to have sex. It encourages them to continue to enjoy sins of the flesh
without worrying about getting caught.

In the eighties, the dialogue between moralists and
those attempting simply to cope with present realities
was a dialogue of the deaf. Ann Landers assured Deeply
Disappointed that she was in favor of old-fashioned
morality and repeated once more, "The only way to help
these people is by trying to educate them to be less
promiscuous and urge them to take precautions against
pregnancy and VD. And that's what I'm doing."

The introduction to the column of Planned Parenthood
and other agencies intending to demystify the shadowy
parts of sex carried with it a heavy semantic load which,
by the midseventies, had completely changed the self-
censored language of the family newspaper. And once a
word like *contraceptive* had become pronounceable, the
subject became important—and not only within Ann
Landers's column.

In the early days of 1975, From Massachusetts wrote, "I
am a Catholic and several years ago, after having five
children, my husband and I visited a cousin who had just
gotten his master's degree from Boston College. He told
us that using artificial birth control was not considered a
sin. . . . I then wrote to a priest who answered questions
in a Catholic magazine. His reply came (along with a
letter) saying 'it is NOT a sin.' He said the Church
preferred that Catholics not interfere with birth, but that
it was a 'personal decision.' " A hopeful Ann consulted
"one of the most knowledgeable Jesuits in the country"
for her response and was told in no uncertain terms that
contraception was not permitted according to Pope
Paul's Encyclical Humane Vitae (1968). But Ann added
that there was much dissension among the clergy and

that, according to recent studies, "almost as many Catholics use contraceptives as those of other faiths."

She thus continued to push this line long and hard, and by 1984 was able to report, "Recently, Father Theodore Hesburgh, president of the University of Notre Dame, let me know that he has heard from several Catholic women who had undergone abortions and want to be forgiven. They had read in my column that the Catholic church does not forever turn its back on such women. All priests will hear a confession of this kind and give absolution."

Of course, once the gates were open, there was always the possibility of a swift reader running ahead of Ann. We have already quoted from the letter of F.M., a high school senior who, in 1976, had questioned the law that kept contraceptives out of the hands of sixteen- and seventeen-year-olds. Ann agreed, "The law is a bummer." The month after From Massachusetts, A Reader wrote in response to a letter writer who should have been "told that birth control information and contraceptives were legally available at the time she got pregnant." But A Reader was after bigger game: "As for you, Lovey, your notion that premarital sex can be very bad for a young girl if there is a lack of sincerity and caring on the young man's part is perfectly valid. But do you honestly believe that marriage removes those dangers? Sometimes it makes them worse. Even though the divorce rate is zooming, Ann Landers says 'Get married first.' You gotta be nuts." Ann turned her answer into a rondelet by saying once again that "premarital sex can be plenty damaging, especially to the woman."

In repeating her concern for the jeopardy of young women engaged in premarital sex, Ann may have been preoccupied with the thought that "the moral standards of this country are falling through the basement." Nevertheless, it was safe to say that by the midseventies their plunge was no longer accelerated by knowledge or use of contraceptives.

During those same years, masturbation was another

word whose utterance made possible discussion of that aspect of sexual practice as a means of birth control. Kansas City congratulated Ann Landers in 1982 for having assured Middle American with a Serious Problem that he really didn't have one: "How much better to relieve the tensions solo than to mislead some vulnerable woman or beget an unwanted child." But Kansas City also remarked parenthetically, "I'm sure that by the time this letter reaches you, your mailbox will have been fire-bombed at least a dozen times by readers who are enraged." Ann confirmed him: "You are right about the fire-bombed mailbox!" even though by this time the subject was widely discussed.

The "fire-bombing" had of course been intense upon the first appearances of the word a dozen years earlier when it provoked letters like one in 1970 from Orange County (California?—if so, a part of the land not exactly on the cutting edge of social experimentation): "I am shocked and disappointed in you. I refer to your answer to the teen-ager who wrote to ask about the harmless effects of masturbation. . . . Your answer has virtually given the green light to millions of young people to go ahead and indulge in this rotten, shameful, disgusting habit."

When Kansas City sent in his belated congratulations, there were few aspects of sexual mores that could not be discussed in the family newspaper, from impotence to penile implants (about which Ann Landers printed several precise explanations). By the mideighties, even the Catholic Church in America had come a long way along that road. In January 1985, a less sanguine Kansan (Guilty in Kansas) wrote about her "terrible pangs" of conscience about continuing to masturbate in spite of "an excellent sex life." Ann turned that one over to a then-Provost at Notre Dame, the Rev. Edward A. Malloy, who assured Guilty in Kansas that many moral theologians now viewed masturbation "as a relatively common form of sexual release." Ann continues routinely to publish some of the protests that follow in the wake of such letters, but one suspects that she does so more to give examples of persistent ignorance than to present a cross-section of public opinion. Different and more serious aspects of sexual life have anyway claimed her readers' attention for the last ten or fifteen years.

The word *rape* was not a fit word for the family newspaper of the sixties. But at the start of 1970, Dumb and Lucky wrote to warn other teens about the danger of riding with strangers: "One cold night I decided to save the bus fare and hitch a ride. I got into the first car that stopped. A middle-aged man was driving. . . . Suddenly, he stopped behind a clump of trees, dragged me out of the car and tried to rape me." After that, the word and explicit discussion of the subject became frequent. Typical of a culture that prefers to address the symptoms of a problem rather than the problem itself were debates that followed, such as how women would be best advised to act in the event of a rape.

In 1975, Avid Ann Fan wrote, "You have printed two letters in the last several weeks advising women on how best to protect themselves against rape. The last letter advised screaming, kicking, karate chops, etc. . . . According to Mr. [Frederic] Storaska [founder of the National Organization for the Prevention of Rape and Assault], a woman should never scream, struggle, run or try to kick the rapist where it counts. If she does, the rapist is likely to silence her by strangling her or cracking her skull open." Ann still preferred the advice of Dr. James Selkin, Director of the Center for the Study of Violence at Denver General Hospital: "Scream, kick, yell your head off." But she allowed, "It's up to each woman to decide which makes the best sense."

The associations to which Messrs. Storaska and Selkin belonged, as well as other support groups that had sprung up by then, were further evidence of our temperamental tendency to accept social aberrations by focusing on their consequences. This tendency led to letters like Proud in N.C.'s, in 1985: "I would like to send a message to all the young girls who were raped last week and who are going to get raped this week. Go to the nearest hospital emergency room or the nearest police station and tell them what happened. The medical evidence needed to get a rape conviction must be obtained within two hours. . . . The next thing you should do is get help. Phone the sexual assault center. You are going to need emotional support and they are trained and willing to give it."

Changing sexual patterns contributed to other attempts at self-protection. The subject of sexual harassment comes up infrequently during the fifties. Ann Landers had urged women readers from the earliest to assert that their body was theirs alone to dispose of, but the Ann Landers of the fifties was inclined to feel that childish as men might be, it was still a man's world, and that those grown-up children were to be indulged.

At the end of 1955, Unhappy wrote, "I am a stenographer in a large office which employs 35 men. I am the only woman. Several of the men have asked me out, but I have refused. My boss (who is much older) asked me to have coffee with him, but I knew what his intentions were, so of course I said, 'No.' " The times allowed Ann to read a certain complacency in that letter, and her answer was accordingly sarcastic: "Oh you poor miserable rose among all those nasty old thorns! Did it ever occur to you that one lone baboon in the midst of 35 buffaloes would 'attract attention' too?"

The point is not that Unhappy did not get what she deserved, but that a few years later changing times would force Ann to modulate her answer. That time had not quite come in 1957 when Helpless, a young bookkeeper, wrote, "I don't want attention from married men but how can I avoid it? They trick me into working late, coming in early, and having lunch. They call me by my first name (which I detest) and chuck me under the chin. I feel I'm being robbed of my dignity." Ann responded,

"No one can rob you of your dignity—but you," acknowledging only, "Your chin is private property and surely you're a big enough girl to know how to intercept a pass!"

But over the years, Ann became distinctly more aggressive. In 1974, Beet Red told her, "Recently, while on a school business trip, one of the male faculty members put his arm around me while I was speaking with the host of a college we were visiting. I was deeply embarrassed by his unprofessional conduct and tried to pull away. He deliberately kept a firm grasp on me." Ann responded in a most unladylike fashion, "I would have wrested free of the clod, even if it meant landing him on his head. The embarrassment would have been HIS, not mine."

Ann's feisty advice to Beet Red may have been due to the fact that by then she was sensitive to more serious forms of harassment and abuse. Complaints about abuse received mixed receptions during the fifties and sixties, in part because the complaints sometimes sent mixed signals. In 1957, Mrs. Upset said of her husband, "He's been six and eight hours late for dinner, and has actually sneaked out of bed at night and returned in time to change clothes and go to work. He's never beat me, but he has hit me a few times when I tried to straighten things out." For this fairly standard kind of letter, Ann Landers had a fairly standard reply: "What does [your marriage] have that justifies living together? You casually mention that he has hit you a few times and sneaks out of bed at night. I can't see that he contributes a single thing to the marriage except money. This you can get without the abuse, deceit and heartache. Tell the heel to send the support checks in the mail until he gets straightened out."

During the innocent fifties, Ann could assume that a woman as weak as Mrs. Upset might actually leave a husband, or force him to leave, and then depend confidently on support checks. Since Ann Landers did not countenance divorce in those days, she could also assume that such action by the woman, however unlikely, would have a salutary effect on the man who would eventually get "straightened out."

But during the sixties, within a changing sexual climate, one finds a different kind of letter about, and from, women who were doing little to resist abuse. In April 1965, Still Shaking wrote, "A lovely woman I've known for years (we're both in our middle 30s) confided that her husband spanks her when she displeases him. She asked if my husband ever spanked me. When I told her I would never tolerate such an indignity, she looked at me as if I was crazy. Then she went on to defend her husband by saying he never spanked her unless she deserved it. 'And,' she added, 'I usually feel a lot better after it is over.' "

Ann opined that "it's both strange and interesting how these physical kooks seem to find each other." Seven months later, there was a letter signed B's Wife (as Eppie had once been Jules's wife): "Every once in a while he loses his temper and socks me. But I accept it as a compliment. If he didn't love me he wouldn't get so mad. Even though he has his little faults I would follow him to the end of the earth, because I love him. Well?" Ann responded, "No. Sick."

Letters like those of Still Shaking and B's Wife were bringing to the fore the sexual component of abuse, but from a peculiar point of view inasmuch as women likely to reveal their part in it were also likely to assert their enjoyment. But as child abuse, this once forbidden topic became one of the most explosive of the seventies and eighties. In the earlier days, it was still partly disguised under the relatively jocular designation of the "funny uncle"—but was very widely documented. In 1972, One You Saved took note of Ann's column on "funny uncles" and described "a step-father who took indecent liberties with me for about four years, starting when I was six. I didn't know what it was all about until I reached my 10th birthday and was put wise by my playmate who was a couple of years older than I was. Her step-father was 'funny' with her and she wrote to you about it. You told her to tell him if he came near her again she would immediately go to her mother and ruin him. She took your advice and he never bothered her after that. I decided to do the same with my step-father." The following year, Freud Was No Fool remembered the column after being forced to confront her daughter's misadventures with her second husband. She requested, "Please repeat the advice. I blocked it out of my consciousness and now I know why."

The advice will be repeated frequently over the following years because the subject elicits a great number of letters. But increasingly it is the father, and incest, that is their real focal point. Sometimes, the letter is strangely casual, as when Mother of Three writes in 1975, "My husband and I are having a disagreement and we want you to settle it. . . . I work evenings and Harry is supposed to watch the children. That's the problem. He watches them too well. Especially the girls. When my daughters take their showers, Harry always finds some excuse to putter in the bathroom. The younger girl complained to me about this. When I mentioned it to Harry, he said the older girl didn't mind it at all, in fact she seemed to enjoy it."

At other times, and more frequently, the letters refer to a category that now has a label, the sexual exploitation of children. By the end of the year, A Victim relates an encounter "with my own father when I was 11 years of age. I would rather not go into the details of that soul-searing experience. I never told anyone about it because I was afraid it might destroy my mother." Toward the end of 1975, Been Through It surmised why Mother of Three's older daughter might have kept quiet: "Maybe she has been threatened into silence—like I was. You should have told Mom to get her crazy, sick husband out of the house before one or both of her daughters got raped." Ann admitted, "I was chilled by the number of letters I received from young girls who wrote to say they had been sexually assaulted by their fathers."

At the end of the sixties, Ann Landers had been using a word previously as unmentionable as the act it designates. Concerning the case of "a brother-sister relationship that was much too close for comfort," she had said the two should be separated because of the danger of emotional and/or physical incest. This prompted No Identification Please to inquire in February 1970: "I have never heard of emotional incest. I would like to know more about it because of some odd and peculiar relationships in our own family."

The identification of the category had the usual dual effect: It brought the aberration out of its former shadows, but it induced a kind of toleration through a nearly exclusive attention to ways of dealing with it. In 1979, Rope's End in New England discovered the "improper advances" her own father had made to her daughter, and though "in a state of shock," she went to the *Ann Landers Encyclopedia* for help, but could find it neither under "Funny Uncles" nor under "Molest." Ann assured her it was there, both under "Child Molesting" and "Incest."

Letters in the eighties are more and more open about sexually abusive fathers and victimized daughters. Their tone tends to be more clinical than indignant. Many sound like Feeling Cheated in Florida (not exactly a vengeful nom de plume) who wrote in 1980: "I feel I must add to the letters from women who were sexually molested by their fathers when they were young. It wasn't until I was 45 that I learned my father had fooled around with my two sisters as well as me. (I am the oldest.) Two of us are now divorced and one is still married. None of us has ever had any sexual feelings. I wonder if this was caused by our early experiences with our father."

As she had been doing all along, Ann advised therapy. The usual support and treatment groups had already sprung up. For the Greeks, the horror of incest was the gods' supreme vengeance visited on that wretched descendant of the house of Laius, Oedipus. By 1981, in California, a similar occurrence called for recourse to Parents United and Daughters-Sons United. Consciousness of child molestation had become sufficiently widespread by 1983 for twenty-two thousand people to correct Ann Landers, who had advised a teen-age girl it would be all right for her to go on a trip to Washington with her bachelor uncle whom "She once liked a lot but [whose] kisses were getting a little too mushy." Ann telephoned the girl and dissuaded her from taking the trip.

Such widespread awareness eventually contributed to swinging the pendulum too far the other way. In August 1984, Wrongly Accused in L.A. wrote about a spanking he had given his recalcitrant son that resulted in "yelling" heard by neighbors: "An hour later, when the kids were sound asleep, the police and a child-abuse investigator arrived and took control of our lives for the next three hours. This tied up the services of social service, police and medical personnel. It left our children fearful that they could be separated from us by some unknown agency." Ann gave the outraged father little sympathy: "I'm glad to know the Los Angeles folks responded so quickly. Four cheers for them!"

In 1984, Burned at the Stake wrote: "This is to address another side of a problem on everyone's mind these days—the sexual abuse of children. In a recent column you advised those who suspect something wrong to report their suspicions to the proper authorities. Are you unaware of the damage that can be done when a person is falsely accused of a crime of this nature?" Ann responded that "children almost never lie" about that subject.

But under such constant and widespread scrutiny, the subject was bound to prove more complicated. Two weeks after Burned at the Stake, Frustrated wrote, "OK— I've molested the beautiful, willing 11-year-old blond nymphet next door. Now what? The gamey little sexpot is returning every afternoon for more. I would like to stop but see no way other than to move out at midnight and leave no forwarding address." And an even more chilling letter came in 1980 from No City, No State, Just Dead-End, USA: "You have yet to address yourself to another sex-related illness: pedophilia—attraction to young children. . . . Please do not recommend that I seek psychiatric care because I have already gone that route with two psychiatrists and a clinical psychologist. 'Treatment' has cost me more than $6,000 and I received no help whatsoever." Ann could only respond, "When people are sick the only advice I can give is 'See a doctor,' and you are among the sickest."

Then there were those for whom this new permission to speak was a chance to make hitherto unspeakable revelations. In 1975, Blood Is Thicker wrote, "I'm in love with my brother, and he is in love with me. X is in his early 30s and I am in my middle 20s. We've felt this way about each other for years but it's become more difficult because of our bad marriages. . . . The physical desire for one another makes us feel weird and unnatural." Ann Landers picked up the words: "Incestuous relationships are weird and unnatural."

In 1983, it was twenty-year-old S.L., Mo., writing: "I've never been in love, until now. The guy, well—he's my 23-year-old brother." And in the first days of 1985, No Name, No City, Please contributed, "I am in my early 60s, divorced and retired. My sister is in her late 50s and widowed. We go to bed together twice a week. This has been going on since her husband died eight years ago. . . . We both enjoy these escapades and they always produce a good night's sleep. No one knows about this and no one is getting hurt." Ann commented: "Sick, sick, sick." Then, proving that, for her at least, incest still retained a measure of awe, she reverted to a rare moment of censure: "The fact that neither of you sees anything wrong with such behavior suggests a moral dead-spot that is unnatural and revolting."

Child abuse and incest may have been the most serious

sexual aberrations discussed in the column, but there were others—some of which Ann Landers found equally unnatural, if not revolting. At the very start of the sixties, homosexuality surfaces timidly. For example, Saved wrote that his mother brought him up as a girl until she died, when he was eleven. He then had to go through "a small fortune for psychiatric care" in order to find "the road back to normalcy." Ann Landers printed that particular letter, but without comment.

Five years later, the topic was current. In 1965, M.V. wrote that she had married and had a daughter by a homosexual from whom she had separated. She had now noticed her daughter "dating a young man who is startlingly like her father." Ann was not yet prepared to take this kind of problem too seriously—it sounded at the time like one more assertion of rebellious youth. She advised a three-way confab with a psychiatrist, but said, "Don't be surprised if your daughter marries the young man anyway. People who feel strongly about romantic involvements seldom listen to reason."

A few months later, Ann was called on to make a distinction for Stymied: "Several weeks ago my boy friend, Dale, asked me if he could dress up in my clothes just for the fun of it. . . . When Dale dressed up and put on make-up, he looked like a very pretty girl. I couldn't get over it." Still for the fun of it, they then went out for a walk. "I know this sounds crazy, Ann, but Dale got more whistles than I did—and he loved it." Ann specified, "Dale is a transvestite. This does not mean he's a homosexual, but it is a deviation, nonetheless. If you want to marry a man who enjoys wearing your clothes and getting passes from men, go ahead. But please urge him to get professional help right away."

The column's early references to homosexuality derive mainly from readers asking for a definition. Within a week of Stymied's letter, Desperate wrote about having raised her son alone after asking his homosexual father to leave. She had now discovered under her son's mattress the pictures of nude men and wanted to know if the aberration was hereditary. Ann assured her that it wasn't and again advised treating the problem as a psychological disturbance.

In 1969, Aunt wanted to know whether there was anything wrong with her cousin's six-year-old daughter. When she played house with her doll, she took the role of the father. Ann told Aunt that six was too young for tendencies to be determined. But those being the days before role playing was questioned, Ann suggested a psychiatrist once again, since "little girls usually imitate their mothers."

The end of the sixties also brought lesbians into the column. Tarsus noted in 1968, "There are many more lesbians than most people suspect. . . . I know, because I am one." And lesbians, like male homosexuals, were starting to speak about themselves. Two years later, Good Memory in Cincinnati, a 74-year-old woman, wrote to tell of the affair that she had at twelve with a woman of thirty, that "lasted several years."

Tarsus also suggested that a decade during which the aberration had been discussed was time enough to acknowledge that it remained beyond the reach of psychoanalysis: "My main purpose in writing is to tell you that your suggestion 'seek professional help' won't work. I sought professional help and I also prayed fervently. I begged God to remove this burden from my shoulders. But, five years later, I still am a lesbian." Ann agreed and changed to the tack she would use henceforth, "I suggest professional help because therapy can give these tortured people some insight into their problem. And hopefully, with understanding can come a measure of self-acceptance and peace of mind."

Until the troubled late sixties and early seventies, Ann could still confuse jokingly such sexual dilemmas and what she considered to be outlandish adolescent behavior. At the beginning of 1970, Concerned Mother expressed her fears, "We have a daughter in college who writes that she has fallen in love with her roommate. We are just sick about this and don't know what to do." Ann answered, "Are you sure your daughter's roommate is a girl? These days one shouldn't assume anything—especially when the under-25 group is involved." But she then reverted to the standard answer for such parents: Urge counseling and then stay out.

As previously mentioned, the rebellion of the young sometimes strained for deliberate excess, and it was sometimes difficult for Ann to distinguish a genuine aberration from the many that were contrived. A few months after Concerned Mother, Mrs. No Name Mother wrote about her lesbian daughter who wanted her to sign forms authorizing a sex change. Ann opined, "Individuals who so desperately desire to be of another sex that they are willing to have their bodies mutilated are severely disturbed." She then told Mrs. No Name how she had refused to discuss transsexual operations on Dick Cavett's show because she "could say nothing supportive."

Indeed, traditional assertions color some of Ann Landers's discussions of the subject during the seventies. In 1973, she was asked by One, "Why are homosexual relationships considered illegal? Why is it considered a sex crime when there is no victim, such as in rape or child-molesting? . . . Why must people like me sneak around behind the backs of parents and relatives so that we don't shame or 'disgrace' them?" Ann answered, "Because homosexuality is unnatural. It is, in spite of what some psychiatrists say, a sickness—a dysfunction. In our culture, in the year 1973, we are not conditioned to accept homosexuality as the normal human condition."

In 1970, homosexuals were only starting to be accepted. A poll conducted that year by the Institute for Sex Research found that about two-thirds of those asked would not accept a homosexual as a doctor. But seven years later, when the Harris poll asked the same question, more than three-quarters said they would. (Even on the more sensitive issue of whether they could accept a homosexual teacher, the opposition dropped from over three-quarters in 1970 to just over half in 1977.)

As homosexuals and lesbians began to come out of the closet during the seventies, they would write with varying degrees of indignation about the mislabelings to which they were subjected. In 1975, One in Evanston wrote, "I'm beginning to wonder if you know the difference between a homosexual and a bisexual"—and went on to analyze a number of differences. Ann retorted, "That whole scene is like playing tennis without a net. It's too far out and totally incomprehensible to me." In 1983, A Truth-Seeker, USA, wrote, "You often use the word 'normal' in a back-handed, liberal manner when writing about homosexuality. . . . Does this mean you belong to an elitist segment of society that knows the true meaning of the word? Will you, once and for all, explain why you consider homosexuals abnormal?" Ann obliged:

> While homosexuality seems normal for those who are physically drawn to members of their own sex—in fact, to them heterosexuality seems abnormal—I stand firm in my contention that homosexuality is not normal.
>
> It is my belief that when God made man and woman He instilled in them sexual desires for one another so they would procreate. That was His divine plan to people the earth. Homosexuals do not experience desires for intimacy with members of the opposite sex. They are turned on by members of their own sex. Since their sexual behavior does not square with the plan for procreation, I believe in that sense they are abnormal.

And she added, "I do not use the word in a pejorative or judgmental manner. For 25 years I have fought for the civil rights of homosexuals and I shall continue to do so."

An earlier Ann might have occasionally been a little more judgmental than she was willing to remember. Only a year before her answer to A Truth-Seeker, USA, Ann's

206 *The Forbidden Topic Everyone Discusses: Sex*

pen had run off with her, when she referred to homosexuals as "side saddle tenors." Nevertheless, it is a fact that she remained more enlightened than a large number of her readers throughout her discussion of homosexuality. In 1970, at about the same time as the appellation "gay" was finding its way into the column, the defenders of a traditional morality started to be heard from. In February, Resident of the World's Largest Open-Air Lunatic Asylum—Los Angeles wrote, "The way the homosexuals are taking over the country, a straight person is considered an oddity. . . . And now, I see there's a church out in Hollywood (natch) that has a fairy pastor and a congregation composed of nearly 300 fags and lesbians. . . . This clergyman recently announced that he will 'marry' homosexual couples." Ann read danger signs in the writer's derogatory language and responded, "If homosexuals want to pray as a group, it's all right with me. I'm more concerned about the violent people in our society." She repeated those words five years later to Mortified, who had complained that there were now seventeen such churches in Los Angeles.

Later that year, Dumb Dora went "to a public library and asked the librarian for a book on homosexuality and she nearly fainted." Ann told her, "Go to another library where the librarians don't faint so easily. Ask for a copy of *Sex and Gender* by Dr. Robert Stoller." The following year, she received a letter from Another California Earthquake (homosexuality in the early seventies seemed to have affected Californian heterosexuals especially hard): "I am all for human rights, equality and all that jazz, but the queers are taking over the world and I resent it." He then went on to tell how his sister who was applying for a marriage license had been asked by the Court House clerk, "Are you sure you're a female?"—and had then explained, "Last week we had two gay couples in here trying to get marriage licenses. Lord knows how many of those characters have fooled us." The letter writer wanted to know "How can decent people be protected against such insults?" Ann turned her answer into a libertarian assertion: "Government is already doing too much prying. The County Clerks should take the marriage applicants' word for it."

In 1973, Straight in Corpus Christi recounted how, in a depressed mood, she went for a cry to the ladies' room of a cocktail lounge; her worried friend found her there a short time later: "When she saw me, she became upset and asked if I was angry with her. I told her my depression had nothing to do with her and that I loved her like a sister. She put her arms around me and said 'I love you too.' At that very moment a woman came in. In a voice filled with disgust she snapped, 'I wish you Gay Libbers would stay in your own homes.' "

Ann assured Straight in Corpus Christi that "those who are the least tolerant and the most critical of homosexuals invariably have doubts about their own sexuality." The warning fell on many deaf ears. Two years later, Orlando Observer was "convinced the American woman's obsession that men be good dancers is breeding the masculinity out of them. Dancing is a woman's game. A truly masculine male was not meant to glide a woman gracefully across the dance floor. . . . Not so with the gay element. They are invariably marvelous dancers." Ann called the letter "hogwash."

In February 1980, Name Deleted by Request came up with a theory not unlike the one Ann herself would propound three years later in answer to A Truth-Seeker, USA: "I believe they are a third sex, created by nature to control the population." But Ann was not buying: "There is a great deal of controversy among psychiatrists on whether or not homosexuals are 'born' or 'made.' I side with those who believe they are 'made'. . . . This rules out the third-sex theory as a method of population control."

A month later, Ark from N.J. expressed his disgust: "I am 68 years old and have been reading your column for 20 years. I used to love it, but lately you've been running nothing but letters about faggots and queers and lesbians.

I am sick of the garbage. TV is no better. Nothing but adultery and murders. Please put those oddballs back in the closet where they belong before you lose your readers." Ann answered, "Sorry if you don't like me anymore, but I address myself to all aspects of human behavior—some of it isn't very pretty. There will be more letters on homosexuality—and rape and incest and child abuse and alcoholism and drug abuse." Her correspondent was right; homosexuality claimed a large part of the column throughout the seventies. And so was Ann; the debate was far from over, and readers like Ark from N.J. continued to resent it.

That resentment, first voiced with such anger in the early seventies, may have derived its strength from the fact that gays were becoming more visible. Fewer and fewer were, like One, willing to "sneak around." Gays were walking out of the closet and right into the family living room, the board room, and the locker room. In January 1971, Sue of L.A. wrote one of the earliest letters expressing this refusal and laying claim to the dignity of acceptance. It was also one of the best of the many letters Ann Landers published on the subject:

> I am a homosexual woman. I do not want to be a man. I have the body of a female. Since no one has been able to prove that the mind has gender I will say I have the mind of a human. My emotions are those of a homosexual woman. This is my only deviation. I am not sick. In fact, I am healthier than most straight women who insist on hanging the "sick" label on me.
>
> I do not want a man or a straight woman or a bisexual woman. And most of all, I do not want to be bothered by curious straight people who view me as a freak or a conversation piece. I enjoy a pleasant life with a single lesbian like myself. We do not bother anyone and we would appreciate it if people wouldn't bother us.

That letter, for all its forcefulness, did not achieve the

desired effect. In the eighties, other voices, in other words, were still repeating the same message to a world that wasn't listening well enough—even in the person of Ann Landers. In 1980, Another One found fault with the practical and antiseptic quality of a previous answer:

> You could have been a lot more helpful. Why didn't you speak of the despair over "one-night stands in cheap motels"? You should have told him that sex is not the sum total of a person's existence. While society generally sees homosexuals as just that and nothing more, I wish to state that I am a useful person, a good citizen and I also happen to be gay. . . . One last comment—as to whether homosexuality is a fault of the genes or psychological conditioning: it is neither, since it is not a fault. God made me and HE does not make mistakes. If one person in 10 in this country is gay, there must be a reason as well as a cause.

In his letter, Another One listed some of the groups that then existed to assist homosexuals: "Dignity is the organization for gay Catholics. The Metropolitan Community Church serves Protestant gays. And here, in Ohio, I know that each group is open to gays of all faiths." Ann listed many more on her own. And under the heading of equal time, A Wasp from McLean contributed that same year the information that there existed in Washington, D.C. "a synagogue for homosexuals, both male and female. It is called Bet Mishpachah, which means 'House of Family.' They meet in a Methodist church, and it is one of nine such groups for Jewish homosexuals."

The thrust of A Wasp from McLean's letter is not altogether clear. She ended her letter with a kind of challenge: "Several years ago you gave a lot of coverage to Dignity, an organization for Catholic gays. You have also referred to Methodists and Unitarian gay groups, but never a word about Jewish gays—as if they didn't exist. I shall watch with interest to see if you print this." The reader is left to wonder whether she felt the Jews had been slighted or whether she resented Ann's having left unmentioned the stigma that tainted Jews as well. Whatever her intention, the customary cultural ethos had taken over. Homosexuals were tolerated, if not quite integrated nor quite understood—but the usual palliative for this passive ostracism was in place. The support groups were there.

For ten years, during the seventies, homosexuality became a genuine concern among many people, instead of the usual stag-party joke. Based on the letters of straights (and of those who were not quite sure whether they were actually straight), what Ann Landers perceived as an abnormality was perceived by many others as a threat. But reading the column over the years shows that the sexuality of these "normal" people was often as unsatisfactory.

From the very start, even before readers could express themselves clearly, couples had complained about being sexually mismatched. In 1956, a fairly typical letter would be M.A.Q.'s: "My husband shows me no affection except on rare occasions when he feels he is doing me a big favor. . . . Believe me, I've tried everything to interest him but nothing works." Ann had no trouble reading through the vague terms and advised M.A.Q.'s husband to visit a doctor.

In 1962, Ann gave statistics after keeping tabs: "The letters from unhappy husbands . . . complaining about icicle wives (they call them 'cold tomatoes') outnumbered the women 20 to 1." What changed over the years was the explicitness of the formulations, leading to a progressively more detailed analysis.

By 1968, Mrs. Content could write, surveying a decade of such letters, "I never realized so many women were married to 'dead batteries' until I read about them in your column. It might help if someone told these frustrated females that sex is not THAT important. I know, because

I used to have the same problem. Then one day I decided to quit making both of us miserable. I looked at my marriage objectively and discovered I had a hard-working, faithful, honorable husband with no bad habits. . . . The only thing wrong with him was no interest in sex. So what?" At the time, Ann thought the letter writer was an unfortunate exception, unaware that she was contemplating in Mrs. Content the mere tip of a huge iceberg. She answered, "Not all women are willing (or able) to make the accommodation you have made."

Starting in the sixties, the problem of masculine response was going to be complicated by one of the forms of youthful independence—the increasing sexual aggressiveness of females. A fairly typical letter in 1961 is Worried's: "Our 13-year-old daughter is a problem. She is physically mature and could pass for 17. Lila has a mad crush on a family friend who is 25, married and has two children. He drops over several evenings a week just to visit. . . . Lila hangs around, sits on his lap and kisses him. He encourages her by telling her she's cute. . . . I've told my husband this is not good but he insists she's just a kid and that I'm out of my mind. Am I?" Ann, who had been getting a hefty dose of such letters, replied, "Your mind is working much better than your husband's."

In the seventies, the number of these accounts increases. In April 1970, Oklahoma wrote, "There's this woman, Ann, whose name I couldn't even spell. Suddenly she picked me out for her husband. If she spots me in public, I'm finished. She has eyes like a hawk and can find me in a stadium that holds 30,000 people." The following month, Ann was asked to arbitrate the family feud presented by Mother Maggie: "Our 14-year-old son Paul left the dinner table last night to answer the telephone. We heard him say, 'Yes, I'm going to the track meet but I'm eating my supper right now and then I've got a lot of homework to do. Good-by.' " She felt Paul had been rude; his older brother felt he had handled things right. Ann acknowledged the problem brought on by changing times: "Ten years ago I would have sided with you. Today I'm with the boys. Young girls have become so aggressive since you and I were young, Maggie, it's enough to scare a kid out of three years' growth."

It was only a question of time before males began associating their poor sexual performance with this kind of female aggressiveness. By the midseventies, their number had grown to the point where No Nostalgia for the Fifties wrote, "I'm not exactly a women's libber, but if I read one more 'expert opinion' implying that aggressive females are responsible for male impotence, I think I'll go to the nearest busy intersection and burn my bra." Ann stood her ground, arguing from the evidence that crossed her desk: "Based on what I have read, heard, and seen these past ten years [one] can no longer typecast the male as the hunter. The game has changed, dearie."

That same year, Experienced shared a memory: "I was interested in your statement that health departments of colleges report many young men now complain of impotency. I'm a man of 75. Although I heard of no such complaining when I went to college, I had an experience that may explain the plight of young men today. . . . One young lady . . . surprised me by letting me know she expected the evening to end with sexual intercourse. This made me think how humiliating it would be if I were unable to perform. The thought became a fear, and the fear became a self-fulfilling prophecy." Ann thought Experienced might be right, but impotence was fast becoming a topic that could not be kept within such simple bounds.

That same year, Battling Betty's analysis of the consequences resulting from a husband's impotence gave a measure of the extent readers had progressed since the fifties in their perception of these difficulties. She said, "It's a vicious circle, Ann. When a man becomes incapable of functioning sexually, the natural response of a wife who loves him is to feel rejected. The more rejected she feels, the more he is turned off by guilt and fear of failure."

But open discussion of the problem in the columns does not seem to have eliminated the problem. In the eighties, Unfulfilled up in D.C. asked Ann Landers once again, "Please address yourself to the growing problem of healthy, middle-aged men who are sexually impotent." And the letter writer then demonstrated how much sex per se still meant to some, even after all the ink spilled because of that topic: "If these males know they are unable to perform, why do they put a woman through the embarrassment and frustration?"

Ann was not prepared to reopen that one, but she did answer another part of the question: "How do you account for what appears to be a national epidemic?" She said, "According to Dr. Domeena Renshaw, a psychiatrist at Loyola University and an authority on sexual dysfunction, male impotence is not a new problem. People are simply discussing it more openly." That openness, like any other, was supposed to be therapeutically beneficial, according to the wisdom of a post-Freudian culture. In fact, all the frank talk about impotence appears to have achieved little more than did Experienced's date when she, perhaps for the same reasons, likewise attempted straightforwardness. The image of this young lady's straight-from-the-shoulder approach and of the coyness (verbal and psychological) of readers in the fifties suggest a culture forever trying to do the right sexual thing without realizing that this very effort destroys a fundamental part of sex—its spontaneity.

Like their obsession with the right procedure, many Amerians were obsessed with the ideal body. In particular, the female breast was an obsession for many writers, even in the days when it was referred to only through gesture or the euphemism of numbers. Even during the sexual revolution and the assertion of adolescent independence, one finds letters like the one Little Eva wrote in 1965: "I am a 15-year-old girl, and I just die when I have to shower after physical education. . . . It's not that I am overly modest, it's just that I wear a size 32A brassiere, and I am ashamed of having so little to put into it. A flat-chested girl is like a peacock without feathers."

Ann remembered the countless other such letters and told Little Eva, "Our society has become dimension wacky in the last 25 years, and it's nonsense. Some of these top-heavy movie stars look like pasture animals." The year after Little Eva's letter, Ann described a "revolting" doll whose breasts swelled when her arms were turned.

Alongside those with breast fixations were others with their own hang-ups, among them the wife-swappers, the pedophiliacs, and the incestuous—all of whom experienced a confessional need of Ann Landers. And in the midsixties, the column was agitated for a surprisingly long time by yet another question—that of women who undressed in the closet; it generated hundreds of letters.

One of the comments, in February 1965, came from Statue of Liberty: "I don't undress in the closet. I undress in a different house. For over a year I was mauled, pinched, squeezed and patted until I was on the verge of a nervous breakdown." Ann pointed out that her husband might not have been the only sick one in that relationship. Ann's response notwithstanding, From Georgia returned to the same point three months later: "Of all the silly squabbles in your column, the one about the wife who undresses in the closet takes the cake. . . . Do you feel, Ann Landers, that it is a wife's duty to put on a nightly strip tease for her husband?" Ann told her, "If you haven't tried it, Honey, don't knock it." Those letters showed, though Ann didn't yet know it, that the practice of sex for its own sake was not thrilling everyone quite as much as it did Unfulfilled up in D.C., and that, in fact, it was becoming a positive annoyance for a substantial number of women.

Even in the emancipated eighties, feelings ran high whenever an apparently trivial subject about the bedroom surfaced. A flap of some magnitude developed in 1980 about women sleeping in their underpants, sparked by a letter from Odd Ball in Ohio. The free-spirited Ann

Landers was surprised that anyone should do such a thing, and then was surprised again by the large numbers who did and were willing to bear witness to the fact. And three years later, the business of undressing in the closet flared up again—prompted once more by complaining husbands, and defended once more by wives who were tired of their husbands' sexual appetites.

Recall here the letter from Mrs. L. She was the widow who wrote in 1955, brooding because she and her "very nice widower" friend "somehow . . . lost our heads"—leaving Ann to guess just what that meant. Having correctly guessed, Ann asked this forty-nine-year-old woman, "How come no one thought of getting a ring on your finger and that piece of paper in your hand first?"

Alongside this might be placed Paradise Lost's letter in 1981: "My wife and I were engaged for nearly three years. During that time we had a wonderful sexual relationship. It was almost as if we had invented it. We were both convinced that no one in the world enjoyed sex as much as we did. Almost immediately after we married, my wife lost all interest in bedroom activity." And Ann's answer (interesting even though it neglected its own Freudian implications): "It is called the Madonna-Whore Syndrome. Illicit sex is exciting. Respectable sex is dull." Considering that the word *sex* appeared only very rarely in the column before 1960, and in light of the floodgates it opened thereafter, one is struck by the curious objectification of sex in our culture. It seems to persist as a strange icon, one that must be either hidden away or incensed, but which, one way or the other, many find difficult to assimilate.

Attempts to remedy this situation seem to have been futile for the most part. The women's movement had as one of its aims to draw attention to sex roles in order to eliminate them. In so doing it contributed further to sexual self-consciousness. What Ann Landers used to call the sexual chemistry between a man and woman was further mentalized and worried through analysis and moral prescript. To say that a woman should not wrap herself in cellophane for her husband's benefit made little more sense than to say that she should.

And Ann Landers, with her liberal belief in the healthy virtue of sex leading to practical advice on how to promote it, even Ann Landers contributed to the distancing of that fearsome icon. She deplored on several occasions the extent to which the culture was sex-oriented — listing as contributory causes the pill, modern forms of popular music, peer pressure, and other culprits. But one cannot omit from such a listing her own column and the ongoing sexual dialogue with millions of readers.

That objectification of sex finally led to a huge expression of fatigue and disillusionment, especially on the part of women. On January 14 and 15, 1985, Ann Landers published the results of her poll, which asked simply, "Would you be content to be held close and treated tenderly and forget about 'the act'? Reply YES or NO." For a second time, Ann was forced to publish results she had not expected: "Seventy-two percent said YES, they would be content to be held close and treated tenderly and forget about the act. Of those 72 percent who said yes, 40 percent were under 40 years old. That was the most surprising aspect of the survey."

Ann received over a hundred and thirty thousand responses. Even though she had asked for a simple yes or no, an indication of age, a postcard, and no signature, "a surprising number of women felt compelled to write letters." More deeply felt than the need for women's rights or sexual proficiency itself was the sense of a lack in the most intimate contact between two people. In spite of our worship, one of our gods had clearly failed.

8
Dangers of the Times: Drinking, Drugs, Disease

In July 1971, It Happened in Billings wrote:

> My husband and I went to dinner at my sister's house. . . . The conversation was made more lively by the martinis before dinner and the wine with the meal. After dinner . . . my husband reached over and helped himself to a pear which was in a bowl of fruit on the coffee table. Before I could get to him he took a bite. His partial plate came out right there and then. The pear was wax.
>
> My husband blew his top. He insisted that my sister put the artificial fruit out as a gag. [I] say if he hadn't been so loaded he would have known the fruit was wax before he bit into it.

Ann replied, "I suspect your hunch about the martinis is correct. Artificial fruit might fool the eye, but a reasonably sober person would have been able to tell when he picked up the pear that it wasn't the real thing."

If Ann admits that a wax pear might fool the eye, one wonders what would have given away this particular pear before it was bitten into. If the man's dentures stuck in it, it was presumably not hollow (or at least not completely hollow) and therefore its weight should not have been substantially less than that of a real pear. This leaves the texture: the surface of wax fruit would be smoother and more slippery than the real thing.

But in the excitement of a convivial evening, could not a guest forget his sense of touch without being drunk? Maybe not, and perhaps the fruit in the bowl was obviously spurious—but the point is that Ann didn't much worry about whether the man had an excuse or not. She agreed with the wife that he must have been "loaded." For Ann, in 1971, there was a strong presumption of drunken guilt in a man who lost his dentures trying to take a bite out of a wax pear. Many reasons account for this. The first is that there was indeed a lot of drunkenness before, during and after dinner parties. Another was that, for Ann, the drawbacks of drinking sprang to the eye ahead of quite a few other drawbacks.

Anyone reading the 1955 column with the eyes of 1985 would be struck by the fact that for every letter mentioning sex as a problem, seven or more mention drinking. From the very start, alcoholism is a recurrent and serious perplexity. Figures on alcoholism in the United States are difficult to gauge, since alcoholics do not always define themselves as such. However, it might be worth noting that in 1955, when Eppie first sat in Ann Landers's chair, Alcoholics Anonymous had risen from a prewar membership of 800 to 150,000. By the midseventies, their membership had topped a million in 28,000 groups. Over a quarter of a century, Ann's constant referral service helped many seek out the group.

Ann Landers identifies alcoholism early on as one of the threats to the home. Using a line of reasoning already analyzed, she makes the woman responsible, if not for the culprit, then at least for limiting damage that might be done by the culprit. In her second week on the job, Eppie received the following letter from Troubled Friend: "I have a friend who has a real problem. She is married to a man who likes his beer. They have a 3-year-old son. The husband works such irregular hours it is impossible to check on him. He comes home very late at night (smelling of the spirits)—with lipstick on his shirt. When asked about this, he says 'Some old bag asked me to dance.' "

Either the times allowed a more superficial approach to human dilemmas, or Eppie had started out in her new job with the determination to keep it light and optimistic. She answered, "Since your friend's husband likes his suds, tell her to order a case of his favorite brew and surprise him. She should offer to dance with him to his heart's content and put as much lipstick on his shirt as he likes." And Ann ended this bit of flippant advice on a note that resonates strangely today: "If more men were able to get what they want at home, they wouldn't spend so much time in the ginmills."

Curious though that conclusion may seem, Ann stuck to it for a surprisingly long time—at least until the midseventies. In 1960, Last Ditch Stand complained, "My husband simply will not come home from work like other men. He always has to stop off at a bar near his office and have a few drinks." Ann's reply: "I'd like to ask a question of you, as well as the thousands of wives who have complained since time immemorial about this same problem. What does your husband find at home when he gets there? . . . When a husband stops off at a bar every night after work it's an admission that he must fortify himself with a little bottled 'courage' to face the wrecking crew at home."

This got Ann a columnful of irate letters a couple of months later, including this remark from On to You: "I knew it all along. You are a man." Other than to say that she did not mean to encourage men to drink ("A few husbands wrote to say 'Thank you' "), Ann offered no retraction. But when she got into the same hassle in 1973, she printed a very long rebuttal by Voice of Experience, who disagreed with her statement that "some boozers go to bars not so much for the booze, but for the companionship that is missing at home." Voice of Experience offered instead the advice received from Al-Anon. That particular discussion abated thereafter.

One assumes that Ann's persistent defense of the bar-oriented husband results from what we have already recorded as one of her earliest and basic assumptions— her belief that a lot of the male sinners were nothing more than oversized children who needed to be taken in hand by a forceful mother-wife. Three days after the letter from Troubled Friend, Wife's Dilemma wrote about how she kicked out her abusive and alcoholic husband and then took in her aging father, who had helped with a down payment on the house. Now the sobered husband was back, but was starting to resent the presence of his father-in-law. Wife's Dilemma did not think she could decently put him out.

Ann told her, "Your husband, sober though he is, shows clearly one classic symptom of the alcoholic— immaturity. He is acting like a child. . . . Certainly, your father stays (in the home he made possible!), but you must insist that your husband begin acting like a grown-up." And in 1966, Thanks for Listening reported "a lethargic, indecisive guy. . . . The only thing my husband does on his own—with no prodding—is drink. He is gassed every weekend." Ann told her, "Wives who are the movers and shakers in the family were that way before they married. And they went out and found a man who needed to be both moved and shaken."

But drinking was of such proportions that it could not long be passed off as simply the result of a wife's dereliction and/or a husband's childish behavior. Ann, a teetotaler, made enemies early—amongst others of beer drinkers who were sure their brew could not contribute to alcoholism. These legions were later to include such refined palates as white wine drinkers. She also antagonized those libertarians who didn't like to feel guilty by association. ("Both my husband and I are sick and tired of listening to you knock liquor. You are probably a lush yourself," wrote Moderate Mixers in 1960.) And there were always those who saw as social rudeness a party without drink or drinkers (as did, for example, Civilized Moderates in 1972). It is interesting to note from their similar pennames the importance drinkers so often attach to an appearance of sobriety.

In 1984, responding to a letter on accidental deaths related to drinking, Ann said, "More and more I see the wisdom of my decision, at age 15, never to touch the stuff." That conviction resulted in Ann's sympathetic hearing for those who were socially browbeaten by people like Civilized Moderates. Time after time, she told them that it was all right to abstain even in public. Myself and I who, in 1960, had said that his nondrinking made him stand out like a sore thumb, was told, "I say what this world needs is more sore thumbs."

In 1965, Social Drinker admitted, "I am a poor drinker and two drinks make me feel dizzy and I get rather foolish. Will you please give me the name of some mild drinks that I can order with safety." Ann gave her "soda pop, fruit punch, orangeade, iced tea, ginger ale, orange juice, tomato juice, pineapple juice, grapefruit juice and of course, there's always plain ice water." And ten years later, Ann heard from Odd Ball, a woman who wondered whether she was crazy because she seemed to be the only one never to have felt the need for a cocktail hour. Replied Ann, "No, you aren't crazy. And chances are a lot of those boozers aren't crazy either. They're just insecure, troubled people who can't face their own inadequacies and anxieties."

But the sympathetic Ann was only one side of the teetotaler. In the face of the many who were nettled by her attacks on John Barleycorn, she showed very early that she could be nettled, too. Tappa Keg grumbled at the end of 1957, "In my opinion, any guy who's afraid to join his buddies after work because his wife might yell at him may just as well be dead. I think you should stop off for a short beer or two yourself now and then. Maybe it would improve your disposition, and you'd understand a little more about life."

Considering that Ann had been largely on the side of the men in this debate, Tappa Keg's letter was less than gracious. But Ann gave him as good as she got: "I don't need to go to taverns to 'understand about life.' I understand plenty from just sitting at my desk and reading letters from men who can't get their wives off bar-stools. And I've learned a little from the women who write and tell me the kids have to get their winter coats through the welfare agencies because father gets full of hops and blows his paycheck. I say, if the shoe fits, put it on. If it doesn't, what are you yelping about?" And the following year, when Marv wrote about the wife he couldn't keep "away from liquor," Ann actually said, "Take a flash camera along on the next 'big night' out. Get some choice shots of your wife while she's in the process of making a fool of herself. A pictorial record could do more to dry her up permanently than all the sermons in the world."

Through conviction or counterpunching, Ann very soon turned her letters on drink into a crusade. Whether or not Ann Landers was a prime contributor to the phenomenon, the quarter of a century following the start of her editorship was increasingly a time of talk during which people sought to exorcise with words the skeletons that had been hiding in their closets. After only two years on the job, she began referring her problem cases to AA and knew more about what she steadfastly called a disease than did a number of her readers.

The term *disease* raised the expected hackles, but Ann never relented. As late as June 1980, she was rebutting a letter written by I'm from the Show-Me State, "The experts whose opinion I respect say alcoholism IS a disease." This rebuttal came at a time when a study by the Rand Corporation was reversing one of its previous studies that had found alcoholics could drink in moderation.

In May 1957, Mary Ann wondered, "A friend of mine hasn't touched a drop in years. But she still feels it necessary to announce in a social group that she doesn't drink because she's an 'alcoholic.' This sounds as if she's confessing she's a drunk." Although Ann Landers would normally have placed a premium on social discretion, she was sufficiently in the know to set Mary Ann straight: "Many fail to realize that an alcoholic can never be 'cured.' The disease can lie dormant for years and in some cases it takes only one drink to set the entire treacherous cycle going again."

That knowledge and her short fuse sometimes combined with her liberal sensitivities, as when Fidelis Semper wrote at about the same time as Mary Ann, "You keep saying alcoholism is a sickness. I am getting pretty tired of this hooey. Heredity is the prime factor in all types of behavior. It's no accident that the heavy drinkers usually come from a long line of lushes. The tendency is in the blood. As a student of genetics, I learned very early that good cattle cannot come from poor stock. It's all in the genes, Mrs. Landers. Haven't you heard?" Ann said, "Yeah, I've heard—but I don't buy it. People aren't cattle. Haven't you heard?"

Interestingly, the side of an earlier Ann Landers that was geared to the world of business sometimes saw things in a slightly different light.

Early in 1960, H.T.H. complained, "Every year the board convenes at a local hotel. My husband packs a suitcase and spends three nights in the hotel which is less than 15 minutes from our home. His excuse is they don't finish the meetings until the wee hours of the morning and since they must start again early he gets more sleep if he stays right there. They buy enough liquor to loop an army so I know they aren't working every minute." Ann suggested on that occasion, "Give in graciously. You can't beat the board. The hotel stay is business-connected so hubby holds all the trump cards. Have his ice-pack waiting."

As we said, such bantering faded when drinking was

discussed with sufficient openness to allow recognition of the problem in its full magnitude. Already in 1957, Ann's answers were nuanced by a shrewd sense of the drinker's psychology. In November, B.H. asked her about "a very attractive and eligible man [who] makes violent declarations of his love while he's under the influence of liquor, but is cold as a mackerel when he's sober." Ann responded, "If you wonder if this man cares for you, the answer is probably yes. Alcohol sets free the censoring agents of the brain." She added, however, "But who wants a man who has to get himself oiled up in order to express genuine devotion?"

In 1970, for those like Vino la Difference who were hopeful of performing better sexually under the influence, she distinguished between lowered inhibitions and action: "The shy guy sometimes finds 'liquid courage' a help in overcoming his inhibitions. But the experts say that in most instances, liquor and sex do not mix. While alcohol often increases the desire, it tends to hinder the performance." And, as the discussion of impotence grew, alcohol was given its due. For example, Too Late noted the same year that "alcohol can be an important factor in impotency among men between 35 and 50."

In 1965, Ann Landers was advising Sinking Fast, who was sixteen and drinking, "Alcoholism is a symptom of a deeper problem. You must learn through therapy why you are so unhappy that you must get bombed out of your mind." And ten years later, the results of such therapy were starting to appear in letters like the one from Showing Off Less and Enjoying Myself More. Showing Off confessed his former drunken willingness "to be the butt of any joke in exchange for attention." Ann Landers was contributing to that therapy with at least two pamphlets, *Alcoholism—Hope and Help* and *Booze and You: For Teen-Agers Only*.

A couple of months after Moderate Mixers had written to criticize Ann Landers for her "relentless and boring" tirades against liquor, she published a column of letters supporting her position. If the country had always been one of hard drinkers, it had also always had its quota of those who were opposed to drink on religious, ethical, and health grounds. That column, however, added a few new weapons to the dry arsenal: Almost $5 billion (in 1960 dollars) were spent annually on liquor, and approximately one thousand Americans a day crossed the line that divides the social drinker from the addict.

And as indicated by Sinking Fast's letter (and the *Booze and You* pamphlet), a number of these were teen-agers. In 1976, Ann confirmed that one million high-schoolers (about one in twenty) were getting drunk on an average of once a week. Those figures were going to get worse. Counselors were hard-pressed to face the children of a drinking culture. That same year, An Adviser Who Is Seeking Your Advice wrote, "A question frequently asked by students (the majority are girls) is this: 'My mom gets bombed every night, double-bombed on weekends. . . . Does she have a right to keep me from doing things she says are bad for me when she doesn't practice what she preaches?' " By now, the crest of the adolescents' assertiveness was starting to abate, and Ann wrote, "It's a cop-out to use their parents' weakness as an excuse to take the low road." But in the wake of assertiveness, addiction remained and Ann relied consistently on AA, telling Niagara Falls Reader that year, "They have a far better record of success than the religious groups and the psychiatrists."

AA and Al-Anon were the prime support groups. But other groups like RID (Remove Intoxicated Drivers) and MADD (Mothers Against Drunk Driving) appeared in order to cope with problems related to alcohol. Since the midsixties, the column had been sensitive to the dangers of drunk driving, and Ann never stopped stressing this particular concern, right through the eighties. In 1982, she responded to a letter from A Chicago Reader, who had asked her not to let up on her campaign: "To my way of thinking, one drunk driver is equivalent to one potential murderer. The people they kill are just as dead as if they had been shot or knifed to death. The fact that they didn't mean to do it doesn't change anything."

Dangerous as it was, drunk driving was a derivative problem; however diverse and specialized the support groups, alcoholism is one case where the root cause was not displaced by remedies addressing specific consequences. As An Adviser's letter had shown, the problem was particularly acute in that it affected the young as well. In demanding the adults' world, adolescents had inherited one of their parents' major weaknesses. The statistics were grim, especially considering that by the midsixties, alcohol had been displaced as a prime concern and statistic by drugs. In September 1982, Ann Landers published an open letter showing how far society's fabric had frayed and to what extent both scourges were intertwined:

> About 25 percent of all fourth-grade children in the United States say they feel pressured by their friends to try drugs and alcohol.
> By the time children reach the seventh grade, 60 percent say they feel pressure to try liquor and 50 percent say they feel pressure to try marijuana. . . .
> The motivation for trying drugs and alcohol among young children was the desire to "feel older." Among those in the middle grades it was a desire to "fit in" with peers. Among high school students it was "to have a good time."

In 1984, Fan in Richmond, Va., noted a lessening of the drug culture: "In the 14 to 18 year range, the users have shown a sharp drop in numbers. Government statistics, compiled in 1983 from 17,500 high school seniors, indicated that 28.5 percent smoke pot. The figure in 1978 was 37.1 percent." Ann commented, "That's the good news. The bad news is that teens are turning to alcohol. And the percentage of students who drink regularly would knock your socks off." After some twenty years, the circle—more vicious than ever—was starting to bend back upon itself. But henceforth, even on the upswing, drinking would remain bound up with concern over drugs. Once drugs had entered the cultural mainstream, they could not be wished away. If there was fluctuation in the number of those who depended on them, it was only because of a shift in dependencies. The dependency itself remained.

The United States had long been a nation of pill poppers. Letters during the fifties made quaint references to "nerve medicine" and pills of various kinds. However, the dreaded word *drugs* was hardly ever used before the sixties and, conforming to a pattern we have already seen, a full airing of addiction had to wait for linguistic openness—as if the topic could not be discussed before it had been named. While drinking was still a social vice eliciting sympathetic laughter or outright admiration, dependency on medication tended to remain unmentioned, and the difference between medical prescription and addiction was seldom gauged.

On one of the rare occasions that Ann Landers encountered the equivalent of the word *drug* during the fifties, she reacted ferociously.

In 1956, Miss D wrote, "I'm positive my boy friend is taking dope. He has several little marks on his left arm and they are unmistakably from needles." Ann told her that the boy needed professional care and added, "A law was passed at the last session of Congress calling for the death penalty for anyone found guilty of peddling dope. In my opinion, the death penalty isn't strong enough."

In the early sixties, letters from readers indicate that dependency was becoming recognizable. Mrs. Hooked wrote in 1963, "My husband is a junior in college. Last semester he was introduced to some 'stay awake pills.' The kids call them Bennies. From Bennies he went to other stuff. At first he took pills only when he had to stay up and cram for finals. Then he began to take them when he needed a lift. It wasn't long before he was taking pills just to keep going." And Mrs. Hooked then went on to identify the one who would be known eventually as the pusher. "The man who started him on the pills provided them free at first. Now they cost $14 a dozen." Ann urged again professional advice for the husband but focused on the pusher: "The man who is peddling the junk should be reported to the police. I hope you have the courage to turn in the scoundrel and spare other young people the agony you are now suffering."

As the effect of drugs starts informing letters written to Ann Landers, one notes for awhile, alongside the firmness of Ann's responses, a certain hesitation in identifying the central difficulty. Three years after Mrs. Hooked, Lucky to Be Alive confessed, "Two years ago I went into a deep depression when we lost our only son. Our physician prescribed sleeping tablets along with tranquilizing pills. The night of the funeral I took two sleeping tablets and left the bottle on my bedside table. I was awakened at 4 p.m. the next day by my panic-stricken husband and a concerned physician. During the night I had taken four sleeping pills, although I had no recollection of doing so." Lucky to Be Alive treated this as a warning not to keep medicines out of the medicine cabinet. And without any allusion to the psychological implications of the letter writer's action, Ann simply added that "Partly used bottles of medicine should be stored in a locked cabinet to eliminate the danger of getting the wrong medicine during the night."

A couple of years later, the language of the drug world began to be used in the column, and the discussion got started—even though the exact center of the problem could still remain imprecise. In 1968, as student rebellions were starting to break out, one of Ann's "Confidentials" read: "To Puzzled Paul: So am I. Your story sounds like something you dreamed on your last psychedelic trip. If you are on the level, send me your name and a self-addressed, stamped envelope and I will try to help you."

The following year, in May 1969, when campuses had erupted into full-blown conflagrations, Gapped wrote a letter that disclosed many of the times' realities—starting with a signature marking the distance between generations to which children were sensitizing their parents: "Our 17-year-old son has admitted he smokes marijuana 'socially' on weekends but insists he is not a habitual smoker and can quit any time he wants to. . . . I know my boy needs professional help but when I suggest it he says he has no problem—that he is just adding enjoyment to his life." At this point, Ann referred to the law that said marijuana is "an illicit drug and anyone caught with the drug can be charged with a felony. And the penalties are stiff." She admitted that the government studies would not be in yet for years to come, but said her experts identified marijuana as "a dangerous way to get kicks." And she added, with the toughness that was usual for her on these questions, "Moreover, it's a cop-out and a gutless approach to living."

By 1970, letters relating to the drug scene are among the most frequent, and daily language has been affected by it. In January 1970, Dunmore asks, "How does one free himself from the clutches of friends who have been on a trip? I don't mean LSD. I mean Europe, the Orient, Hawaii, Puerto Rico, or, heaven forbid, an African safari." As noted in Chapter 4, some adolescents were still in the former mold of those who wrote to Ann Landers for counsel, and they could be sufficiently in the know to ask her about drugs with which it might be safe to experiment. And the usual support centers were in place.

In September, A Stockton, Calif., Mother and Volunteer wrote, "Most county hospitals have detoxification clinics where patients are physically taken off drugs. . . . The county hospital can also put callers in touch with organizations that help addicts get free treatment and follow-up counseling." And confirming the way drugs had become woven into the social texture, Lived Through It wrote two years later to disagree with Ann Landers's advice to remain silent after learning about the addiction of a friend's child. Ann updated her social manual on the issue: "I have checked with others who also 'Lived Through It' and the consensus is the same. Close friends are expected to call—as they would if they heard of an accident or a death in the family."

Meanwhile, Ann Landers was continuing her own war on drugs. In June 1970, Flower Power wrote about the importance of long hair: "Hair is an effective means of nonverbal communication. When I show up any place, I don't need to tell my brothers and sisters, or my enemies, 'Hey look, I'm against the Viet Nam War, racism, poverty and pollution. I dig grass, black power and revolution.' They look at me and they know."

Perhaps because of the letter Flower Power had written, when the self-confidence it displayed indicated that he should not have done so, Ann did not mince her words: "I doubt I can get through your hair but I'll try. . . . A parasitical, cop-out approach to life adds up to an empty and meaningless existence, as so many of your breed have already discovered. After a while you will be sick of yourself and sicker of the leeches around you. If you have the guts you'll admit your experiment was a flop. You will then rejoin the human race, get off the mind-bending junk, take a bath, cut your hair, put on your shoes and be counted as one doing something about the lousy state of the world instead of contributing to it."

In 1969, Ann had told Gapped that in the absence of comprehensive studies, her experts thought marijuana was a dangerous way to get one's kicks. By 1972, that evidence was still not in and Ann remained cautious in the medical part of her advice, as when she told Concerned About the Future, "One of the principal reasons I advise against all mind-altering agents is that we do not yet know the effects it may produce over a period of several years. So far there are no definitive findings." But in the moral part of her advice, Ann remained as tough as

she had been with Flower Power. She continued her war
on drugs by publishing throughout the early and midseventies the testimony of teens who had been victims and
were trying to warn their peers away.

In 1956, a wrathful answer of Ann to Miss D had said
that death was not punishment enough for drug pushers,
but it was soon apparent to her that stemming the huge
inroad of drugs would require more than moral outrage
and grand pronouncements. Her strategy changed; she
enlisted the assistance of the usual ad hoc groups (now
pressing even AA into this service) and began stressing
the psychological damage of addiction devolving from all
drugs, while accepting the inevitability of pot. Twenty
years after her anger following Miss D's letter, she came
out for the decriminalization of marijuana—and ran into
the usual barrage of accusations.

In March 1975, she responded to Sunrise, Florida,
"Letters like yours drive me up the wall. I have been one
of the earliest and most outspoken critics of marijuana,
having stated my views categorically in this column at
least a dozen times. Please look up the word 'decriminalization.' That's what I am for. I don't believe young
people who are caught with pot should be labeled
criminals, put in jail and deprived of many of their
constitutional rights." Exactly a year later, she specified
that she was not for the legalization of pot, but felt that
casual users should not be fined or sent to jail. On that
score, the moralist in Ann maintained her strong objection to drugs, while the pragmatist recognized that
marijuana had become so much a part of our customs that
it seemed pointless to deal punitively with its use.

By 1980, the studies on marijuana were in, and Ann
could use a balanced and unemotional evaluation of pot
in order to maintain her opposition to harder drugs.
Answering Shaker Heights Student in January, she wrote
about the psychological aspects of addiction: "Marijuana
does not create physical dependency, like heroin or
alcohol. In other words, a person can get off pot without

suffering withdrawal symptoms. BUT—and it's a big one—marijuana can be psychologically addictive, which is just as bad. The desire to revisit a dream world can be crippling if the person enjoys it so much he decides he wants to live there."

Five months later, she addressed the physical jeopardy in answering Just Plain Mom and Dad (a typical signature reflecting the bafflement of well-meaning people trying to keep up with an alien and alienating world):

> Dr. William Pollin, director of the Drug Institute, said, "Many young people view marijuana as a simple herb with the power to enhance their lives. Research is showing it is a complex drug which can interfere with learning and motor coordination and may eventually lead to serious health problems."
>
> There is also scientific evidence that heavy pot use can alter the chromosomes, produce a lower sperm count and in some cases cause sterility.
>
> I have said it before, and I will say it again. Any mind-altering drug can be dangerous. If some creep mixes a little angel dust with the grass, an unsuspecting smoker could get spaced out permanently.

As we saw, there was among the young some lessening of drug consumption in the eighties and a concomitant return to alcohol. (This picture might have started to change again late in 1985 with the introduction of crack.) But the shifts in dependencies were less important than the reality of the dependencies themselves. Recall also the letter from Plenty Worried in Arizona in 1984 with the following statistics: "According to a study based on a survey of 960 eighth-graders in the Tampa-St. Petersburg area, 25 percent have tried marijuana, 5.4 percent said they smoke pot about three times a month, 22.7 percent said they use alcohol about once a week, and 3 percent said they have tried heroin. When one considers that most eighth-graders are 13 years old, such statistics are nothing short of frightening."

Those statistics may indeed have been nothing short of frightening, but their reality had become so much a part of the social warp that the threat, for many, had lost some of its edge. Hard drugs were creating different kinds of problems that further removed pot from the central position it had occupied in the consciousness of the sixties and a large part of the seventies. We recall that in 1984, Ann was also deluged with mail because of "roach clips"—those pliers used in the smoking of marijuana—when "a few thousand readers" wrote in to set her straight. There was something good-humored and even amusing about the episode. In contrast, other and newer jeopardies had begun to frighten Ann Landers's readers: A complacent reliance on the ability of medicine to cure most ailments was being shaken by the appearance of previously unknown and dangerous diseases that seemed to be grotesquely appropriate emblems of the times.

Health had always been one of the concerns of readers writing Ann Landers for help. But in the fifties, such questions tended to address the esthetics of health rather than its substance. People, especially young people, would write because of something about their body that made them less popular or not as attractive as they would have liked to be. They would write about acne, or about hair problems (Ann never registered any objection to women dying their hair), or about their shape. These concerns are related to an interest in plastic surgery that started in the sixties, and of which Ann generally approved—provided the surgeon was competent. The most common complaint by far was voiced by those who were overweight.

In 1955, someone like Mrs. H.M. would write, "I can't get a job because I am overweight. Fat people have to live, too." And Ann would answer, "Of course, fat people have to live, too. . . . get on a diet, and then consult the

want ad section of this newspaper." Or a teen would
pour out her tale of woe: "I'm 18 and have never had a
date. . . . I'm quite heavy and think maybe a boy would be
ashamed to be seen with a girl my size." And Ann would
hardly consider this to be a problem at all: "Ask your
doctor to put you on a diet—and stick to it. Lean toward
the larger fellows and when the fat begins to melt away,
they'll start to lean toward you."

But typical of other kinds of innocence that would be
gone with the fifties, this breezy approach no longer
obtained in the sixties. By then, the problem of weight
had become a medical fact, and dieting the start of a
national institution (soon to be followed by jogging).
The column stressed the dangers incurred by the minds
and bodies of the obese. A typical letter in 1968 was that
of Columbus, Ohio, Blues: "I hate you because you are so
unsympathetic to fat people. In your column today you
insulted us again. . . . I refuse to spend any more money
on doctors because I don't have the willpower to stick to
a diet. So what do I do? I eat myself sick and cry myself to
sleep."

In ten years, both Ann Landers and her readers had
learned to dig at the less obvious roots of what was no
longer merely a cosmetic problem. She answered, "Sorry,
I refuse to pity you and I don't buy the idea you can't help
it. . . . You need more than medical advice, my friend, you
need psychiatric help. Your sense of worthlessness and
self-pity are destructive impulses that have been with you
for too many years. Only when you rid yourself of these
feelings will you be able to eat like a normal human
being."

But alongside the simply unhappy fat people of the
early days (and the plain hypochondriacs who wrote
during the first ten years and for whom Ann Landers
prescribed frequent check-ups as reassurance), there
would appear occasionally a more interesting case. In
1960, Concerned wrote about her niece: "20 years of age
. . . 5'6" and weighs about 100 pounds. She's still dieting

so she can be 'slim like the models.' . . . I tried to tell her
that malnutrition could lead to serious illness but she
says the models in the ads look pretty healthy to her. Am
I old-fashioned as she says?" At this point, Ann merely
confirmed that "Your young relative will never be an old
relative if she doesn't cut out the foolishness." But ten
years later, what Concerned and Ann had seen as merely
the crazy ideas of a peculiar young woman, would emerge
as anorexia. In 1970, Alice's Mother wrote a nearly
identical letter about her five-foot five-inch daughter
who weighed eighty-seven pounds and who "practically
starves herself to death because she is afraid she might
gain an ounce."

Ann informed her, "[She] is compelled by something
stronger than the wish to be stylishly slender. Your
daughter may be suffering from an emotional problem
called anorexia nervosa. Girls who starve themselves into
emaciation are often fearful of facing adulthood and sex.
By starving themselves and remaining small and childlike
they feel as if they are not a part of the grownup world
and therefore exempt from adult responsibilities."

Ten years further down the line, still another variant
had emerged, described in 1983 by Healing Slowly and
Ever So Grateful: "Thousands of women . . . rely on self-
induced vomiting as a means to deal with food binges. It
is commonly known as 'gorging and purging' and is as
deadly an illness as anorexia nervosa." Thanks in part to
the column, the medical name of that illness, bulimia,
would soon become something of a household word.

Thus were obesity and dieting caught up in the pro-
gressive frenzy of the sixties, in order to emerge some
twenty years later as full-fledged diseases of the body and
mind. As we have seen, the sixties were also the years
during which sexual constraints were being loosened
with equal abandon. One of the results was that in the
first ten years of Eppie's tenure, VD in the United States
tripled, with more than two-thirds of the cases being
among those aged thirteen to nineteen. Starting in the

midsixties, Ann began calling the disease by its name and citing statistics.

Throughout the seventies, syphilis remained largely a concern of adolescents, and much of the information Ann imparted had to do with the fact that the disease could indeed be contracted through kissing. Other age groups were less concerned with the disease, the big preoccupation of sexually freer adults during the seventies being vasectomies (which Ann Landers endorsed). Also getting its share of intensified attention was cancer, especially breast cancer and—reviving an old phobia of Ann's—smoke-related lung cancer.

But another kind of venereal disease was soon going to get everyone's attention. In January 1976, Bad News asked Ann, "Want to perform a real public service? Tell people about the latest V.D. bummer. Most folks think only of gonorrhea and syphilis. Antibiotics can handle these, but this new-fangled infection from sexual contact causes clusters of blisters and is extremely painful. What's worse, it is incurable. There are already 300,000 reported cases."

Ann named it as she had named anorexia six years before: "The latest 'V.D. bummer' is called Herpes Simplex II. A vaccine has been produced to combat Herpes Simplex II and it is effective in about 50 percent of the cases." Ann was being optimistic. The failure of the hoped-for cure caused herpes to be the disease most frequently discussed during the first three years of the eighties. Emphasis shifted from recovery to control—abstinence during the times when the diseased person became infectious.

The reason herpes finally became a topic of less than nearly daily concern was that in 1983 it was replaced by an even more urgent preoccupation—AIDS. As she had done for herpes, Ann was able to move into high gear nearly immediately and with remarkable accuracy. From the first, she told her readers about the etiology and symptoms of the disease, and also sought to dispel the myths connected with its spread, contagion and moral implications. She tried to help gays like Distressed Uncle who found himself cut off from nieces he loved the day the disease was perceived by the general population as a "gay plague": "Ignorance can be a terrible thing. Your brother and his wife need to be educated." And she then attempted to do so.

Ann Landers's knowledge and efficient communication may have had something to do with the fact that the eighties were a time of increased preoccupation with health, and she was getting frequent practice in the dissemination of information relating to a wide spectrum of medical novelties. People were suddenly conscious of frighteningly new diseases like herpes, AIDS, and Alzheimer's disease, an illness previously confused with senility. Along with these was the rise among women of health hazards that had once been the privilege of men, along with the jobs that occasioned them. Not the least of these was lung cancer induced by smoking.

Some, who were less concerned with health than with the incomprehensible disappearance of a familiar world, saw in the rise of these terrifying new diseases God's dismay at an awful new world. AIDS was the punishment inflicted on homosexuals (and drug users) just as, one assumes, hypertension and lung cancer were now visited in increasing numbers on women who no longer knew their rightful place. It was all very confusing and terrible—and certainly different from those faraway days when all an overweight woman needed in order to achieve social acceptance, economic well-being, and general bliss was a better diet and a little willpower.

9
The Not-So-Great Controversies

Ann Landers always enjoyed a large, growing, and faithful readership. And on occasion, that readership asserted its size in a sudden groundswell of letters pertaining to a specific subject. These periodic upheavals were of two sorts: They either developed spontaneously because of a topic that expectedly or unaccountably seized a great many imaginations, or they were generated by Ann herself. Whether or not they deal with consequential questions, such moments of special and collective excitement are of interest because they provide a sense of what concerned large numbers of people at a given moment. If they are significant, they also help us see where Ann stood in relation to such nodes of interest.

Ann described one such epistolary tidal wave (one she set in motion herself by asking women whether they would be satisfied to have tenderness without sexual intercourse): "The mail room looks like a disaster area. We have put on extra help. The employees are working double shifts and weekends." At the time of that letter, she had received 90,000 responses and would get over 130,000 before the flood crested. She noted, "Since I

238

have been writing this column the only time the response was heavier was when I asked my readers to clip the column, sign it and send it to President Reagan. That column was about nuclear war. This sex survey beats the meat loaf recipe, the lemon pie and the poll asking parents, 'If you had to do it again, would you have children?' "

Her own figures thus give an idea of what the biggies were. But other such nodes occurred periodically, starting very soon after Eppie took over the job, and sometimes with a volume of response seemingly out of proportion to the trivial issue that generated it. The previous chapter described the continuing worries of Ann's readers over drinking, drugs, and disease. Yet, through them all, life somehow went on. As Ann herself said (in reference to yet another flood of interest generated unexpectedly in 1983), "With all the serious problems in the world, I was stunned at the hundreds of people who wrote at once to rescue that poor woman from her dilemma. This week, no one seemed to care about unemployment, inflation, the national deficit, kids on drugs, drunken drivers or cheating spouses. The major concern is to help that woman turn out perfect deviled eggs." In 1983, Ann remembered the time she "printed a letter from a woman who was having an argument with her cousin. Should the toilet paper be hung so that it goes OVER the roll and hangs down in front—or should it go in the opposite direction and hang close to the wall? When I received more than 15,000 letters from readers with opinions, I knew it was an OK subject." The reason why so many people felt compelled to share their wisdom on this subject is not immediately apparent. But then, there never seemed to be any way of predicting how widespread might be a quirk that was thought at first to define only a single individual. The United States is a nation of well over two hundred million people—on any day of the week, a few thousand of them can catch fire over an idea or an occurrence and not even be representative.

But heavy mail was elicited, of course, by more serious issues. Some were indeed concerns that affected more people than just those who wrote about them. We have already examined a number of these.

Those who had an especially sensitive ear to the ground might have detected as early as 1958 the way in which the voice of the young was already resonating within the awareness of certain adults. In April of that year, the column was given over to letters prompted by Ann's urging the mother of a ten-year-old girl to make her daughter wear the ugly dress her grandmother had crocheted for her. A respondent, Buffalo Reader, demonstrated at the time generational preferences and child-oriented sensitivities that would be mandatory ten years later: "In my opinion, this was clearly a choice between hurting the grandmother's feelings and crushing the little girl." Even though Ann didn't quite give in, she picked up the writer's argumentatively loaded verbs in her response (perhaps because she seemed to phrase her answers whenever possible by using the very words of the question): "As 'Buffalo Reader' pointed out . . . it's clearly a choice between hurting the grandmother's feelings and crushing the little girl. I chose to spare the grandmother. Hundreds of you said I was wrong. Take your choice, Mother."

And while still on questions of sartorial importance to the young, she gave some ground the following year: "Confidential to all you teen-age gals who raised the roof because I said 15 was soon enough for nylons and heels. OK, kids, times have changed—14 gets my blessings if you behave like ladies! (Haven't had so many teen-age blasts since I knocked Kookie!)"

The year after that, readers who were feeling the first effects of the economic pinch let Ann Landers know they didn't like her advice allowing a step-daughter to put away for college a $40 a month inheritance received from her father's estate. Ann faced up to "a blizzard of complaining letters" like that of Richmond, Va.: "I say the

step-father should use that money to support the girl. . . .
The mother said they were having a hard time financially.
Although $40 a month is a drop in the bucket toward
total support of a 16-year-old, it would help some."

But that "blizzard" was small alongside the one that hit
ten years later, in 1970, at a time when some adults had
heard all they cared to hear from their children. A bride
(who signed herself Generation Gap for rather obvious
reasons) wrote to complain about parents who did not
want to give her a fancy church wedding because she was
in the fifth month of her pregnancy. Two thousand
parents on the other side of the gap let her know via Ann
Landers what they thought of her. And three years later,
Ann made the mistake of advising a father to buy himself
a second paper instead of complaining that he always
received his after it had been mangled by other members
of the family. Another two thousand dissenters availed
themselves of that opportunity to state their newly re-
kindled feelings about family hierarchies—and Ann
concurred.

In the course of fifteen years or so (starting in the
midsixties and going through the seventies), attitudes
toward children changed from something like fear to
simple fatigue. Along with this, women's attitude
changed, and they became increasingly reluctant to accept the roles in which they had been traditionally cast.
This was noticeable in several instances. One occurred in
1975: Speaking more with an ear to conventional sentiment than to the times, Ann told Feeling Rotten in
Denver that she would get over her anger and resentment
at a second pregnancy "the minute the new baby is
placed in your arms." Ann didn't exactly back off on that
one, but did acknowledge, "I can't recall such a barrage
of angry letters since I told American housewives they
were lazy if they didn't iron their bedsheets and
bathtowels."

In 1976, the growing impatience of women, the fatigue
of browbeaten parents, and the economic realities that

were putting more theoretical questions in a realistic perspective, all combined to swamp Ann with one of her largest mailings in response to her poll asking, "If you had it to do over again, would you have had children?" The 70 percent who said they would not floored her. Four years later, she told a reader she could still see "the evidence right there in huge piles on my desk."

Most of what we have recorded elsewhere resulted from such flare-ups of interest. They might be due to an awakening of public awareness through media reports—such as the discovery of a new disease or statistics on drunk driving, or even family problems, provided they were shared by a sufficient number of families to attain national visibility. Others might arise from concerns voiced by Ann Landers (on gun control or smoking, for example) that ran up against the beliefs of organized or nonorganized constituencies. Such letter swells vary in duration. They range from those that focus reader attention for a few weeks or months (as did the question of tight jeans in the fifties), to more enduring issues, like those resulting from sexual concerns—be they concerned with the Other Woman, abortion, incest, or homosexuality.

Other questions with a sexual core occasioned periodic bursts of intense interest. We have previously alluded to what appears to have been a long and recurrent fear of sexually aggressive women. During part of 1975, a multiletter discussion centered on whether a woman could be found guilty of rape (to which the legal answer appears to have been no). This became, during the exchange, a discussion about whether or not a woman could rape a man (to which the physiological answer appears to have been yes). About this, Ann said, "My mail indicates that the female of the species has become so sexually aggressive these last few years that, while 'rape' might be too strong a word, it describes rather well what goes on in today's society."

The question of female rapists paled, however, alongside another discussion that had taken place ten years earlier about women who undressed in the bedroom closet. It began in 1964 and was still going strong the following year. Thereafter, it seemed to die down for awhile, only to surface again in the late seventies. This time, however, it continued off and on through 1983. As that protracted discussion dragged on, what had been perceived at first to be a personal quirk began to appear more and more sensible as people tired of the great sexual revolution, and as others who had not enjoyed much of a voice previously—housewives, senior citizens, singles—began to find one. Middle-aged women, for example, found that on aesthetic and other equally valid grounds, undressing in the closet wasn't such a bad thing to do after all.

The newfound voice of some who were hitherto silent may have derived, paradoxically, from the new conservative social mood. Like its political counterpart, that conservative mood had as one of its consequences a kind of isolationism—the feeling among many that it was time to do what they felt comfortable doing, rather than accept the outrageous freedom or the embarrassing openness that had been preached for such a long time. Recall that even though Oddball in Ohio had worried about being a freak because of her sleepwear (see Index), it turned out that she was actually far from singular. As Ann acknowledged in March 1980, at the start of a full column devoted to the subject, "All week I've been inundated with letters on underpants." She concluded, "What you've read here is a small sampling, but the results, when tabulated, looked like this: One third of the females out there do, indeed, sleep in underpants and two thirds don't. I am amazed that the percentage of 'do's' is so high. The things I learn from my readers!"

Withdrawal from the great sexual emancipation of the previous decade occasioned, as we know, some of the heaviest mail the column had ever seen. On March 9, 1985, Ann wrote, "Yesterday's column dealt with letters all critical of my statement that 'Sexuality is a divine gift from the Almighty, and to give it back, unused, would surely disappoint Him.' The angry mail is still pouring in." She proceeded with a second, consecutive column on the subject.

Much of her mail was obviously from religious bigots and conservatives who were fearful that she had "given encouragement to countless teen-agers who think they are 'solid, sane adults' to participate in premarital sex." But more reflective observations came from others like L.A. Friend, who concluded nevertheless, "There are many reasons a solid, sane person could have a life without sex. For a woman who is usually sensible I don't know how you lost your way so completely on this one." And this fatigue with sexual blatancy reached its apogee the following year, in the avalanche of over a hundred thousand letters—letters mainly from women, almost three-quarters of whom said they would prefer tenderness to sex.

The great issues generated great volumes of mail, but, as we have seen, lesser issues did, too. What seemed to preoccupy an inordinate number of people during the fifties was the question of the office party. It was a problem that arose with some regularity during the months of October or November in anticipation of Christmas festivities. In 1956, Ann Landers's generally probusiness outlook favored the office party. This did not sit well with spouses like Wise Up Wife who wrote, "Plenty of trouble gets started at these liquored up get-togethers. They ought to be discontinued." But husbands, like Horace, Boris and Morris, were sufficiently delighted to give some color of legitimacy to their wives' objections: "You're a living doll! Your piece on Office Parties appeared just in time to give us a badly needed assist." There is some doubt whether the Horaces, Borises, and Morrises of the office world improved their subsequent behavior, because wives' mail against the office party continued.

The following December, Ann gave in. Responding to

the complaint of Seven-Year Itch ("Well, it's THAT time of year again and my husband and I are having the same old fight"), she changed her tune without warning: "The annual Christmas office party has gotten to be more of a sickness than a social event. For this reason, many firms have cut it out." But the firms and Ann notwithstanding, the battle continued with renewed acrimony, climaxing the following November when A Reader accused Ann Landers of being a man (which, as we have seen, happened on more than just this occasion) and lambasting a ritual that evidently kept her spouse hung over clear through Christmas Day. Ann invited A Reader to read more carefully, but it seems evident that at a time when the world appeared to be freer of dire apocalypses, the Christmas office party aroused greater passions than words or reason could stem.

Other topics of the fifties that excited people in large numbers were the awful mien of women in the morning, according to the testimony of mailmen, later substantiated by icemen (such people were evidently still around at the time). This controversy arose in 1956 and spilled over into the following year. Another topic of concern was how to deal with a snoring spouse. This topic was actually never quite laid to rest before the great crises of the late sixties and seventies. Ann defended the wives whose task it was to get a family out of the house rather than to beautify themselves, and tried to give some common-sense advice about snoring before she was overcome by the ingeniousness of antisnoring remedies and just offered them for what they were worth.

Mothers-in-law were another topic that began in the fifties and picked up sporadically every time one of them was linked to a family upset that found its way into the column. Each such event was bound to provoke constant comment, pro and con, for at least a few weeks. Ann praised her own mother-in-law and tried to discuss each subsequent case on its merits.

For the sake of completeness, one should mention that there seems to have been a considerable number of amateur acne specialists around at the time. Ann recorded in April 1960 that a letter by a boy who wrote for help because of a bad case of acne "produced an avalanche of mail from readers . . . with home remedies for getting rid of skin problems." Even though Ann told her readers, before it was generally known, that acne had nothing to do with eating sweets, she took no chances here and repeatedly advised seeing a dermatologist.

And a few days later, A and B wrote, "My husband's aunt lives with us but she has always been pleasant and easy to be with. Last week she almost broke up a dinner party in our home by announcing to one and all that she is intercepting radio messages between Red China and the Russians through her bridgework. This woman is not a fool. She has a master's degree and has taught school for about 15 years. She is active in civic organizations and has headed some big groups in her day." Ann's initial response was more in pity than in anger: "Urge her to see a doctor. She may have been a community leader in her day but she is sick now and needs professional help."

That dismissal did not dispose of the question. Three months later, letters were coming in from others, among whom was Richmond, Va., who wrote, "I work in a small plant. For several months I thought I was going out of my mind because I imagined I heard voices. I was afraid to tell anyone for fear they'd put me away. One day the voices became so clear I decided to see the plant doctor. You can imagine my relief to learn that small particles of metal filings were getting between my teeth and I was receiving radio waves." From San Juan, Puerto Rico, a writer speculated on even more extended modes of short-wave reception: "Very often when my hair is up in metal curlers a familiar tune goes through my mind. When I turn on the radio the same tune is being played. Could I be receiving through my curlers?" Ann, whose aversion to electronic possibilities we have remarked on already, mustered sufficient fairness to print those letters, but did not comment on them.

In her listing of the larger writing convulsions that

seized her readers, Ann mentions a lemon pie incident. This refers to a "best-ever" recipe she printed in January 1980. Even though she once "swore off recipes," for very good reasons, she tested and ran this one—only to discover that the *Muskegon Chronicle* set it with a typo that caused some of her readers to experiment with "13 cups of lemon juice" (instead of 1/3). This incident was still a vivid marker of reader indignation a full year later: "I haven't read such angry mail since . . . the lemon pie recipe."

This was only one of the vexations Ann suffered at the hands of a kitchen devil that seemed to plague her over the years. There was, for example, the great gelatin debate of 1960. That year, a woman wrote to bemoan the fact that she couldn't make a successful gelatin dessert. Ann admitted that her own molds wouldn't win any prizes either. At the beginning of May, she gave the column over to some of the responses that poured in afterward: "Apparently thousands of women in America are making perfect gelatin dessert—and I feel more stupid than ever. . . . Here's what the mail has been like— and it's still pouring in!"

It poured in for a long time, and was still trickling in during the month of July. Though Ann had identified thousands of women who could make gelatin molds, there appear to have been a number who could not. In May, Louisville, Ky., wrote, "My molds used to flop too, especially when I had guests. My psychiatrist said to accept the fact that I would never be able to make a successful mold. He urged me to switch to custards." Panhandle Pete had the last word: "Warm a tray of ice cubes, throw in some gelatin, add fresh pineapple and marshmallows shaped like stars. Bring to a furious boil. Dump into a bowl which has been greased with mutton tallow, then throw the whole mess out."

The following decade, it was a method for the painless peeling of onions that drove the amateur cooks of America to their writing desks. And once more Ann was surprised at how so many could be distracted from so much by so little. She introduced the subject in September 1975 by saying, "With everything that is happening in the world, do you know what people are concerned about this week? Would you believe it's how to peel onions without crying. Recently, I printed a letter from a reader who had the thing licked. . . . 'If you start at the root of the onion and peel up you'll never shed a tear.' Well, I did a little home research and ended up with bloodshot eyes and a runny nose." She then proceeded to contribute to what she had identified as a slight concern in a tormented world by devoting the bulk of the column to other and, one presumes, equally ineffectual ways to peel an onion cheerfully.

But by far the greatest of the culinary crises was the other to which she referred—the one she still remembered ten years later as the "meat loaf disaster" of 1970. This generated forty thousand letters before it died down and gave Ann pause, but not enough, before running her lemon pie recipe. In 1969, she published a recipe for that particular dish. The first rumblings occurred early the following year when Disappointed in Adrian, Mich., wrote in:

> You should stick to advising people who have problems and not get into things you don't know anything about. We had company for dinner Sunday and my wife decided to try a recipe she clipped from the *Detroit Free Press*. It was Ann Landers's meat loaf.
>
> My wife has been making meat loaf for years and it has always turned out just dandy. Since we were having guests for dinner, she decided to give Ann's recipe a try because she thought somehow it would be better than her own.
>
> Well, Ann Landers's meat loaf was very mediocre. Nobody said anything but there was plenty left over for the dog.

Even though Ann Landers managed to keep her sense of humor, she was clearly puzzled and pained: "I am terribly sorry my meat loaf was a flop. How is the dog? Please let me know. I worry about things like that. For the life of me I can't understand what went wrong. I have given my meat loaf recipe to several friends and no one ever complained until now." She then repeated the recipe "on the chance something was left out." That restatement mollified some but left others as cold as they had been after the first one. They all got their say in a column given over to the question the following month.

But this was far from enough: The letters came in for several more months. In May, she printed what she thought was the last of the letters, availing herself of the opportunity to give credit to her sister, Mrs. David Brodkey of Omaha, whose recipe it had been in the first place. For reasons that defy explanation, this suddenly reawakened the meat loaf issue that had apparently been only dormant and, in June, constrained Ann to address an open letter to her readers, if for no other reason than to save the sanity of Mrs. David Brodkey:

> Now Mrs. Brodkey isn't speaking to me. In fact, she isn't speaking to anybody. She is not answering her telephone.
>
> I had sent out thousands of copies of the recipe and was sure that every housewife in the United States, Canada, Mexico, Puerto Rico, Tokyo and Bangkok who wanted it, had asked for it.
>
> I was wrong. When Mrs. Brodkey's name appeared in the column she suddenly became the most popular woman in Nebraska. No address was given, but that didn't discourage the meat loaf lovers. Her mailman is exhausted. He keeps asking, "When is this going to stop?" Letters have arrived addressed to Ann Landers's Sister. One letter was addressed: MEAT LOAF, Omaha.
> . . . I hereby take an oath on Julia Child's head that you have heard the last of my meat loaf. If anyone wants the recipe, please get it from a friend. Do not write to Mrs. David Brodkey, or to the Brodkey Jewelry Company or to me. I have had it.

Letters addressed to MEAT LOAF, or to Ann Landers's Sister, Omaha, may understandably have annoyed Mrs. Brodkey, but they are evidence of the formidable presence and resonance of Ann Landers across the land. Just as the screen close-up once magnified to the point of caricature what had been previously the emoting of theater actors justified by the distance between stage and spectator, so was every word of Ann Landers magnified, intensified and scrutinized by millions of diverse sensitivities. It is a credit to her considerable skill and tact that flaps like the one about the meat loaf occurred only infrequently during the third of a century she has been in the public eye. It is even more to her credit (since she did after all serve as a strong and constant educational force) that the greatest response after the sex survey was to the column in which she voiced her fear of a nuclear nightmare and invited her readers to express their own fears to President Reagan by sending him copies of the column. That one aroused such response that the Great Communicator himself sent her his endorsement, which she printed a little less than a month later.

Nor was a nuclear holocaust the only important concern to which she leant her very considerable influence and her seemingly boundless energy. Her entry in *Who's Who in America* lists her work on behalf of the Anti-Defamation League and the National Foundation for Infantile Paralysis even before she assumed editorship of the column. Thereafter, she worked for the Christmas Seal Campaign, the Mayo Fund, the American Cancer Society, the National Cancer Institute, the President's Commission on Drunk Driving, the Menninger Foundation, and many more. In recognition of her efforts, she received, among others, awards from the National Family Service Association, the National Council on Alcoholism, the Golden Stethoscope (for her contributions to medical health), the Lions Club (for humanitarianism), the American Cancer Society, the American Psychiatric Association, the National Kidney Foundation, the Epilepsy

Foundation, a citation for distinguished service from the American Medical Association, the Margaret Sanger award, and the Stanley G. Kay medal from the American Cancer Society.

There is hardly an area of public service to which she did not contribute—while at the same time concerning herself with someone like Wit's End in Charlottesville, Va., in 1982, whose twenty-two-year-old daughter appeared to be suffering from personality alterations due to a neurological disorder. After having suggested a psychiatrist, Ann ended her advice with, "Do try. And please let me know how she is doing. I want to hear from you."

That intimate expression of care reverberates in a frequently deaf world that promotes many kinds of self-insulation. Ann Landers's "please let me know how she is doing" is more than just a remarkably audible and intimate voice.

At a time when many of the taboos have dropped away that once induced letter-generating fears, the comforting and socializing rituals afforded by those taboos have disappeared as well. There is no longer as much call to write a syndicated advice column; and along with the taboos, approval of authority has lost its importance. The freedom resulting from the loss of taboos also created a multitude of constituencies with a babel of voices across which it is proportionally difficult to speak with assurance.

Such anguishes as have replaced the dilemmas of a more innocent age require an immediacy of hot lines and specialized attention commensurate with the intensity, the privacy of the individual crisis. Alongside this urgency, the slowness and public nature of a letter to a recognizable mother figure are the obsolescent emblems of less frantic and less alienated times.

The audibly human voice of Ann Landers rising above our collective impersonality, reaching out to the daughter of Wit's End, may well be the last form of help available at the end of advice.

Ann Landers Says: An Interview with Eppie

This interview was taped in the living room of Ann Landers's home in Chicago in May 1986.

David Grossvogel: Your column is the most widely syndicated in the history of American journalism. How many letters do you receive a day?

Ann Landers: I receive about a thousand pieces of mail a day. One-third are requests for booklets. Another third is mail with names and addresses of people needing personal responses. The last third, without addresses, yields most of the letters that make up the column.

D.G.: What is it like to have the largest reading audience in the world? What thoughts run through your mind when you sit down to respond to eighty-five million daily readers?

A.L.: I never think about those numbers. I simply address myself to the person with the problem.

D.G.: Have you ever stayed up nights worrying that maybe you gave the wrong advice?

A.L.: Nothing keeps me up nights. I realize that no one is infallible. It would not be humanly possible to come up with the right response every single time. I accept my limitations. When I make a mistake, I admit it. I don't believe admitting a mistake damages a person's credibility—in fact I think it enhances it.

D.G.: Have you ever been sued for giving the wrong advice?

A.L.: No. I am quite safe in that regard. A reader would have a difficult time winning such a suit, because he or she came to me for my advice. Also, the advice is free. No one can claim he didn't get his money's worth.

D.G.: To what do you attribute your extraordinary success?

A.L.: I have been fantastically lucky. When I fell into this job thirty years ago, there was nobody else around. I mean nobody. Dorothy Dix had been dead for seven years, and hundreds of papers were hungering for someone to fill that void. The timing could not have been better. And then, of course, I was trained by one of the world's best editors—Larry Fanning. He knew how to bring out the best in people. Larry convinced me that I could actually help those troubled souls—that I could really make a difference—and that is what motivated me to give it my best.

D.G.: What criteria do you use when you select letters to publish in the paper?

A.L.: I view the column as an opportunity to educate, and I select the letters with that in mind. I try to run three letters every day. Those letters must be on three different subjects. If one letter is sad, the next letter should be upbeat. If one letter is from a teen-ager, the next letter will probably be from the underappreciated wife of a clergyman or a man who wonders if he should marry a woman with herpes. Variety is extremely important. Some days, if there is a hot issue, I will devote the entire column to it. I did this when I wrote a letter to President Reagan about the possibility of a nuclear war and what the world would be like if some nut pressed that button. I also wrote a column urging my readers to write to their senators and insist that they vote for the National Cancer Act. I felt issues of such monumental significance rated special treatment.

D.G.: I know you received enormous responses to those columns.

A.L.: I certainly did. Over nine hundred thousand people wrote to their senators about the National Cancer Act. That was the heaviest mail they had ever received on any issue, including the war in Vietnam. Soon after, Congress voted to spend $100 million on the fight against cancer. It was, I believe, my single most important achievement.

D.G.: And you also received a response from President Reagan.

A.L.: Yes, I did, and a very good one. He asked if he could use my column to respond to the American people about the arms buildup. I said, "Yes," and I printed his letter. The President suggested that instead of my readers writing to *him*, they should write to Brezhnev.

D.G.: How much rewriting of letters do you do?

A.L.: As little as possible. Too much alteration destroys the flavor of the letter. Most people write too long, so I must do some trimming. Also, the letters that are not literate must be fixed. Sometimes I launder the language. It does on occasion get pretty raunchy.

D.G.: Are you ever tempted to alter a letter in a way that gives you an opportunity to put forth your own point of view? Undoubtedly you have some pet causes that you would like to promote.

A.L.: It isn't necessary. I know if I wait long enough, I'll get exactly the letter I want—the perfect letter that will allow me to speak my piece.

D.G.: You have, however, gone out on a limb and spoken on behalf of causes that you knew would get you in trouble with many of your readers.

A.L.: Yes, I have.

D.G.: What issues generated the most trouble?

A.L.: The issue that brings in the most hate mail is

abortion. My position is prochoice. The runner-up is gun control. Then comes Planned Parenthood and sex education in the public schools. Since I support the use of animal models for medical experimentation, several animal groups are screaming for my scalp. Without the use of animals, we could never have conquered polio, diphtheria, mumps, hepatitis, and measles. Cancer research would come to a screeching halt if researchers were prohibited from using animals. You would not believe how many people insist, "A dog is a rat is a child."

D.G.: How much of the mail do you answer personally?

A.L.: Very little. It just isn't possible for me to write seven columns a week, 365 days a year, make speeches all over the country, attend board and trustee meetings, and respond to a great number of letters personally. Fortunately, I have an extremely competent staff. Three of my eight assistants have degrees in social work. Sending people to the appropriate social service agencies so they can get the continuing help they need is terribly important. I believe one of the finest compliments I have ever received was from Dr. Robert Ebert, former dean of Harvard Medical School. He said, "Ann Landers runs the most effective social service agency in the country."

D.G.: How much help do you get from your staff in preparing the column?

A.L.: My staff does the typing and routine research. I select all the column material, and I do all my own writing. This means not only the column but booklets, magazine articles, books, and speeches. Now and then, the women who type the final copy will challenge my judgment, and we'll discuss it. On occasion they persuade me to soften an answer or change the advice completely (I've really been blessed with a marvelous staff), but the column is pure me.

D.G.: Some people—I would guess most people—are not actually looking for advice. They find your column amusing. They read it for entertainment. Does that bother you?

A.L.: Not a bit. I don't care *why* they read it, so long as they read it. A great many people have told me that they started to read the column for laughs, and after a while they realized it was a lot more substantive than they had thought. No one can read that column day in and day out and not learn something. In fact, I have learned a great deal from writing it. It deals with every conceivable facet of life. That column has taken me into areas I had never thought about before. Incest, genetic diseases, rape, drug abuse, schizophrenia, battered wives (and husbands), donating organs for transplantation, women who do their housework in the nude, what happens to missing socks. It has stretched my mind in a thousand different directions.

D.G.: I think a great many people read you in order to second-guess you. Match their wisdom with yours.

A.L.: Yes, of course. They tell me they put their hand over the answer to see if my response lines up with theirs. If it doesn't, sometimes they write and complain. I have printed some of those responses and told them, "Thank you. Your answer was better than mine."

D.G.: You do more than simply give advice. It seems to me that the column is also the means of a wider dialogue.

A.L.: It certainly lets people know they aren't alone. And often the problems they read about make theirs look like a piece of cake. It makes them feel better.

D.G.: I know that in some instances, you have contacted your readers personally.

A.L.: Yes. If I believe a person is deeply distressed or suicidal, I will pick up the phone. This is always a great surprise to the person on the other end of the line. They simply can't believe it. The shock of hearing my voice. The fact that I would care enough to call often gives them a tremendous lift and motivates them to seek professional help.

D.G.: You have often written, especially in your end-of-the-year columns, that your work does not depress you. As I talk to you, it is obvious that this is so. But what about your view of the world being colored by the people who write? After all, you do hear mostly from those who are troubled.

A.L.: I have learned to separate myself from the problems that cross my desk. I also realize that there's a big difference between being troubled and having troubles. Everybody has something in his or her life that isn't as wonderful as it could be.

But not all people write to me about problems. As we were saying, they often write to comment on someone else's problem. Or they write to tell me my advice to Tortured in Toronto was terrible and that I am ignorant or stupid or crazy.

D.G.: How do you respond to such criticism?

A.L.: Sometimes I agree with the reader and take my twelve lashes with the wet noodle. I am not always right, you know. There is a great deal of wisdom out there, and when I goof they let me have it.

D.G.: Has your readership changed over the years?

A.L.: Yes, it has. I'm getting less pornographic mail, less nutty stuff. I'm receiving more letters from men. Also, the quality of the letters has improved. More thoughtful and better educated people are writing. I'm getting more serious and substantive mail, more letters from the chairmen of the board, bankers, physicians, senators, and college professors.

D.G.: Occasionally, you start an avalanche of mail by saying, "I'll ask my readers." When do you feel the justification to start such a groundswell?

A.L.: I go with my gut. I have a visceral feeling about the topics I should take to my readers. Like the one about how to hang toilet paper. What an extraordinary response! Imagine fifteen thousand people writing about *that*!

D.G.: Why did you pick that letter to publish?

A.L.: I trust my hunches. I knew it was not an earth-shaking issue, but it was something everyone could relate to. And I often wondered how many people, when they hang a roll of toilet paper, place it so the paper goes over the top and how many want it to hang down along the wall. When I ran across that letter, I knew at once it was a subject thousands of people would want to say something about.

D.G.: I can relate to that. I wouldn't like to see my toilet paper hanging away from the wall.

A.L.: You see? Another sleeper was one about hard-boiled eggs. I got ten thousand letters after printing a letter from a woman who was having trouble with her hard-boiled eggs. She could never get them peeled right. They would be nicked and ugly because they stuck to the shell. No way could she use them as garnishing. Know what the trouble was? They were too fresh!

D.G.: I suppose that kind of exchange comes under the general heading of public service. But occasionally you print a letter that seems to have little meaning—it may even be mildly insulting—but you print it, seemingly, only to dismiss it.

A.L.: Controversy heightens reader interest. I never arbitrarily pick a fight with my readers, but when they get nasty I let 'em have it.

D.G.: Important issues often become the subject of polls. Do you refer to polls when you do your work?

A.L.: I don't refer to anyone else's polls. I think the polls I take are right on the money. I have the best polling mechanism in the world. I hear directly from the people, and they tell me exactly how they feel. There's no reason for them to lie to me.

D.G.: And you don't think that you may simply be getting a nonrepresentative sample, no matter how large, of people who just happen to get excited about the same issue at the same time?

A.L.: What you are saying is that I hear only from malcontents on a particular issue, therefore my polls are skewed. But the eloquence of the letters on opposite sides of the issues never fails to impress me. My column serves as a national soapbox, a forum if you will. People tell me exactly how they feel about everything. When I run a poll, I believe the results are amazingly accurate.

D.G.: So you think that when seventy percent of the parents who write to you saying if they had to do it over again they would not have children, that actually represents a cross-section of our culture, even though other polls that I have seen say the level of discontent you found was too high?

A.L.: On that particular poll, a great many people wrote to say, "You're off base, Ann. I don't believe it." Well, *I* believe it. The parents who responded had children of all ages. Parents with infants, for example, said, "We used to have a lot of freedom. We went to parties, we entertained, we went to the theater. We loved to travel. Now we have four children under nine years of age. They demand a lot of time and energy. They get sick. We walk the floors at night. We can't afford the things we used to do. Our social life is zero. If we had to do it over again, we certainly would not have had four. Two, maybe. But not four."

Then there were those with teen-agers. Many said, "Our kids are driving us crazy. They don't listen. We worry every night when they go out. Our son has wrecked the car twice. Our daughter is sleeping around. She's had one abortion, and we think she's pregnant again. These kids are always in trouble. They're expensive and demanding. They're sassy; they've got big mouths. They don't appreciate anything we do for them. Our lives would have been better without them."

Then there are the older folks who said, "Our son the doctor . . . we worked hard to put him through medical school. Do you think we ever hear from him? Forget it. And our daughter, she lives in California. If we see her for two days out of the year and she sends a plant for Mother's Day, it's a big deal. We get very little pleasure out of our children. When I think of how hard we worked, and the sacrifices we made to educate them and give them the best of everything, it makes me wonder how we could have been so foolish."

D.G.: You think dissatisfaction with the second group, the teen-agers, might be less now than at the time you took that poll in 1976? Reading you, I feel the parents are trying to reassert themselves.

A.L.: Well, they're trying. And I'm trying to help them. I keep repeating that discipline is the greatest gift you can give a child. If you let your children do anything they please, they get the feeling you don't care about them.

D.G.: Do you feel optimistic about the family structure?

A.L.: No. I cannot say truthfully I believe the family structure is getting stronger. We now have in the work force a record number of divorced women with young children. Their ex-husbands duck their financial responsibilities by moving from one state to another. These women try to fill the emotional gap created by an absent father, and it's tough sledding. Many mothers tell me they must work outside the home because the family can't make it on one paycheck. "Even with both my husband and me working it's hard," they complain. And then there's the career woman who wants to have it all. She lets us know she earned her MBA at Harvard and it cost a lot of money. She's not about to forget it. She feels she has no status if she stays at home.

Societal pressures can be heavy. The woman who *does* stay at home is asked, "Do you work?" She replies, "Damn right, I work! I've got three kids. Do you think that's not work?" Then she is asked, "I mean do you have a *real* job?" Lots of people don't think staying at home and being a mother is a real job. The result is that many of these women feel inferior if they are not holding down an impressive position—or practicing law. Somebody's paying the price for this.

Another problem is competitiveness between husband and wife, especially if she has the more prestigious job or brings in more money. So this business of women doing their own thing isn't always one hundred percent terrific. It has hatched a multiplicity of problems. This is a very long rebuttal to the notion that the family structure might be stronger than it was ten years ago.

D.G.: So you feel that the family has undergone significant changes in the last several years?

A.L.: Indeed. The family structure has changed. It is much more fragile.

D.G.: What concerns you most about those changes?

A.L.: The moral fiber of family life is coming apart at the seams because there's nobody home. Parents are not spending enough time with their children. They can't. The rat race is highly competitive, and children aren't valued the way they once were. They are put into day-care centers, or they are left with a sitter who may be too young, too old, lacking in patience, or highly incompetent. Children are not getting proper parental discipline or the knowledge of proper values. Small wonder so many teen-agers are stoned on pot, snorting coke, smoking crack, and crashing cars. And this generation of young people will be running our country in twenty years. I find it scary.

D.G.: Do you believe the loosening of family structures is more important than even, say, the sexual revolution?

A.L.: I do. You can't say to women anymore, "Stay at home and raise kids." Society is telling them something different. Fifty or sixty years ago, when a woman was a lawyer or a doctor (there weren't many, but there were some), they also managed to pay attention to their children because children were considered at least as important as a career. But no longer is this true. The career gets the quality time, and the kids get what's left over.

D.G.: Since you consider a large part of your mission to be education, a great part of what you write is the result of research. What proportion of your column is personal experience?

A.L.: I've had a relatively trouble-free life. The only thing that rocked me was my divorce. And even that didn't slow me up. I walked right through it. It was traumatic—thirty-six years of a very good marriage finished. But I was never depressed. I carried on without missing a beat. My divorce changed the direction of my life and gave me some valuable "fringe benefits." I must say, I am a very happy woman. Two years before, I never dreamed I would ever be a single woman—a widow, maybe, but never a divorcee.

This may sound trite, but I believe all trouble has some built-in blessings. I always knew I had a loving family and a lot of good friends, but I never knew how loving and good they were. Incredible—the emotional support that came my way, the affection and the caring. But my whole life has been that way—positive and good. I was never discriminated against careerwise because I was Jewish or because I was a woman. Life has been kind to me. I have been blessed with excellent health, boundless energy, and a pretty good head. I learn from people who are smarter than I—and the world is full of them. I know how to pick brains, and I know how to pick friends. I don't waste my time on nonsense. I'm not a drinker or smoker or a party girl. Those things never did appeal to me. I have always saved my energy for things I thought were worthwhile.

D.G.: If not personal experience, what then? Common sense?

A.L.: It's mother wit.

D.G.: Mother wit?

A.L.: Mother wit. Maybe that's just another word for common sense. I was never flighty or foolish. This is not to say I never made any mistakes in my life, but more often than not, I seemed to make good choices and go in the right direction. Maybe it's the way I was brought up. You might say I was raised with solid, Midwestern values.

D.G.: In addition to mother wit, you frequently rely on authorities. How did you develop these resources over the years?

A.L.: As the column took on a more serious tone, I realized I just didn't know enough. I had to call on experts for help. In the process, I developed a stellar stable of first-rate authorities. The organizations and institutions I became involved with were excellent vehicles for enlisting consultants—and they have helped me grow as a person as well. Harvard Medical School, the Menninger Foundation, the National Cancer Institute, the Hereditary Disease Foundation, the Mayo Foundation, the Rehabilitation Institute of Chicago, the American Cancer Society, Meharry Medical College (a black medical college in Nashville). Being a trustee at Meharry gave me wonderful insight into blacks and the problems they face. It opened a whole new world. Although I've always been a liberal, I didn't grow up with blacks and I didn't know what it was like to be black in America.

D.G.: What about the areas that are nonpolitical? Have you grown more liberal or more conservative over the last thirty years?

A.L.: I believe as we grow older we all have a tendency to move to the right. I know I have. I am not as liberal as I used to be.

D.G.: I consider you to be in many ways a feminist. You have long fought for women's rights. You have come out against harassment, you have been prochoice, and so on. You obviously feel strongly about women's issues.

A.L.: Certainly. But I don't know if I'd call myself a feminist.

D.G.: I didn't mean a militant.

A.L.: I believe women should have the opportunity to do whatever they are capable of doing.

D.G.: Clearly, you are prime evidence of a woman who has become a corporate success. I realize that you don't go into the street carrying a banner, but you have been quite articulate on behalf of women's rights for a very long time.

A.L.: Today, women make up 40 percent or more of the student population of the Harvard Medical School. The same is true at Yale, and most of the medical and law schools around the country. We are going to have more women physicians, dentists, and lawyers out there than ever before. And more women will be in executive positions—presidents and vice presidents of corporations, and I say, "Hooray! It's about time."

D.G.: You don't believe in turning what one might call

a logical feminism into an ideological feminism?

A.L.: The issue I am most interested in is equal pay for equal work. For years, business and industry have been getting away with murder. They have been getting women to do the same job for a lot less money than they pay men. A man will get $45,000 a year, but they'll pay a woman $30,000 for the same position. They can't do that anymore.

D.G.: You are a Jew dispensing advice to a Protestant culture. Has this anomaly affected the advice you give or your relationship to your readers?

A.L.: My sense of ethics is based on Judeo-Christian principles. My readers know I'm Jewish, but I am not considered "a Jewish columnist." I am rather a columnist who happens to be Jewish.

D.G.: Over the last 30 years, you have won a great many awards, citations, and honorary degrees. You have been named the most influential woman in America by the Women's Almanac. Of what bit of recognition are you proudest?

A.L.: I believe it is the Albert Lasker Award for Public Service, which was presented to me in November 1985.

D.G.: The inscription on that award reads, "To Ann Landers for her thirty years of tireless commitment to improve the physical and emotional health of the American people, and for her unique ability to relate to individuals on every intellectual, economic, and social level." That must have been a thrilling day for you.

A.L.: It was indeed. Governor Mario Cuomo was the speaker at that luncheon. It was a glorious day!

D.G.: What do you plan to do when you retire?

A.L.: Who said anything about retiring? I can't imagine life without work. I would be bored out of my mind and feel useless to boot. I plan to keep on doing what I'm doing as long as I have all my marbles and the good Lord gives me the physical strength to carry on.

General Index

Index of Letter Writers